An Insider's Guide
to Political Jobs
in Washington

AN INSIDER'S GUIDE TO POLITICAL JOBS IN WASHINGTON

William T. Endicott

JOHN WILEY & SONS, INC.

Published by John Wiley & Sons, Inc., Hoboken, New Jersey.
Published simultaneously in Canada.

For general information on our other products and services please contact our Customer
Care Department within the U.S. at (800) 762-2974, outside the United States at (317)
572-3993 or fax (317) 572-4002.

Wiley also publishes its books in a variety of electronic formats. Some content that appears
in print may not be available in electronic books. For more information about Wiley products, please visit our website at www.wiley.com.

Library of Congress Cataloging-in-Publication Data:

Endicott, William T.
    An insider's guide to political jobs in Washington / William T. Endicott.
      p. cm.
    Includes bibliographical references and index.
    ISBN 0-471-26819-4 (pbk. : alk. paper)
      1. United States. Congress—Officials and employees—Selection and appointment.
2. United States—Officials and employees—Selection and appointment. 3. Government
executives—Selection and appointment—United States. 4. Presidents—Staff—Selection
and appointment—United States. 5. Political parties—Employees—Selection and
appointment—United States. I. Title.

JK1083 .E53 2003
320.973′023—dc21
                                               2002026723

*Dedicated to all those who gave
me a chance to serve*

CONTENTS

ACKNOWLEDGMENTS

I want to thank a number of people for helping me with the book. First, there are John Noble and Mary Beaulieu, director and associate director of career services, respectively, at Harvard's John F. Kennedy School of Government, who gave me encouragement and ideas at many stages of the project.

Jennifer Blanck, director of career and alumni services at Georgetown University's Georgetown Public Policy Institute was also extremely important. Not only did she offer many suggestions of her own, she also organized meetings with Georgetown students, which allowed me to "road test" the book. The students in this group included Nina Boughton, Tom Cassels, David Coffey, Michael Craig, Dan Feltes, Julie Giardina, Erik Glavich, Allison Hansen, Jon Nomachi, Mike Nemec, Jamie Reim, and Rebecca Walton. All were helpful, but Craig and Glavich were especially helpful.

I would also like to thank Jon-Christopher Bua, Mario Buil-Merce, Don Ediger, my wife, Abbie Endicott, my son, Sam Endicott, Michael Grant, Cherylyn Harley, Nick Johnson, Eric Kline, John Maclean, Roger Majak, and Danny O'Brien, who gave me much editorial assistance and other kinds of advice. Finally, there are the countless colleagues with whom I have worked during the last three decades who have given me many insights and a greater appreciation for those who serve in political jobs.

INTRODUCTION

➤➤✕✖

➤➤ An Honest Discussion ✕✖

Some years ago, when I was working in a political job, I noticed a recurrent theme. By day, I listened to people complaining about how terrible politics was in this country. But by night, I showed foreign dignitaries around my organization and listened to them say how wonderful our system was and how they wanted to copy it. How could both be true at the same time?

I realized the answer was contained in the phrase "compared to what?" Compared to perfection, we don't do so well. There are always stories of excesses or inadequacies coming out in the press, and the system sometimes seems creaky at best. In a way, this is probably a good thing because it forces us to regard our democracy as a work in progress. It forces us to realize that there is always plenty of work to do for people of good will. But it also creates an atmosphere of cynicism, an atmosphere that I think the facts do not warrant.

Compared with anyone else's system, we do pretty well. Permit me another personal anecdote. I remember in 1987 being in East Germany when a man said he wanted to talk to me about the United States. Our conversation was in German. I said, "Sure." "Let's go over there," he said, pointing to an open field where it would be impossible for anyone to bug us. Shortly after

1

we started talking, a group gathered around us—"like tsetse flies," the man quipped—sensing what was about to happen.

"Tell us about America," they said.

"What do you hear?" I asked.

"We hear about poverty, AIDS, crime, racism."

"Well, we have all of that, and we can talk about them, if you want," I said. "But we have a lot of other things, better things, and we can talk about those too."

"Stop right there," someone said. "The mere fact that you are willing to admit to us that you have those problems and that we can talk about them, that must mean America is the best country in the world."

I was stunned. Such a little thing, having an honest discussion, something we take so much for granted in this country. But it was the major issue in East Germany.

The discussion went on, of course, an honest discussion of what things were really like in our two societies. It's the kind of discussion I hope we can have in this book—a rigorous analysis of politics, but politics the way it really is, not the way it is imagined. A discussion of both the good and the bad.

Why It's Worth It

Let me confess my optimism up front. In large measure, this book is a defense of politics. I believe in political parties and in campaigns. I believe in debating ideas, in voting, and in elections. Politics is how we meld together competing interests—private interests, sectional interests, business interests, the interests of those who cannot fend for themselves—and come up with the national interest, the ground rules by which we operate our society. Human nature being what it is, I accept that individuals will fight hard for their side. I accept that people will take the issues very seriously, for indeed, the stakes are enormous: how just a society we live in, how long we live, how safe we are, what the opportunities will be for our children and grandchildren. For all these reasons, I believe politics is not only an important undertaking; it is a noble undertaking. Engaging in the U.S. federal political system is a great opportunity for a number of reasons, including the following.

➤ *There are vast resources.* The federal government commands vast resources, resources that can be marshaled to do great things, such as building the nation's interstate highway system, rebuilding Europe and Japan after World War II, and implementing a G.I. bill. Or passing Medicare or the Voting Rights Act, winning the Cold War, reducing disease, landing a man on the moon, and coordinating and funding early Internet development. Okay, maybe it's not always quite as grand as that. Maybe it's just helping to increase the number of loan guarantees the Small Business Administration makes to women and minorities in this country. Or helping a town get a federal grant to improve its sewer system. Or helping someone win a case for Social Security disability. Big or small, you have a chance to serve and help people.

➤ *You work at the fulcrum of history.* Working in our national political system means working at the center of American history and even world history. As more and more of the world's traditional societies wrestle with modernity, it is to our secular, scientific, and industrial society that they look, approvingly or disapprovingly. They look especially to our political democracy, which places such a premium on the force of ideas over the force of arms. They look to our political democracy, which fosters the free exchange of ideas and the emancipation of women and of men. Should they embrace us or resist us? Our political democracy sets the framework for our entire system of free-market capitalism and cultural pluralism. Our achievements become models for the rest of the world—and our mistakes serve as warnings. To work at the very crossroads of these earthshaking events at any age, and possibly change them, even just a little, is the chance of a lifetime. To do this in your early 20s is even more than that.

➤ *You have a public mandate.* A politician elected to office usually has won a public mandate to pursue certain objectives, usually the ones on which the campaign was waged. Prevailing in the most open, democratic election system in the world creates a great moral authority to get things done.

➤ *It's exciting.* The chance to work on implementing public policy is an exhilarating mental challenge; it's just plain fun. Furthermore, in many fields, the people who are the best at what they do often have two things in common: talent and a fascination for the process that is almost as important to them as the final result. People who have these skills are exciting to work with. If you are an extrovert and are intrigued by interpersonal relationships, politics may be the profession for you.

➤ *It's good preparation for running for office yourself.* Working as staff is an excellent preparation for running for office yourself. Bill Clinton started out as a clerk on the staff of the Senate Foreign Relations Committee to help pay his way through college. A number of representatives, such as Leon Panetta (see Chapter 8, the case studies section of this book) started out on the staffs of representatives and senators. The knowledge you get about the issues and the process can be a great help. So can the contacts you make.

➤ *It leads to other jobs.* The knowledge you gain here can also help you later in getting jobs in the private sector. Look at the following examples from the case studies: Richard Armitage, Catherine Bertini, Jon-Christopher Bua, Andrew Card, Wendy Greuel, Susan King, Roger Majak, Sylvia Mathews, and Roger Porter. For some young people, working in government steers them in directions they weren't sure about before. Take the example of Jason McManigal, who was once a White House intern working on President Clinton's health care initiative and is now a medical school student. As he explained to me, "Working on health care gave me an understanding of how the system worked. It made me more of an activist. I decided to get into it by first learning the medicine. Down the road I want to be part of the group that figures out where medicine goes."

➤ *It teaches you how to be a democratic leader.* Becoming proficient in the U.S. system of politics teaches you valuable leadership skills, such as organizing, coalition building, bargaining, negotiating, and reaching compromise, all of which are useful in many other settings.

Living Inside the Beltway

Although this may come as a surprise to some, I believe that living in the Washington, D.C., area, "inside the (Route 495) Beltway," as it's called, is a huge added benefit of working in a Washington political job, especially for young people. When I first came to Washington, people warned me, "You're not going to like it; there's nothing to do here." I discovered that just the opposite is true. It's hard to find anywhere else such a good mix of exciting work and fun things to do outside of work, especially out of doors.

In a nutshell, Washington has many of the advantages of a big city, such as New York (metro area population about 20 million), London (7 million), or Paris (10 million), while actually being a much smaller city (D.C. metro area is 3 million; D.C. itself is 600,000). Washington is the only major planned city in the United States, and it has an international, European style, reminiscent of Paris. Washington is an astonishingly beautiful, open, airy city, where one can always see plenty of sky—no skyscrapers are allowed to overshadow the Capitol dome or the Washington Monument. The Washington Mall is like the Champs Elysée in Paris, and like Paris, Washington is full of monuments. It has wide streets and many trees—and gorgeous pink cherry blossoms in the spring. It has parks and waterways. The air temperature is warm enough to make outdoor sports possible year-round, and air conditioning has taken care of the problem of being indoors during the summer.

In the last 20 years, the quality of Washington dining has risen dramatically. Although a few Washington restaurants are on a par with the excellent ones in New York, there are scores and scores of very good restaurants in Washington. They represent cuisines from all over the world, including French, Italian, Indian, Thai, Vietnamese, and many others. But at the same time, Washington has many bars and pubs that young people prefer. It also is home to the National Symphony, the Kennedy Center for the Performing Arts, the Smithsonian museums, the Folger Shakespeare Theatre, and a broad spectrum of dance and music shows. And it has plenty of intellectual activity because of its many colleges and universities, such as American, Catholic, Georgetown, George Washington, George Mason, Howard, and the University of Maryland.

Also important is the easy access to rural areas. You can drive 10 miles outside D.C. and feel as though you were 150 miles away. Take my own case. I live seven miles from the White House, but it is a 90-second run from my home to the rapids on the Potomac River where I coached world and Olympic champions in whitewater kayaking. I can bicycle 35 minutes to the White House or 45 minutes to the Capitol. And most of the trip is on the Chesapeake and Ohio Canal towpath, on which no cars are allowed, only joggers and bikers. Many of my neighbors are outdoor adventurers—when they are not working for the World Bank, Congress, the White House, or the Pentagon, working as political consultants, at foreign embassies, at newspapers, or running computer companies. Others are students. Many of them engage in such sports as running, sailing, windsurfing, rowing, biking, rock climbing, and hang gliding. A neighbor who recently emigrated from France was even able to find a team handball club.

It is true that Washington remains first and foremost a "company town," unlike New York or London, which have many industries. The primary industry in Washington is the federal government and industries associated with it, such as lobbyists, reporters, and foreign diplomats. It is a fast lane of ambitious, competitive people, "the best and the brightest," the Eagle Scouts, the class presidents, the A students, the high achievers from all over the world, all seeking power to get things done. You have to have something on the ball to be a senator, a cabinet secretary, or a president—or to work for people who are. In Washington, you're not just an individual, you're a VIP, or an assistant to a VIP. Forty-eight percent of D.C.-area workers are in managerial or professional jobs, more than in any other region. And that workforce is the best educated in the nation: in just the District alone, more than 40 percent of adults are college graduates, compared with one-quarter of adults nationwide. For people living outside D.C. in the suburbs, the proportion is even larger.

Unfortunately, all fast tracks, such as New York and Hollywood in addition to Washington, are traditionally easy targets for the media and even for politicians who portray these fast tracks as the real axis of evil, the source of corruption and scandal and big money and elitism and everything else that is wrong with the country and that only they can fix. Campaign consultants rant that Washington is a vast labyrinth of waste and corruption, all financed by high taxes. To cynics living in other parts of the United States, terms such as "inside the Beltway," "K Street" (where the lobbyists have their offices), "The Hill" and "The White House" make people wince. "Congressional page" and "Washington intern" have come to mean scandal and worse.

And, yes, Washington has other image problems. It has one of the nation's greatest extremes in terms of numbers of high school dropouts versus people with graduate degrees, crowded apartments versus expensive homes, and those on public assistance versus those working in the professional ranks. And the disparity of income is growing in the District.

For all these reasons, there is a long tradition in the United States of being suspicious of Washington, starting with founding fathers such as Thomas Jefferson, who believed that the people should always be critical of their government, lest it rob them of their freedom. It is fashionable to criticize those in power, fashionable to knock them off their high horses. Except in times of national crisis, such as during the Great Depression, World War II, and the War on Terrorism. At those times, people drop their suspicions and rally around the flag. At those times, government workers are heroes. At those times, the public is reminded of what binds us together as a nation, that we are all on the same team. Those bonds were reforged by the terrorist attacks of September 11: a new cycle began in which Washington was once again seen as uniquely qualified to shield us from foreign enemies, save the economy from recession, rebuild New York City, and deliver us from skyjackers and bioterrorists.

When you live in Washington for any length of time, you become more aware of this historic cycle, that here, more than in any other place, is America's shared experience. You are reminded of it when you visit the Capitol or the White House and recall that the occupants of this place led us through our triumphs and our tragedies, the Civil War, the Great Depression, and the World Wars. For a moment, it is as if a spell is cast upon you. You realize that here history was made, that here it will be made again—and that you can have your chance to serve. And then the bubble bursts, and you come back to earth again.

There are plenty of other things to buoy the spirit, too. Not just the obvious sites such as the Capitol, the White House, the Washington Monument, and the Smithsonian museums, but the other ones a day trip away, such as the presidential estates of Mount Vernon, Monticello, and Oatlands. Or the colonial village in Williamsburg, Virginia. In Washington, you can find free concerts at all times of the year. The shopping malls are unparalleled in the world. You can find just about any book in the world at the Library of Congress, as well as an expert on any subject at places like the Smithsonian or the National Institutes of Health. You can learn about any country in the world by visiting its embassy in Washington or National Geographic's headquarters.

But most of all there are the people. Washington is full of interesting and colorful people from all regions of the United States and the world. Your neighbor could be a student at Georgetown, a Senate aide, a Marine Corps general, an Associated Press reporter, or the ambassador to Kazakstan—dynamic but practical people who are full of ideas about public policy and how to make things better. Interestingly, Washington is also becoming an industrial town, a technology center, which means there is an increasing number of jobs for former or future government staffers. Only the growth of the military industrial complex after World War II has had as great an impact on the area as the last few years have, starting in the early 1990s with MCI Communications and America Online. These technology pioneers have led to whole new industries, employers—and personal wealth. Since 1998 more than 50 companies in the Washington area have sold stock in initial public offerings, most of them technology or telecommunications companies. In 2000 32 Washington-area public companies had revenue of at least $1 billion, in industries ranging from credit cards, telecommunications, and real estate to health care and hospitality. So, in addition to being a government city, Washington is also a technology center and a diverse and deep corporate community. But above all, it is a beautiful, clean, manageable, international, and outdoorsy city—and a great place to work.

Excellence in Political Jobs

Throughout this book, I will attempt to describe not only what political jobs entail but also what excellence in them entails. I will try to point out the difference between merely doing the job and doing it well. I will try to determine, in short, who makes a difference. Although the exact nature of excellence differs with the job, the following are a few common denominators among people who are excellent in political jobs.

➤ *They help people.* Most politicians who make a difference do it by setting policies that help people. Some help people who are vulnerable because they are sick or old or unemployable. Some help people who are poor or discriminated against and need only a temporary helping hand—a scholarship or a loan, for example—to catch up with the rest of society (and sometimes surpass it). Others protect and defend us through enhancing the police or the military. Other politicians improve the chances for commerce by improving modes of transportation (highways, air travel) or helping to develop new industries (the Internet) or new markets (both at home and abroad). Some set policies that make our food, water, and air healthier. Some make the laws to collect the taxes to pay for all of this and seek to make those laws fairer so that the burden is shared more equitably. Others make their mark simply by correcting these processes when they go awry, getting them back on the right track or figuring out how to accomplish them at less cost.

➤ *They accomplish things that were thought to be impossible.* Fair and sensible laws are not a given. There are always plenty of obstructionists who benefit from the status quo, no matter how unfair it is. These things get changed through politics, but it often takes gifted politicians to do it. Ordinary politicians just go with the flow.

➤ *They do not cost a great deal.* People in political jobs do not get paid as much as people with similar skills and job descriptions in the private sector. Furthermore, people in political jobs do not have civil service job security. For these reasons, people in the political system who are truly excellent at what they do represent a bargain for society.

The foregoing are generalities about what constitutes excellent achievements in public life; the following are some of the methods people use to achieve this excellence:

➤ *Getting elected and staying elected.* In general, the chances of making a difference will increase the longer the politician stays in office. One could say that the chances of hitting home runs go up the more at bats a politician and his or her staff have, the more experience they acquire. So politicians and staffers who know how to win elections are generally going to be more effective than those who do not.

➤ *Leadership.* Excellent politicians are society's leaders. They run the process by which we collectively determine our future. They represent us in the negotiations, the bargaining, and the decision making that will determine our goals as a nation. Any large, diverse group of people is likely to have conflicting needs and desires, and politicians broker solutions to these conflicts. Some leaders are content to merely hold the title and not rock the boat. But it is the leader who is willing to do more than that—to get people to change what they are doing—that really counts. Real leadership is getting people to do what they ordinarily would not do. The ability to organize, motivate, and inspire people to make short-term sacrifices for long-term gains is one of the key characteristics of a good leader. Here are some more:

➤ *Clear vision.* A really good leader begins with a clear vision of the final objectives. It may be possible to win an election and hold a political job without having much of a vision, but it's almost impossible to become a great leader without a vision. By the same token, as a staffer in charge of other staffers, it is a lot easier to get the job done if you have a clear goal. Take soup kitchens, for example. Recent polls have found that college students believe that community service is important but that they don't believe politics is the best way to provide community service. In other words, they believe that working in a soup kitchen is a valuable community service but that being a politician is not. Although I agree that working in a soup kitchen is valuable, I would suggest that the person who figures out how to eliminate the need for soup kitchens and gets it done is providing an even greater public service. A great politician is the one who brings about this change in policy, and this starts with a clear vision of the ultimate goal.

➤ *Ability to communicate.* Some people have a vision but just can't explain it very well. Others can explain it, but they don't do it enough. They assume everyone has gotten the word when they haven't. A good leader constantly articulates the vision, over and over again.

➤ *Ability to motivate.* To get people to do what they ordinarily would not do, one has to get them emotionally involved in the quest. You have to take them through several stages: conceiving, believing, achieving. You have to help them conceive of the change that is needed. Then you have to help them believe that it is actually possible to reach the goal. And finally, you must lead them through the mechanics of actually achieving the goal. Usually, motivating people toward a great goal means two things: showing them how it will improve their lot materially and showing them that it involves a great moral cause, such as fairness or justice. A great leader realizes that either one alone is probably not enough.

➤ *Teamwork.* Everything that is done in a large organization—and a large organization is anything more than one person—requires teamwork. Being able to work well with others is likely to enhance the chances of excellence. Some leaders lead by intimidation and are effective, but they create a lot of enemies, enemies who are looking for a chance to get even—and who often do. Other leaders work well with others, being able to delegate— to describe to others exactly what needs to be done, motivate them to do it, and then stand back and let them do it, without micromanaging them.

➢ *Innovation*. Part of making a difference often means coming up with new ideas or approaches and sometimes recognizing when the time is right to implement an older idea.

➢ *Networks*. People who make a difference create networks with others who have the same objectives and ideals. They find these "soul mates" not only where they all work together but also in related jobs. Good leaders can pool the objectives of all these people, focus on them, and find people in authority that can put them in place.

I would not go so far as to say that engaging in politics is every citizen's responsibility. Some people just have a natural flair for it; others do not. Although the stakes and opportunities are huge, so, often, are the hurdles. You may decide to play a limited, but important, role by simply voting. Or you may choose to avoid both voting and politics altogether—as long as you are willing to let someone else set the rules by which you have to live. But if you want to have a voice in setting those rules, if you want a chance to serve and change history, you can do it in this country. And it is surprising how easy it is for a young person to make a difference.

It happened to me several times in my 20s. In one case, while working for a Massachusetts representative, I did a survey in our congressional district of the effects of the new Supplemental Security Income program that resulted in local improvements that added many dollars to many indigent people's income. Another time, during the gasoline shortage in the early 1970s, I took a scientifically based poll of the federal gas allotments to Massachusetts stations. The poll found that Massachusetts was not getting an equitable gas allotment and led to an increase in that allotment.

Later, when working for an Iowa representative, I had an even more dramatic incident. We started receiving a lot of constituent letters complaining about newly proposed federal regulations to close a number of our district's rural hospitals because they did not have a high enough bed occupancy rate. But if these hospitals were closed, the people in those rural areas would have had to drive hundreds of miles in an emergency. We checked other rural representatives and found that they were receiving similar mail.

My boss directed me to prepare legislation to stop these regulations from going into effect. Working with the lawyers in the House Office of Legislative Counsel, I helped to write a bill that my boss introduced. I then started helping my boss recruit cosponsors for the bill. We ended up with scores of them. At first, the bill went nowhere because, although my boss was a member of the majority party, he was a junior member and not on either of the committees that had joint jurisdiction over the bill. The committees refused to even consider the bill. One of the committees was the powerful Ways and Means Committee. Meanwhile, the mail was piling up.

At that point, I consulted the House parliamentarian to see whether there was any way to force the committees to consider the bill. One of his assistants told me about the Discharge Petition—get a certain number of members to sign it, and House rules required that the bill be brought straight to the House floor, thus circumventing the committees altogether. The required number was high, and most members were reluctant to sign a Discharge Petition because it meant going against the chairs of powerful committees, chairs who could cause problems for those members later if they wanted to. In the end, we not only got the required number of signatures, but the bill came to the floor and passed unanimously. The very next day, officials of the Department of Health Education and Welfare showed up at my desk to have me assist in rewriting the regulations, which I did.

I learned from that experience as a young man that our system moves only when it perceives a widespread consensus on an issue—but then it can move remarkably quickly. This usually means, however, that before you can get anything done, you have to build a consensus for it. You have to be able to show that you are not the only one who cares about changing something, but that a lot of other people also care—people who can do something about it, like vote.

Because of what I've seen, I believe that the people who are effective in our political system are admirable people. They possess rare skills, determination, and persistence, which allows them to accomplish important tasks that help millions of their fellow citizens and even more millions around the world. Collectively, they make up a system of politics that has served this country, and humanity, well. I vehemently disagree with those demagogues who irresponsibly bash politics and government. Sure, government has problems, and there is always room for improvement. That's why we need you, the reader, to get involved. But the glass is at least half full, not half empty, and this is reason to be optimistic about our system, not pessimistic about it.

After all this praise of politics, I do not want readers to think that I am saying that government, indeed, just the federal government, is the most important aspect of living in the United States. Far from it. Even more important is the private sector. Government may set the ground rules and act as referee, but most important is what's happening on the field of play, the making and selling of goods and services. People engaged in these pursuits, especially the ones who do well at them, are also admirable people because of the skills they possess, the skills that are crucial for producing goods that people want and making a profit year after year and using those profits to grow their businesses, to employ Americans, and make charitable and philanthropic contributions.

My own belief is that the most interesting life involves engaging in both worlds, working in both the private sector and the public sector. And as you will see in this book, there can actually be a lot of carryover from one to the other. But this is a personal choice, and each individual must determine the appropriate path. Some may be more comfortable specializing and staying in one area; others may want a broader approach. My objective here is simply to get more young people to go into politics for at least part of a career. I firmly believe they will be better for it, and so will their country.

This book grew out of two things. On one level, it is a response to the questions young people ask me, questions they can't get answered in high school, college, or even in graduate school. They all want to know what political jobs are like. They want to know how to get those jobs and where they lead later. Maybe someone has told them that political jobs hold the most power to make change, or that knowledge of how the political system works would later help them in their law career. Or maybe they like the idea of serving the country, or maybe politics just seems exciting to them. But many have told me that they find the whole process of politics mystifying. They don't know what it's really all about, how to get involved, and they can't find anyone to tell them. They don't know where to start. So I have tried to give them a place to start. I've attempted here to demystify politics, present a road map of what it's all about, at least at the federal level.

On another level, I hope this book will motivate energetic young people to serve in politics. During the last three decades, people have approached me with their worries about the system, wanting to know whether it was really as bad as the press made it out to be. Many were cynical. Even more were apathetic. It reminded me of how in the 1980s I would ask people in communist countries—East Germany, Poland, Czechoslovakia, Yugoslavia—"Do you believe in your system? Do you have any friends who do?" Surely, I thought, there would be such people, misguided, perhaps, but sincere believers nonetheless. I never found any; they were all apathetic. In view of this, it was not so surprising that a few years later the whole thing collapsed: no one cared enough to stand up for it. I don't want that to happen here, and I hope that in a small way, my book can help avoid it. I look around today and see all bastions of authority—medicine, business, the law, the church, politics—under fire, and I worry.

Finally, I believe this book will be of interest to the general reader who simply wants to know how political service works in the United States. This includes not only Americans wanting to know more about their government but also foreign readers who would like to know more about the most influential country in the world.

A word about what this book is and isn't. It is a book about political jobs in Washington, D.C., in other words, jobs in the federal government or having to do with the federal government—jobs that you get directly or indirectly by winning elections at the national level. There are about twenty thousand of these jobs: about thirteen thousand in Congress, about eight hundred in the White House, about fifty-six hundred in the administration and about eight hundred between the two major political parties in Washington. In addition, there are untold thousands of jobs in lobbying groups, think tanks, and the press located in Washington and that interface with the other twenty thousand.

This book does not look at jobs in state and local governments, making that, perhaps, a good subject for another book. I wanted to focus on the "Washington experience" because it is unique. Nor does the book look at permanent civil service jobs or judicial jobs. In the case of the latter, one could argue that they are part of the political process because an elected official nominates judges and legislators have to confirm them. But to me, because judges are supposed to conduct themselves in a nonpartisan manner once in office and because most have permanent job security, I do not consider them to be in the same category as the other jobs I discuss here. Finally, the book does not deal with presidents, cabinet secretaries, senators, or U.S. representatives—only the people who work for them.

Federal Issues

If you are going to work in political jobs within the federal government, one of the first things you will have to learn about is federal issues and how they differ from state and local government issues. Federal issues are the ones the president, the White House, the administration, the Congress, the national political parties, and the lobbying groups, think tanks, and national press deal with.

State issues include personal income tax, corporate tax, property tax, auto insurance rates, school issues (funding, vouchers, performance), welfare, national guard, use of tobacco settlement funds, state environmental laws and regulations, state prisons, and state highways. The officials handling these issues include the state governor and the governor's administration, the state legislature (usually called the state house of representatives, or the assembly, and the state senate), groups that lobby them, and state chapters of the national political parties.

Local government issues include property tax, police and fire departments, schools, snow and garbage removal, water and sewers, and local road maintenance. Local officials include the mayor and the city council.

One of the best ways to get a quick grip on federal issues is by looking at Table I.1, which shows both receipts (income from taxes) and expenditures of the federal government in fiscal year (FY) 2000. Although it may not represent a typical year, FY 2000 is interesting because it represents an optimum year—high employment, great economy, no war, and a surplus to pay down the national debt. I have ranked items according to their dollar value and calculated their percent of receipts (taxes) and outlays (expenditures) as appropriate in order to better show the nation's priorities in good times.

As Table I.1 shows, the greatest source of revenue for the federal government is the individual income tax at over 49 percent. Next is the Social Security tax, which pays for Social Security retirement and disability benefits and Medicare benefits. These are both personal taxes and together represent more than 80 percent of the annual revenue to the federal government. Income from corporations is only 10 percent. These taxes and what they pay for are a constant source of debate: Are the taxes too high? Is the burden spread equitably among different income groups? Are the benefits from the programs worth the money we are spending on them?

Now look at the expenditure section of the table. Together, about 34 percent of the entire federal budget goes to Social Security and Medicare, an amount that is projected to grow in the future, not only in absolute terms but also as a percentage of federal expenditures. This is a big federal issue. Is it fair to demand that young workers pay a higher and higher tax to finance benefits for the elderly? Should the benefits be cut (and thus throw some elderly back into poverty)? Look at defense: it is not much larger than interest on the national debt. Some people say that is wrong and that we should pay down the debt so we can lower those interest payments. Others say we should pay more for defense. What kind of defense? Strategic nuclear weaponry or antiterrorist defense? Foreign aid (under "international affairs" in the table), which is thought by some to constitute an unreasonably high percentage of the federal budget, is in reality less than 1 percent. And so it goes: each item on this list is a large collection of issues having to do with the nature of the benefits versus their cost. In addition to the merits of the programs themselves is the issue of the jobs they create. All these issues impact millions of people, often in dramatic ways. And each issue has

Table I.1. The Federal Budget: FY 2000

Receipts by Source	Amount (in $ millions)	Percentage of Total (%)
Individual income taxes	$1,004,462	49.6
Social Security	652,852	32.2
Corporate income taxes	207,289	10.2
Excise taxes	68,865	3.4
Deposits of earnings by Federal Reserve	32,293	1.6
Estate and gift taxes	29,010	1.4
Customs duties and fees	19,914	0.9
Others	10,533	0.5
Total receipts	$2,025,218	100.0

Expenditures	Amount (in $ millions)	Percentage of Total (%)
Social Security	$409,436	22.6
National defense	294,494	16.5
Income security	247,894	13.9
Net interest	233,218	13.0
Medicare	197,113	11.0
Health	154,534	8.6
Education, training, employment, and social services	59,201	3.3
Veterans' benefits and services	47,083	2.6
Transportation	46,854	2.6
Agriculture	36,641	2.0
Administration of justice	27,820	1.6
General science, space, and technology	18,637	0.1
Natural resources and environment	23,031	0.10
International affairs	17,216	0.09
General government	13,454	0.08
Community and regional development	10,629	0.06
Commerce and housing credit	3,211	0.02
Energy	−1,060	−0.003
Total outlays	$1,788,826	100.0
Surplus	236,392	13.2

Source: U.S. Department of the Treasury and Office of Management and Budget.

lobbyists who aggressively push their point of view on elected officials and their staffs.

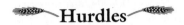

Hurdles

When you work in a political job, you face a few institutional hurdles that make your job harder. They can wear you down. Often the best defense against them is a passionate belief in your mission—and patience. What follows is a discussion of these hurdles.

➤ *Dispersal of power.* This makes for complexity in the U.S. system because in most cases, no one actor has the power to act alone. Although this guarantees that we will not have a dictator, it also means that it takes time and knowledge of the process to get all the actors on the same page. The United States not only has a national government in Washington but also 50 separate state governments. And even within the federal system itself, there is redundancy and complexity. The House of Representatives has to pass judgment on a matter, then the Senate does, and then the president has to accept it. Then regulations have to be promulgated and enforced. There are many, many actors—more politicians and political staff per capita than in any other country. You have to work with all these people in order to get something done.

➤ *Blocking versus creating.* The U.S. system is particularly good at recognizing the excesses of human nature and controlling them, largely by pitting one interest group against another—"setting ambition against ambition," as James Madison put it, in a grand scheme of mutual frustration. It is a conservative system, often more of a brake than an accelerator. It is easier to block something than to create something. That works fine when you are trying to stop something, but it means that you have to be particularly inventive to create something. That is why, in my opinion, the greatest accolades should go to staffers and politicians who are successful at creating things.

➤ *Creating incentives to do the right thing.* Getting people to do good is often a matter of providing them with tangible incentives for doing it. It's not always enough to expect them to do the right thing just because it is the right thing. In public policy, figuring out the right thing is often much easier than getting people to do the right thing. People may know intellectually that a certain policy is best for the nation, but they may be more motivated by what is in the best interest of their constituency instead, or by their own self-interest. Producing incentives to induce people to do the right thing is the key—but it takes ingenuity and time. You have to become proficient at figuring out what people really want, even if they tell you it's something else.

➤ *Constant pressure of elections.* Not only does the United States have more politicians than other countries, those politicians have to face the voters more often and more directly than in most other systems. In addition to the president (and by extension, the president's administration) having to run for election every four years, every U.S. representative has to run every two years and every senator every six years. On top of that, most states have a house of representatives, a state senate, and a governor, all chosen directly by the people, all having to reside in the area they represent, and most having to run every two to four years. Then there are local races. All in all, there are more than five hundred thousand elected offices in this country. All of these actors have to organize, finance, and run their own campaigns, and they may or may not get much help from their party. In Britain, by contrast, the campaigns of members of Parliament (MPs) are financed exclusively by their parties, not the candidates. MPs do not even have to reside in the district they represent, often voting in one district while representing another one. Campaigns are short in Britain—only a few weeks long, as opposed to months in the United States—and elections are required only every five years (although they can be held earlier if the prime minister wants).

➤ *A struggle for power.* Whatever system of government you have, the leaders are always engaged in a struggle to get power and hold on to it, power to determine who gives out valuable resources and who gets them. It is not human nature to give away power voluntarily; one has to seize it. In the U.S. system, you seize it by winning elections, by winning votes. In politics, even in the U.S. system, you cannot make the mistake of thinking that the righteousness of your cause will carry the day and that you won't have to fight for it. No matter how just you are, there will always be people who will work for your defeat. This is because, while you may be content to do good, there are plenty of others who are content to do bad. Or, more likely, they will just have a different idea of what "good" is—good for whom? So if you plan to work in this system, remember first and foremost, it is a fight for power, the power to implement what you believe in. Furthermore, to bring about really big change, you must continuously engage in this fight. Big change takes patience. American politics is in many respects, I think, about patience. It may not seem so at first glance—politicians and their aides are always in a swirl of activity. They seem like the most impatient people in the world. And total engagement is what it takes to win a victory. But victories are often at the margin. A lot of hustling goes into one little victory; and big change is brought about through the compilation of many such little victories. Quite often issues never really get settled; they just go on the back burner for a while. One must wait for the right time to bring them back again—or be ready to defeat them again.

➤ *Dealing with big egos.* The longer you stay in politics, the more likely it is that you will come into contact with some big egos. Great self-confidence is usually a prerequisite to achieving great things. People have to believe in themselves before they can get others to believe in them. The motives for why people seek power or why they seek to do great things are not always the most attractive aspects of human nature. It takes strong motives to enable people to put up with the hassles they encounter in public life, and emotional insecurities, megalomania, greed, and selfishness are sometimes among the motives. We often just lump all this under the word *ambition*. Ambition can sometimes be so strong that it poses a fearsome obstacle to those simply seeking to do good but who are not prepared for the struggle. They may simply be swept aside. On the other hand, good deeds often come from less-than-perfect people. Whatever the motivation may have been, the good deeds stand. It may not always be about ego, but the higher the job the politician holds, the more likely it is. You need to be prepared for all this in dealing with the egos of your boss, your colleagues, and the staff people you encounter. Sometimes it matters less what is right than who is right.

Metaphorically, it is tempting to view high-ranking U.S. politicians as feudal lords battling each other for power. They may cloak their ambitions in altruistic words—religion, the public good, patriotism—but other more personal motives are probably equally important. These lords have followers who support them because the followers stand to benefit in a material way if the lord wins. The followers have to be rewarded to encourage them to continue supporting the lords. Likewise, lords have enemies who stand to lose in a material way if the lords win, and these enemies have to be encouraged to cease their opposition, either by punishing them or by winning them over.

Loyalty demonstrated over a long time is usually the key factor in determining whom lords are going to trust the most, whom they will select as their most trusted staffers. Willingness to sacrifice for the lords when they are most in need, when they are campaigning for election, is usually the best way to demonstrate this loyalty. Often the people making the greatest sacrifices will get the greatest rewards. Often, but not always: the lords themselves have to know that you made the sacrifice. Triumphant leaders get ego massages through certain emoluments, publicity, and the right to give out resources—and even to do good. Their followers get similar rewards, albeit at a lower level. Their enemies lose the right to these things—but they live to fight again another day.

➤ *Politics or statecraft?* It is convenient to view American politics as a ritualized form of combat, removing the physical violence and substituting verbal violence. That's one reason you often hear fight metaphors used to describe politics—"combat," "boxing," "war," and so on. (The other reason is that it makes for livelier copy.) Although the war motif (or in some circles, sports motif) does explain a lot about politics, it unfortunately also obscures the greater goal of *statecraft*—reaching the common good. As politics gets more extreme, more and more good people tend to leave until only the zealots are left, the left wing of the Democratic Party and the right wing of the Republican Party. And for them, compromise is not an option. Gridlock is the result. But with leaders who are willing to rise above this and compromise, much more is often possible.

Sometimes, however, statecraft means having the courage to stand up for what is right no matter what the cost to oneself. In 1956, then-senator John F. Kennedy wrote a Pulitzer Prize–winning book, *Profiles in Courage*, about this subject. He examined in the book the pressures experienced by eight U.S. senators over history—the risks to their careers, the unpopularity of their decisions, the defamation of their characters—as they placed principle above personal profit and stood up for what was right, not for what was popular. The timeless message of Kennedy's book is that there are occasions when it is the responsibility of an elected official to vote his or her conscience regardless of what public opinion dictates. Kennedy cited such examples from history as Senator Daniel Webster of Massachusetts going against his constituents' wishes and compromising with the South in the Compromise of 1850 and thus holding the Union together. Another is Senator Edmund Ross, defying his constituents' wishes and voting against the impeachment of President Andrew Johnson. One thinks of Gerald Ford pardoning Richard Nixon, or Republican senator John McCain bucking his party's desires and joining Democratic senator Russ Feingold in backing campaign finance reform, as modern-day equivalents. In questing for power, then, are our leaders going to be politicians concerned only with self-advancement or the advancement of some narrow interest group? Or will they be engaging in statecraft, concerned with the advancement of the country as a whole? As you decide who to work for, you need to ponder this question. The truly great leaders are the successful statesmen and stateswomen, and the greatest satisfaction of working in politics is to work for one of them.

➤ *A bum rap.* I don't think politics is explained very well in our society, with the result that the public does not think very highly of politicians or of those who serve them. The public has trouble recognizing when an act of statecraft has occurred. Part of the problem, as already noted, is that our system has all sorts of redundancies and complexities designed to disperse power. But that also makes it harder for the voters to understand. And what they don't understand, they often distrust.

In the first place, real politics—the art of the practitioner—isn't taught at all in our schools, even in courses called "political science." In those courses, the student studies ancient Greek and Renaissance thought about the ideal government, U.S. history and governmental institutions, social history, and economics. These courses are interesting and provide good background, but they do not show the techniques of politics. Other courses, especially the ones on modern politics, try to quantify results such as voting statistics and then analyze them in a scientific manner to spot trends and predict future outcomes. The methodology is sound, and sometimes the findings are useful as far as they go. But usually these analysts cannot get enough data to take it far enough. Worse, other analysts who rely on public explanations and public records arrive at incorrect conclusions because such public sources can be mere window dressing that mask the more important interactions between key actors that really decided the issue.

One of the problems is that not many people are willing to write or talk about how it all works, meaning that there is only sporadic, anecdotal evidence to study. And that may mean that politics will always remain an art and not a science. But I would suggest that in the same way we have art appreciation courses, we could have politics appreciation courses.

Another problem is that even if more practitioners were willing to talk about politics, some instructors fear it would be awkward to teach in schools because it might sound unethical, like teaching Machiavelli. They fear that the types of compromise and bargaining necessary in good politics might sound shabby in the classroom. They fear that teaching the techniques for advocating the wishes of a narrow constituency instead of the common good might sound greedy. But ironically, what I think we need is a new version of Machiavelli, one that is geared to explaining the democratic politics of twenty-first-century America, not the oligarchic politics of sixteenth-century Italy. I believe politics can be dissected in an academic way and then defended as a worthwhile, even admirable profession. This book will do some of that.

Politics is also improperly reported in the press. What does seep into the public domain is usually something gone awry—a mistake, a scandal, something sensational—because that's what sells newspapers. One gets a sense of this in the remark of longtime Washington reporter Helen Thomas about the types of lives politicians should live: "My feeling is, if they want privacy, don't go into public life . . . I've decided that if you aspire to high office, you should decide at the age of five and live accordingly."[1]

People tell pollsters that they want to see less wrangling and more cooperation in government. But as any media representative will tell you, compromise and cooperation do not sell as well as conflict and chaos do. There is no balance. Seldom reported are successful deals and how they were achieved: through artful negotiation and thoughtful compromise. This "only the bad news" approach inevitably gives politics a bad name. The net effect of this, unfortunately, is that those who work in politics have to be ready for a certain level of apathy, mistrust, and cynicism from the public.

How the Book Is Organized

This book is organized into four large sections. Chapters 1 and 2 contain background information on the process of getting political jobs and, in general terms, what working in politics is like. Chapter 1 provides an overview of the general process of getting jobs through networking. Chapter 2 describes the lives of politicians and what working for them is like. Chapters 3 through 7 examine specific political jobs in the political parties, Congress, the White House, the executive branch departments, and related jobs (in think tanks, lobbying groups, political consultants, the media, and state and local governments), respectively. My position throughout this book is that all of these areas constitute a federal network of Washington political jobs, that many people hold jobs in more than one area over the course of a career, and that it is hard to understand any one political job without setting it in the context of this network.

The third major section, Chapter 8, consists of 36 case studies, or short biographies, of people who have held one or more of the jobs discussed in the book. This chapter is meant to give a more human dimension to the descriptions in the earlier chapters and to show the reader what the actual careers are like.

The appendix contains a list of recommended readings, daily and weekly news sources, reference books, and other books that contain glimpses of what working in Washington politics is like. It also provides a list of potentially useful television programs.

Note

1. Helen Thomas, "Personal Presidential Anecdotes and the Press' Function in Society" (Fourth Sondock Lecture in legal ethics, University of Houston Law Center, Houston, Tex., February 2001).

1

GETTING THAT FIRST JOB

If you are reading this book, chances are that the foremost question on your mind is, "How do I get that first job?" Once you are on the ladder, you are thinking, it is easier to advance up the rungs, but how do you first get on the ladder? So I will address that right now. I will talk about variations later in the book, but this chapter presents the essential paradigm. I want to say, however, that in looking for the first job, it helps to have a road map of where first jobs can lead. In my experience, too many people do not look far enough down the road, and then later in their careers they wish they had. So another objective of this book is to show beginners what the whole federal system of political jobs looks like and to get them to think several moves, not just one move, ahead: What skills and mentors do you need to accumulate now that will get you to where you ultimately want to be?

The Intersection of Policy and Politics

This book is based on the following premise: the most interesting jobs in government are the ones at the intersection of policy and politics. One without the other is not enough. I'm not saying that there aren't interesting and even well-paying jobs in either pure policy work or pure political work.

And both are important. To make an important change, you have to start with an idea, and ideas often come from think tanks, academics, or interest groups. But then you have to put the idea in the hands of someone who can do something with it. In our system, this someone is a politician who can win a popular mandate by winning an election. So helping politicians win elections is a crucial skill, too.

But best of all, most important of all, most interesting of all is to sit at the intersection of policy and politics, to understand them both. For example, you can be a policy "wonk" and know everything there is to know about an issue, but if you can't sell your ideas to politicians, you can't make an impact, and this is terribly frustrating. Conversely, it is possible for you to be exquisitely well versed in the mechanics of getting someone elected but then never get to sit at the table and discuss policy matters because you don't know anything about that. So I think you need to be grounded in both. You need to be able to be comfortable in the theoretical world of ideas and in the practical world of getting things done in a political system. That is how you can have the best experience in government.

Working Your Way Up versus Transferring In

There are two fundamentally different routes into political jobs that young people need to think about. The first is the "Entry-Level Generalist" route (which I focus on the most in this book); the other is the "Mid-Career Specialist" route. The first involves gaining experience on the job and working your way up from the lowest positions. The other strategy is to develop some issue and political expertise and experience before entering political jobs with the expectation of going in as a relatively senior executive or staffer. There are advantages and disadvantages to each, and which strategy you choose is partly determined by your age and experience. The following sections give more on this point.

INTERNSHIPS, FELLOWSHIPS, VOLUNTEERING

Internships, fellowships, and volunteering are positions in which one essentially works for a period of time at no expense to a politician. They are tried-and-true entrance strategies. In essence, they give you a chance to "show your stuff" and parlay that into a paying job later. There are both

"junior" and "senior" internship programs. The former include intern programs at the political parties, as well as Capitol Hill and White House internships for high school and college students with little or no experience. Senior internships include such jobs as the Presidential
Management Intern program, the American Political Science Association Congressional Fellowship, the American Association for the Advancement of Science Congressional Fellowship, or the White House
Fellows program. These all require some government, political, issue, or
leadership experience. Many interest groups, lobbying firms, and political
consultants also have intern programs. Then there is just plain volunteering. You can do this at the political parties, on the Hill, and at the White
House. Many people have gotten full-time jobs this way. The disadvantage of all these programs, of course, is that usually you do not get paid,
and you usually have to start out working on more mundane chores before
you can prove yourself. Examples from the case studies in Chapter 8 of
people whose first government job was in one of these internships include
Wendy Greuel, Sylvia Mathews, Sean O'Keefe, Scott Palmer, and Roger
Porter. Even Robert Reich, secretary of labor in the Clinton administration, got his first political job as an intern—in the senate office of Robert
Kennedy.

TRANSFERRING IN

A number of people are able to transfer into political jobs at a higher
level from related jobs. They develop issue expertise through association
with academic institutions or positions in the General Accounting Office, lobbying groups, or think tanks, interest groups, trade associations,
or labor unions. Perhaps they become experts through law practice,
teaching, or policy work outside government. Examples from the Chapter
8 case studies include Richard Armitage, Maria Echaveste, Patricia de
Stacy Harrison, Susan King, and Michael Myers. Danny O'Brien was able
to transfer in because of his political organizing skills. Other people, such
as Roger Majak and Paul Wolfowitz, do some combination of working
their way up and transferring in.

Preparing for the Job

Before you can go out looking for a political job, there are several basic
things you have to do.

FIGURE OUT WHAT YOU BELIEVE IN

You have to decide what you're for and what you're against. Do you have liberal views, conservative views? Why? Have you honestly researched the question, or are you just letting emotion be your guide? Do your views come from theory or from dealing with real live people? How much do you really know about a particular issue? It pays to examine these questions carefully because later you will be tested. You will have to defend your position vigorously against people on the other side of the issue who believe in their case very strongly. If your views are poorly thought out, that fact will probably emerge and limit your effectiveness. To the extent you can determine your beliefs in precise detail, so much the better. What issues do you care most passionately about? Are you interested in certain aspects of foreign policy? Health issues? Defense issues? These are the issues you can become more expert in and thus have the greatest chance to make a difference.

FIGURE OUT WHO YOUR ALLIES ARE

Politics is a matter of mobilizing coalitions of like-minded people. Only by doing this can you build the large groundswell of support necessary to win votes in the democratic process. To find allies, you have to declare yourself, take sides, join a team. Are you a Republican or a Democrat? If you're wishy-washy and say "I don't like politics, I don't like either the Republicans or the Democrats," how can you organize? Where are your allies going to come from? As an independent, it's much harder to get things done because there are not enough independents out there in positions of power to help you. In theory, you can start your own team of independents, and once in a while, for brief periods, on certain issues or centering on certain celebrity candidates, it can be done. But over the long haul, being able to change things as an independent is awfully tough. In the first place, independents aren't allowed to vote in primaries, and primaries are where key decisions are made as to who the final candidates will be. Independents don't donate as much money to campaigns, don't work in them as much, and may not even go to the polls on election day.

FIGURE OUT WHO GETS THINGS DONE

Once you know what you believe in, you need to find politicians who share those views. But more than that, you need to find the ones who are effective in getting things done in those areas. These people are the ones you want to learn from, the ones you want to be your mentors. Charisma is not enough. You need to find politicians who actually have a track record of making positive changes in your areas of interest. What bills have they gotten enacted into law? What programs or regulations have they created? Charisma and public communications skills can be an important part of the package, but what other political skills do they possess? You will have to study these politicians a bit. Start looking into their voting records; don't just listen to what their ads say.

DEVELOP A SKILL SET

Simultaneously with figuring out what you believe in and who you want to work for, you have to develop a set of specialized skills that set you apart. What issue area do you want to be an expert in, and how can you become an expert in it? For example, maybe you want to become an expert in defense affairs. Look at the case studies discussed in Chapter 8 to see how Richard Armitage, deputy secretary of state in the George W. Bush administration, built his expertise in this area. He started out as a graduate of Annapolis, served in Vietnam, and from there gradually worked his way up to higher and higher positions involving defense issues. Or look at the different way Paul Wolfowitz, Bush's deputy secretary of state, did it: as an academic whose first government job was as a management intern at what is now the Office of Management and Budget.

Or take a totally different field, that of communications. Susan King, assistant secretary for public affairs at the Labor Department, started out her long career in broadcast television as an editorial assistant to Walter Cronkite. Jon-Christopher Bua parlayed a career as an actor and acting coach into communications jobs in politics.

Each of these people developed skills that set them apart from others and combined them with belief in a candidate and certain issues to land a job in politics. But there are many paths, as the Chapter 8 case studies show. Almost all the people profiled there have college degrees. More than half have advanced degrees: 35 percent have masters' degrees, 17 percent have law degrees, and 14 percent have doctorates. And the percentage of people in these positions with advanced degrees will probably go up in the future. College majors are all over the lot—international relations, dramatic arts, engineering, psychology, sociology, anthropology, political science, biology, U.S. history, and mathematics. The general background ranges from specific subject knowledge at one end of the spectrum to knowledge about political organizing at the other. You can get subject knowledge through a college major and an advanced degree, but you can't get knowledge of political organizing that way. You have to get it through practical experience.

LEARN HOW TO SELL IDEAS TO POLITICIANS

On top of developing a skill set, you need to know how politicians think so you can sell your ideas to them. And much of what they think about concerns getting elected and acquiring power. One of the best ways to start gaining that insight is through campaign experience. A campaign is a crash course, a close-up look at building a coalition. For beginners, almost any campaign experience will do, but you may eventually want to learn how to run a congressional race, state race, or even a presidential race. Later, when working for someone in office, you will gain more insights on how to sell things to politicians. You will already have a pretty good idea of how to help sell things to your voters, but now you will have to learn how to sell them to other politicians' voters; how does it affect their self-interest?

Look at how many of the subjects in the case studies have had campaign experience: at least 70 percent of them. Look at how people like Sylvia Mathews, a top White House official, started out as a researcher in a presidential campaign. Or Kapil Sharma, who owned his own business at age 29 after having been senior counsel for Senator Robert Torricelli; Sharma started consulting on various campaigns during his junior year in college.

For a first-timer, getting campaign experience probably means volunteering. You figure out what candidate you like and, unless you have a mentor who can get you in at a higher level, you walk in the door as a volunteer. Or you walk in the door at party headquarters; the parties always need help with races they're interested in. Or you seek a position as an intern with a political consultant. Once you get your foot in the door, you put yourself in a position where you can show the decision makers what you can do.

Campaigns are tough work. You may get only four to five hours of sleep per night and eat cold pizza and Chinese food at odd hours of the day and night, all for months at a time. Believing passionately in what you are doing, in the candidate, and in the issues is crucial to getting through all this. If you do not work on a campaign at least once in your career, you will never really understand the bond between people who have undergone this common ordeal. You will not understand why it is that politicians give their best jobs to people who have helped them in their greatest moment of crisis: running for election. There are many other reasons why being in a campaign is important. One is that it gives you insights into the minds of the voters, a subject that is always in your thoughts in any political job. Another is that it allows you to make contacts that will be useful to you later.

➤ Identifying the Job ➤

Start talking to people. When you're looking for that first job, whether it be a paying job or an internship that can lead to a paying job, you have to tell people. You have to create a network. Start with people you've met in your policy area or the campaign you've been in and ask them for advice—advice from everything from what your resume should look like to who to contact to find out more about jobs in your area. One referral leads to another, and eventually you will find out about vacancies. That's how you learn about the best openings in political jobs. They're not posted in newspapers or on bulletin boards.

When you're young and just starting out, the following people can be part of your network:

➤ *Family members.* Who in your family knows anything about politics? When I was looking for my first political job, I told my parents, and they introduced me to Republicans because they were Republicans. But then, my wife introduced me to her uncle who was a U.S. representative and a Democrat. I liked his stance on the issues. It turned out that he needed a campaign staff for an upcoming election, and he offered me a job. Maybe your parents' business networks can help; quite possibly one of their associates knows someone in politics to talk to.

➤ *Friends and neighbors.* Maybe the people who live down the street work in politics. Chance are that if you call them up, say you're interested in politics, and ask whether you could come over for some advice, they'll say yes. If they like you, they'll probably be impressed that you took the initiative to contact them and will want to help you.

➤ *Classmates and coworkers.* Who better to recommend you than someone who has worked with you and been impressed with your abilities and who also has a role in politics? And even if they haven't worked with you or don't know you very well, if you play your cards right, they'll probably talk to you and want to help.

➤ *Teachers.* Hillary Clinton got her first job in politics as a staff member of the House Judiciary Committee. She impressed a law school professor who recommended her to the staff director. I know many people who have followed this pattern. In fact, former labor secretary Robert Reich used to complain that he had students who signed up for his college courses not because they were interested in the subject matter but because they wanted to get to know him because of his political connections.

➤ *School alumni organizations.* One of the main reasons to go to a prestigious school is because of its alumni network. Use it. Even if you went to a not-so-well-known school, there is a good chance that it has alumni working in politics who could help you.

➤ *Local politicians and their aides.* Local politicians and their aides know all sorts of people, including national politicians. They can make introductions for you. Because you are their constituent, their job is to help you, and referring you is an easy way for them to help. Don't be afraid to ask; they're used to people asking for things.

➤ *Donors.* Get a list of donors to a politician you want to work for. You may know some of them, or your family may know some of them. Donors carry special weight with politicians because they provide crucial campaign funds. The bigger the donor, the more clout he or she has with the politician.

➤ *Constituency group leaders.* As you will see as you proceed through this book, all politicians sit on top of a coalition of constituency groups, people who helped them get elected. You need to identify who these people are for the politician you want to work for. As with the donors, you may find that you or your family know some of them.

Get comfortable with asking people for things. Politics is about asking people for things—for votes, for money, for advice, for favors. Most people do not like to do that because it feels awkward, like you're imposing. But if you hope to be successful in politics, you have to master it. There are good ways and bad ways to do it, however: polite ways that make people want to deal with you, and rude ways that make them want to avoid you. Here are the good ways:

➤ *Become a natural networker.* I once worked for a politician who had three giant trays of Rolodexes with the names and telephone numbers of thousands of people he knew in government. If he needed someone to do something, he just whizzed through the Rolodex, got the number, and called. If he got only voice mail, he left a detailed message about what he wanted. That was it; no hours spent trying to locate the person, no time-consuming letters, no wasteful telephone tag—just a quick phone call. Five minutes per problem. Whammo. And he was always meeting new people and putting them into the Rolodex. Not only is the process of getting a political job usually a matter of networking, so is working in politics itself. Politics is a people-person business; personal contact is the key for getting things done. If you're not a natural networker, then you'll have to make yourself into one. Otherwise, politics is going to be a tough road for you. A lot of people who are interested in policy issues are not natural networkers but can train themselves to be adequate ones.

The best time to start building a network is long before you start looking for a job or for help once in the job. Meeting people, doing little favors for them, and staying in touch are the keys, and this can all happen in a relaxed, friendly manner. Look for ways to meet people, eventually to meet people in the area you want to work in. Parties, meetings, and get-togethers can all provide such chances. The more you do it, the more people you will meet. Keep their names, titles, addresses, phone numbers and e-mails in a handy database for future reference.

How much you widen the circle depends on how social you are. Clearly, get-togethers of people working in your area of interest are the most important to your career. But you never know where you might find a useful contact; often a purely social setting, completely outside a professional one, can lead to a valuable contact later because that person happens to know someone in politics.

In these networking settings, you should never ask for anything upon first meeting a person; you just develop a rapport. But you need to leave a clear, favorable impression. When you first meet someone, say what you're interested in and what your skills are, but don't ask for a job or a favor. Try to get the names of other people to talk to, other names you can add to the network. Often it is these other referrals that lead to a job or to help once you are in a job.

➤ *Make a favorable impression and keep it fresh.* You want people to remember you as an interesting, upbeat, competent, and helpful person who is fun to be around. Let's face it, that way, they are much more likely to recommend you to someone else than if you come across as negative and scheming. And to make sure they remember you, when you first meet them you want to give them little anecdotes, or quotes—sound bites, if you will—that are easy to remember you by. Then, every few months, freshen the acquaintance with a contact of some sort—a handwritten note, a post card, an e-mail, a phone call. At first you just exchange pleasantries. As you get to know each other better, you can discuss more personal things, such as the area you'd like to work in or a specific problem that you're trying to solve. You can ask for advice. People like to be asked for their advice; they'll want to help you if they like you.

➤ *Make it a two-way street.* People don't want to feel as if they are being used, so when you network, it's as important to think about what you can do for them as what they can do for you. In fact, you should always be thinking about doing little favors for people because you never know when that person may be in a position to do you a favor later. And always thank people for the favors they do for you. In fact, it may even behoove you to thank them disproportionately for what they've done. They have to leave each contact with you thinking that it was a pleasant experience and looking forward to dealing with you again.

These are the ways that you can find out about jobs and even get interviews for them. If you have a good network, people will let you know when they hear about a job opening. They may even help you get an interview or write a recommendation for you. But these networking skills are also necessary once you're in the job, because the better your network is, the more you will be able to get done.

If you are by nature not a particularly sociable person, you may look at all of this networking as a lot of effort. But think of it as building your effectiveness, an investment in your skill set—and networking is the ultimate skill set in politics.

Applying for the Job

Once you have identified a job you would like, here are some pointers about how to apply for it.

➤ *Get your foot in the door.* If you are applying for your first political job, chances are you will not get the one you would ideally like—because others will be more qualified than you, will have paid their dues longer than you have. So you may have to settle for something else first and work your way up. Be optimistic, enthusiastic, and upbeat, no matter what the assignment. Many political jobs promote from within. But first, you have to prove that you can be trusted; you have to stand out. Take on as much responsibility as you can handle while still doing an outstanding job. You may even want to volunteer full-time initially if you think it could lead to a really great job. Be willing to work extra hours. If you are competent and show this extra level of interest, it won't be long before you are noticed.

➤ *But avoid bad jobs.* As in any profession or job market, there are some bad jobs on Capitol Hill, in the executive branch, and everywhere else, and you need to be able to spot them. Here's how. Look for high turnover among staff. That is usually the first sign that something is wrong, that there may be a controversial or personally troubled boss who is impossible to work for. Ask the people in your network what they know about the office in question. What kind of reputation does the boss have? Do colleagues consider the boss too eccentric, personally abusive? Are the senior aides power-hungry maniacs and too hard to work for? Does the office have a reputation of being inept? What are the hours like? Many political jobs have long hours, but some are 24/7. The aides in the office who are interviewing you may not tell you these things if they are anxious to hire you to take some of their workload.

➤ *Forget the resume drop.* The uninitiated often feel that sending out hundreds of unsolicited resumes to politicians is a good way to search for a job. But people in politics get thousands of resumes, and they usually don't pay much attention to them. The resume is not the most important way to get an interview for a job; the personal referral is. The resume comes later.

➤ *Find your "rabbi."* Whether applying for a position in a campaign that you think might lead to a job possibility later or actually applying for that job now, you have to come recommended. Who will vouch for you, or, as they say in New York, "Who is your rabbi?" Often you can't even get in the door to interview for the job without this recommendation. A "rabbi" is not just someone who knows your technical job competency—a teacher, an employer, for example—although that kind of recommendation is also important. A "rabbi" is a political mentor—someone who is politically connected to the politician in question and whose recommendation is valuable because it means you have been screened for political sensitivity as well as job competency. Rabbis benefit from having their people "on the inside"—that's one way they get information and have influence. Politicians want to cultivate relationships with rabbis, and hiring their people is a way of doing it.

The most logical rabbi is your local representative or senator. How do you get a recommendation from such an august person? You impress the aides. In your "Preparing for the Job" phase, you figure out ways you can do little favors for the congressional office or the senator's office. For instance, they often need help putting on events, press conferences, fund-raisers, hearings back home—that sort of thing. You can volunteer to help out with those and impress the aides by doing a really good job. Don't worry about impressing the representative or senator. He or she will hear from the aides how good you were.

Of course, the more important the rabbi's connection with the politician you want to work for, the better it is for you. An important member of Congress who has business with another member of Congress or a cabinet secretary or even a president is going to carry a lot of weight. But big donors can also be good rabbis. So can the heads of constituency groups integral to the politician's election. Letters of recommendation are one way a rabbi can weigh in, but best of all is getting that rabbi to pick up the telephone and call the politician.

➤ *Sell yourself.* You have to become adept at explaining precisely what job you want and precisely what skills you have and how they can help the person you're applying to. This means both in written form, through a resume and cover letter, and verbally in an interview. It's harder for people to help you if you don't have a specific job in mind. Your resume has to tell a story that supports your claims—education, jobs, accomplishments that buttress your claim of possessing a set of valuable skills.

Exactly how the resume is written is not as important as the fact that it clearly and succinctly highlights useful skills. However, you should keep in mind some resume basics. Be honest with your experience. If not, you can seriously undermine your credibility. Avoid all personal pronouns, and minimize articles (i.e., "an," "a," "the"). Make absolutely sure the document has no spelling, grammatical, or punctuation mistakes—check it over and over, and then get at least one other detail-oriented person to check it, too. It should have a clean, balanced, consistent, and professional look. A traditional reverse chronological format, where you account for each year of work, is best. Functional resumes arouse suspicions; the reader wonders what has been left out and why. You don't have to include everything you've ever done, but now is not the time to be modest, either. In addition to the typical Education and Professional/Work Experience categories, you can include sections such as Volunteer or Leadership Experience, Computer Skills, and Language Skills. Volunteer and other unpaid experiences can be very important in getting a political job because they show your dedication and commitment to a cause. Keep thinking about the reader's self-interest: What skills do you possess that will help the office you are applying to?

When referencing your professional experience, you should include five elements for each entry—title, organization, location, dates, and description—but not necessarily in that order. When describing what you did, use active verbs that communicate your skills, such as "organize," "manage," "coordinate," and "research." Give examples from your experience that illustrate how your skills are relevant for the job you want. Be concise; many readers will just scan the resume, so you want the relevant skills to jump out. Remember, though: a resume may help you get an interview, but it won't get you the job. To get the job, you have to impress people in interviews.

➤ *Give a strong interview.* In interviews, you have to be polite, but come to the point quickly. You have to show that you've cared enough to research the job and know exactly how your skills can help out. You cannot be a shrinking violet. Chances are, you'll have competition for the job, and one of the key determinants as to who will get it will be how adept you are at oral presentation. In the interview, you realistically have about five minutes to make your case. After that, the interviewer takes control of the interview.

➤ *Prepare for the final interview.* Once you have interviewed with the aides, and the rabbis have begun to weigh in, you may get into the final round to be interviewed by the boss—the representative, the senator, the cabinet secretary, one of the president's chief assistants, or possibly even the president. Once you get to this point, you can be confident that the aides like you; they feel that any of the people in the final round can do the job, that not only are your credentials good but that they like you as a person. When you see the boss, he or she will have your resume, as well as the recommendations from your rabbis. But the boss won't be paying as much attention to those items as to trying to size you up as a person. At that point, it's all about personal chemistry. Find out beforehand what the boss likes and dislikes. Talk to the aides and the rabbis. Show the boss that he or she will like working with you.

➤ *Keep trying.* If you don't get the job, try to figure out why, so you can learn from the experience. Keep in touch with the aides; maybe they'll know of other jobs later that you can get. Keep building the network.

Once on the Job

Once you've gotten a job, you want to enhance your chances for getting the next job. You need to cement your relationship with your present employer by getting as much "face time" as you can. But you also want to be known to as wide a range of players as possible, so that they will be impressed by working with you and offer you even better jobs later. If all goes well, you will never have to look for a job again—you'll be asked. What that means, though, is that you get a bye into the final round of the competition; it's between you and a handful of others. From there on, you have to sell yourself better than your competition does. That's when rabbis become important again. So stay in touch with them, and add new ones to the list.

This, I believe, is one of the essential dynamics in politics—the networking, getting to know people, convincing them that you can do things for them and convincing them to do things for you. Learn how to do this well, and you will go far. But along the way, it helps to know a lot of other things, too. That is what the rest of this book is about.

2

WORKING FOR POLITICIANS

Understanding what motivates your boss will increase your chances of success. More important, it will probably be a big factor in determining who you want to work for—who you can learn the most from and who can be your mentor in both the short and long term. There are many different ways to dissect politicians. This chapter will consider a few of the most obvious ones: political party affiliation, legislative or executive branch, and personality type.

Political Party Affiliation

Two key factors in working for a politician are what party he or she belongs to and what his or her position is on the issues of the day. What the parties stand for is explained in detail in Chapter 3, and you need to decide how your beliefs fit in. Some time ago, I received the following in a letter from a college classmate that underscores the need to be honest with yourself about this:

> I am tired of the X Party. I became an X out of sheer opportunism in the first place (I figured there was more room at the top, more chance to have an impact on policy, etc.). Opportunities and desire for self-aggrandizement, however, are not enough to sustain anyone in politics. Far better to follow one's heart and ideals.

This doesn't mean becoming an ineffectual intellectual. One has to get in the gutter and fight it out.

Legislative versus Executive Role

In the U.S. political system, there are essentially two political roles: legislative and executive. Often the former is used as a stepping stone to the latter, for both the principal and staff. Experience with the former is also good preparation for the latter because executives throughout our system always have to work with legislative bodies, whether it be city mayors working with city councils, governors working with state representatives, or presidents working with U.S. representatives. But the nature of a legislator's work is different from an executive's, and staffers will probably want to consider this in choosing the person to work for.

LEGISLATIVE ROLES

The main job of legislators and their assistants is to consider legislative proposals submitted by the executive. As Woodrow Wilson once put it, speaking of the federal system, "The president proposes, Congress disposes." Hence, legislators usually must act in concert with many other legislators, not by themselves. They are part of a majority or a minority of votes on any given issue. Although they are nominally concerned with the national interest, realistically they are usually more concerned with their district's interest or their state's interest, a much more narrow concern than that of the president.

A secondary role of most legislatures, including Congress, is oversight, ensuring that government programs are doing what they are supposed to do. For that reason, Congress often holds hearings or investigations into what the government is doing. But Congress is not ultimately responsible for the running of the entire government; the president is. Congress only looks over the president's shoulder when it chooses, and certainly not on all programs at all times—it doesn't have sufficient staff for that.

EXECUTIVE ROLE

Executives, such as presidents and governors, are responsible for formulating and submitting proposals to the legislature—and then lobbying public opinion and the legislators to get them passed. A president draws on the huge national prestige of being the only official elected by the whole nation to accomplish this. A president also has far more support staff than Congress—thousands of political appointees commanding hundreds of thousands of civil servants.

Personality Type: Career Politician

There are career politicians in both parties. These people connect well with voters because they are inwardly driven to be the center of attention and therefore win personal validation. What seems to drive them is the feeling that there is always somebody else they need to convince, someone else's approval they can get, someone else's vote they can win. The more often they can campaign, the more often they feed the need to connect with people and feel validated. They revel in the process and become expert in it—becoming "political animals." This may be on top of being a "policy wonk," possessing a deep, analytical mind and interest in policy issues. But it may not be. The interest in the political process may be all there is, the only motive. Politicians of this sort are constantly seeking public adulation and risking public rejection. In this sense, they are similar to actors, artists, sports stars, and other public performers who depend on public attention and adulation. They crave the applause.

Most of us feel the need to be validated in some way. But most of us are not willing to choose the increasingly undignified way in which politicians have to do it—constantly asking people to vote for them to prove they are loved and putting up with humiliations, invasions of privacy, and limitations on family life. Career politicians may know nothing else or care about nothing else. They start running for something as soon as they can and are more willing than most to endure the hardships.

To spend your entire life doing what it takes to get elected and then working your way up the ladder to even higher office usually results in a very restricting, narrow life. For these types of politicians, success in politics may be all they have. So for them, losing an election can be even more devastating because, for these people, the reverse of getting validation through winning an election is the sense of rejection caused by losing one, the sense of deep hurt and depression that it can cause. They will work frantically to avoid this.

Paranoids Live Longer

Another thing to understand about politicians is that in a way they are usually quite insecure people. That is, they are constantly surrounded by political enemies or, at least, critics. They must be vigilant to determine where the next attack is coming from and to head it off. So they are constantly probing, testing, asking, and listening. The ones who do this the best generally stay in office the longest.

What the Lives of Politicians Are Like

When I was first exposed to politicians and politics, I developed what I call the "dynamo theory." That is, many politicians are human dynamos of energy, constantly in action. They always have to be working on something. Sometimes it even seems that the sheer need to be moving fast is more important than deciding what to commit all that energy toward. Shrewd constituents and lobbyists pick up on this and take advantage of it, realizing that they can help set the agenda, hitch their cause to the dynamo, so to speak, and watch the sparks fly. They even realize that it is in their best interest to place people from their sphere of influence on a politician's staff to help focus the dynamo.

Most politicians' lives are fast paced and hectic. It takes a lot of energy on the part of a staff person to keep up—or more accurately, to stay ahead, to anticipate. The higher the job politicians hold, the more they exist in a world of minute-by-minute schedules, limited time, aides, briefings, scripts, public events, photo opportunities, fund-raisers—and entreaties for special consideration. When you work for such a person, there is the distinct possibility of getting "event whiplash," a kind of fatigue from too many really interesting things happening too quickly. The following are some of the reasons for this, some of the recurring themes in a politician's daily life.

EXTERNAL POLITICS

External politics means dealing with constituents who bombard a politician with requests. These requests often have to do with what I call the "doctrine of self-interest," which describes what people want from government and which comes in three parts:

> *Most people are motivated by short-term economic gain.* This is because they are beset by money problems. According to the most recent census, the median income for a family of 3.17 people in this country in 1999 was $48,950. That comes to about $15,400 per person and means that half the country is doing worse than that.

In 1972 it was $41,710, adjusted for inflation. So things haven't gotten a whole lot better in almost three decades; huge numbers of Americans have money problems. Now, of course, there are plenty of other people, much more well off, who are also concerned about money. This second group is usually more adept in pressing its case than the first group. One of the quintessential dilemmas of politics is determining how much help you are going to give to the first group and how much to the second group.

➤ *Politics is doing well if it can get people to think about their own long-term economic gain.* This means getting them to make short-term sacrifices in order to obtain long-term benefits.

➤ *Politics is doing extremely well if it can ever get people to think about other people's long-term economic gain.* This is usually a pretty hard sell.

INTERNAL POLITICS

Internal politics means dealing with other politicians. In the federal system, this includes members of Congress and their aides, the president and White House aides, administration appointees, and party officials. It means building coalitions with them, negotiating with them, and reaching compromises with them. To be good at this takes time and patience, among other things.

DEALING WITH THE MEDIA

In essence, politicians try to manage the news so that it reflects favorably on them. They want a good story, preferably with a color photo, all above the fold. The media, on the other hand, wants to catch politicians doing something wrong because that's what sells newspapers. This "gotcha" journalism is essentially a reaction to the Vietnam/Watergate era. With modern technology, the news cycle has sped up. It is now possible to spread a story around the world in a day, which means that politicians have to be quick to react in the same news cycle and get their rebuttal out—"rapid response." In addition, modern politicians need the media to communicate with voters more than in the past. First, voters have access to many more media sources than they did even 10 years ago. Second, politicians cannot depend on a party machine to interpret them to the voters the way they once could. All of this means that media relations (especially looking good on television) are an extremely important part of a politician's life.

RAISING MONEY

Up until even about a generation ago, it used to be that politicians could depend on their parties to raise money for them and provide campaign workers to run their campaigns. Nowadays, with the party structure not as strong as it once was, politicians need to do more on their own. And with costly television ads being the best way to reach the voters, politicians are more and more occupied with raising money for their (media) campaigns. Not only does this mean constantly organizing and attending fund raising events, it means dealing with the requests of the people who give the money.

PERSONAL ADVANCEMENT

Most politicians are interested in advancing to more powerful positions, whether it be within the branch of government they are currently in or moving to a higher office. This means that they are often engaged in extracurricular activities, activities not part of their immediate job descriptions, designed to help them move up. This can include doing favors for other people, such as raising money or speaking on their behalf, or getting a lot of national media attention by organizing media events.

FINDING FAMILY TIME

Unfortunately, working in Washington is not always conducive to family life, especially if you are an elected politician. On top of the burden of work is the problem of having to be in Washington to vote but also back home in your district or state to take care of constituent needs. Most representatives and senators have two residences, one in Washington and one back home. They belong to the "Tuesday/Thursday club," meaning that they work in Washington from Tuesday through Thursday (when votes are usually scheduled) and then fly home for Friday through Monday. It used to be that representatives or senators who were married would have their families stay with them in Washington and would fly back home alone on the weekend. But today, more and more have opted to keep their family at home and commute to Washington during the week. Neither case leaves much time for family life, meaning that most members of Congress are adamant about spending quality time with their families. Close observers also feel that having members live in their districts and commute to Washington makes for a more partisan Congress because they are not in Washington enough to get to know each other as human beings.

In dealing with external and internal politics, the media, raising money, personal advancement, and even finding family time, politicians often use tactics such as the following.

BARGAINING

Bargaining refers to the willingness to compromise, on the grounds that half a loaf is better than no loaf. Most politicians are reluctant to get up from the negotiating table without some sort of deal because it makes them look ineffective. So they engage in a give and take—a tactic that upsets some of their most zealous supporters who think that settling for anything less than total victory is a sellout.

CO-OPTING PEOPLE AND ISSUES

Often the best way to move forward is to involve complainers in the solution—put them on a committee to deal with it, seek their opinion. That way, they can no longer complain because now they are part of what they were complaining about. President Lyndon Johnson used to describe this as "Better to have 'em in the tent pissing out than outside the tent pissing in." Adopting issues from the opposition is another way of undercutting criticism.

BEING A SYMPATHETIC LISTENER

Good politicians come across as sympathetic listeners. They cultivate the ability to make whoever is talking to them at the moment feel like the most important person in the world. They do this by looking intently at the person and asking a question or two to show they are engaged.

PUTTING YOURSELF IN OTHER PEOPLE'S SHOES

Being able to determine exactly what other people want and why they want it takes skill. Often what they want is not what they tell you they want. Being able to look at something from their point of view—often an emotional point of view—is a valuable skill.

NEVER SAYING NO

People hate to hear an outright "no." Thus, politicians often function as lawyers, representing their constituents' interests before someone else who will make the final decision. If a "no" must be said, they try to get someone else to say it, so they don't have to say it themselves.

BOUNCING BACK

Churchill once said that success was going from defeat to defeat "without loss of enthusiasm." Good politicians do this because they instinctively know the truth of the Greek philosopher Epictetus' maxim: "Man is not disturbed by events, but by his opinion of the events." In other words, something may have happened, but whether it is perceived as good or bad is often in the eye of the beholder. The eye of the beholder can be influenced by spin. If you cast the event in positive terms, often other people will accept it. Critics sometimes call this "having no shame," something politicians are accused of all the time.

COMPARTMENTALIZING

In politics, as in any fast-paced activity, there are bound to be plenty of good times and plenty of bad times. The danger is in always being obsessed with the bad times, which makes the experience no fun at all. You need to cultivate the ability to really enjoy the good times and then quickly switch gears to deal with the bad times—and back again.

DEALING ON THE EMOTIONAL LEVEL

Politicians realize that often the best way to attract the voters is by appealing to their emotions rather than their brains—to get the voters to feel rather than think. One needs to find simple, impressionistic issues that appeal to attitudes and create an emotional reaction rather than a conscious thought.

SIMPLIFYING ISSUES AND USING SYMBOLS TO DESCRIBE THEM

Most good politicians and their staffs believe that whenever they engage in lengthy, complex explanations, they have probably already lost the argument. They feel that voters often don't have the time or the sophistication to follow convoluted reasoning and will think politicians are trying to con them when they engage in it (and sometimes the voters are right). Better to make it simple, and the best way to do that is to use something well known to symbolize it, such as phrases like "corporate welfare" or "throwing money at the problem." The media often latch onto these sound bytes.

USING HUMOR

Good politicians make jokes to simplify issues and gain attention for their point of view. Take Representative Barney Frank's quip, "This bill is the legislative equivalent of crack. It yields a short-term high but does long-term damage to the system and it's expensive to boot," or septuagenarian Ronald Reagan debating a much younger Walter Mondale and defusing critics who thought he was too old to be president by saying, "I will not make age an issue in this campaign. I am not going to exploit for political purposes my opponent's youth and inexperience."

What Is a Good Staffer?

Now that you have some feel for the world of the politician, what are the attributes of the successful staff member? This question is independent of what technical knowledge the staffer may need in addition to the political skills mentioned here. Such technical skills will likely have to be considerable. On top of them, the successful staffer will need to do the following:

➤ *Become a student of power.* You need to become expert at determining who has the power to get things done, how they exercise that power, and how you can tap into it. It's not always the person with the title of the top officeholder, not always the "general." The person with the title may be in a position to accumulate and exercise power but doesn't know how to do it or doesn't care to do it. On the other hand, someone with a lesser title, a "colonel," let us say, may have worked out a way to get the power. Furthermore, he or she may use it in subtle or indirect ways, and you need to figure that out. You need to cultivate the "sergeants," too. Sergeants are the clerks and secretaries who work for the high-ranking officers. They often have the ability to act on behalf of their bosses and to make your life a lot easier—or, if you cross them, a lot harder. They don't like to be taken for granted. Learn the first names of the sergeants, and be nice to them.

➤ *Be good at gauging your boss's political needs.* A lot is contained in this sentence, involving a keen understanding of points considered earlier in the previous section "What the Lives of Politicians Are Like." Essentially, you need to cultivate the ability to know what is going to make your boss look good or bad to potential supporters.

➤ *Anticipate the boss's needs.* Be able to anticipate what the boss is going to need and present it before he or she starts worrying about it.

➤ *Avoid surprises.* This means constantly keeping the political antennae up in order to glean information and to forewarn the boss about any eventuality, good or bad.

➤ *Maintain confidentiality.* In general, you owe it to your boss not to tell tales out of school, and you should aim to be known as the person who knows everything but leaks nothing. Now, having said that, it is also true in Washington that a nice controlled leak is sometimes the best way to make an announcement. But that is only seeming to tell a tale out of school, when in reality it's all been carefully orchestrated with the boss's welfare in mind.

➤ *Appreciate the chain of command.* When something goes wrong, there is the temptation to take your complaint straight to the boss, but this is improper staff etiquette. Instead, you are expected to take it up the chain of command. If you don't, the people you circumvent will resent you. The best policy is usually to make an honest attempt at dealing with the problem through the chain of command first. Only after you have made a good faith effort to do that are you justified in taking it to the boss.

➤ *Know how to present bad news and good news.* Politicians may say that they always want the unvarnished truth. But this can easily lead to their being overwhelmed by bad news—and wanting to shoot the messenger. Maintaining self-confidence is key to success in politics (as it is in many areas), but Washington is full of assaults on self-confidence such as demoralizing newspaper and television reports, every day, day after day. The temptation is to stop looking at them. On the other hand, telling bosses just the good news risks isolating them from reality. Basically, you report all the good news and only the bad news they absolutely must hear now. Try to put out fires yourself before they rise to the level of needing the boss's attention.

➤ *Be on the lookout for ways to get your boss good publicity.* Politicians usually want to remain in the pubic eye because it helps them get reelected and even run for higher office later. Thus, one of the ongoing jobs for all politicians' aides is to generate favorable press for the boss. Activities that could get in the press include problems solved, grants obtained, or visits to some part of the congressional district, state, or country.

➤ *Be a good oral briefer.* Know your stuff so well that you can give quick, accurate, verbal answers, with the important information up front. Busy elected officials can't give you much time to make your point. They look to shorthand explanations and validators. What's the bottom line?

What do their friends think about the matter? How do the organizations they know rate it?

➤ *Be a concise memo writer.* Written memos often take too long, and verbal briefs are better. But if you need to write a memo, make it short and use newspaper style, with the important things up front and the less important things either lower down or in an attachment, because they may not get read. Confine the memo to what the boss really has to know. Use short paragraphs and headers to break up the text.

➤ *Return phone calls promptly.* Even if you do not have a final answer for someone calling for your boss's attention, you need to get back to that person promptly, even if it is with an interim response. If you can't call, get someone else to do it for you.

➤ *Don't procrastinate.* In most cases, it's better to deal with an assignment right away, even if you were given no specific time frame for accomplishing it. In politics, no specific time frame means "now." Putting off an assignment will (1) probably disappoint the boss and (2) mean that you will have to handle it during a time when more things have piled up and you have even less time to deal with it. Dealing with it quickly often means having good instincts and being able to whip through your Rolodex to get the number of the right person you can call for help.

➤ *Be outwardly optimistic.* The last thing a busy office wants is a naysayer, someone who constantly complains and looks for ways to do only the minimum amount of work. What they want is someone who is always eager and willing to help no matter how hard the job, someone who looks for ways to get things done, rather than reasons they cannot be done. Someone who makes their lives easier, not harder. By the same token, a busy office is not going to be impressed by someone who panics all the time. Bad things will crop up, but first of all, there are usually ways of handling them. Second, showing panic scares everybody else in the office, including the boss, and makes them less confident in the staffer's ability to do the job. This does not mean that you should lie about your abilities to do an assignment—the only thing worse than complaining is an embarrassing failure. But think very carefully before complaining.

➤ *Be careful whom and how you criticize.* Young people are often taught in school to participate in public discussions, voicing their opinions and criticisms freely. In one sense this is good: they need to have opinions on things. But what they may not realize is that if they do this in political jobs, it can hurt them badly. You have to weigh the egos and interests of the people involved in the discussion. If you are frequently critical of others, you may not only alienate them, you may also alienate onlookers who fear you might criticize them later. One rule of thumb is praise in public, criticize in private. But in politics, one has to be even more circumspect than that. For example, if you praise people publicly and it then turns out that they are wrong, you have gone on record as having shown a lack of judgment. And although criticism in private is certainly better than criticism in public, even private criticism is often resented. Criticism behind someone's back is also bad because the listeners will fear that you will criticize them later behind their backs.

➤ *Be a creator and collector of chits.* If the key to success in Washington is building relationships, then the key to building relationships is "chits," as the late Republican operative Lee Atwater used to put it. A chit is a favor. If you do a favor for someone, that person technically owes you a favor in return, a chit. The best favors are the ones that are done when they are not needed, when you didn't have to do it. You never know where chits are going to go, or from whom you can call them in, so it is best to place them everywhere.

➤ *Be anonymous to the public and the press, but not to your boss.* A good aide is expected to give all the credit for an achievement to the boss. But an aide should also make sure the boss knows the work the aide has done; a busy boss may not realize it. So the aide tactfully needs to find a way to make sure the boss knows.

➤ *Be ready to work long hours.* Most political jobs require long hours. Part of the reason is that a lot needs to be done. But another reason is that it is often difficult to measure or quantify a work product in politics, so working long hours is used as a substitute for gauging a staffer's abilities. People will probably notice the hours you put in, and word will get around. Furthermore, often the most interesting things start to happen after normal work hours, when the pace slows down a bit. At those times, you can often get more face time with the boss, when he or she kicks back and starts telling you really interesting things.

➤ *Deal in ethically gray areas with integrity.* The reason most people don't like politics is because they think it is sleazy, that all politicians lie, take bribes, make unseemly compromises, and care only about themselves. The real truth is more complicated, but the bottom line is that even if a politician is honest—and most are—most politicians and their staffs will probably be confronted by ethically gray matters from time to time. Examples are requests for special consideration from someone whose case is weak, offers of campaign contributions in exchange for doing a favor, or an invitation to "horse trade," that is, support someone else's position even though it has little merit because doing so will get you that person's vote later for one of your pet projects. In most of these instances, political pressures will dictate that you have to do something with these requests; you cannot just walk away from them and still expect to maintain a valuable relationship with the person making the request.

It is the staff's job to handle these requests in such a way that nothing improper is done but that the person making the request is satisfied that something helpful was done. This often takes a lot of ingenuity. Sometimes you can modify the request to a point where it is possible to do something helpful yet honorable. Sometimes it means doing a favor for a third party who, in turn, will then help fulfill the original request. Sometimes you can get by with an answer that is true as far as it goes but that doesn't answer questions not asked. Whatever the situation, you will be judged by how well you have advanced your boss's interests while keeping everyone else happy, including public opinion and the law.

➤ *Don't be the scapegoat.* In some cases, a politician may indicate, subtly or otherwise, that he or she wants nothing to do with certain requests but that it's all right for staff to handle them as long as the boss can maintain deniability, that is, be able to claim no knowledge of the request and what was done with it. Thus, if something goes wrong later, the politician can report that a "rogue aide," acting totally alone and unauthorized, chose to pursue the request. If you are tempted to enter into such a situation in the belief that you are being loyal to your boss and that somehow you will be rewarded for it or that some higher-up will rush in at the last moment to save you if it goes wrong, you may be mistaken. Everyone might just distance themselves from you, happy there is a scapegoat they can point to. You have to protect your own reputation; you can't rely on others to do it.

➤ *Have something else you can do if you are out of office.* Working for elected officials means that you could lose your job abruptly for a variety of reasons. Your boss could lose an election. Or you may decide that you've had enough of politics for a while, that it's taking too great a toll on you and your family. Being able to walk away from it gives you a lot more freedom. That's one reason a lot of staffers are lawyers or political consultants or teachers or run businesses that they can return to.

➤ *Have a good sense of humor.* Politics can be pretty intense, and it can grind you down. A good laugh is an excellent antidote, and the staff person who can create one is a prized asset. But you need to know how to do it, walking the fine line between ridiculing an absurdity and offending someone's sensibilities.

➤ *Start as a reporter; end as an advisor.* A politician is likely to have two kinds of assistants, those who round up facts and a smaller number who interpret the facts and give political advice based on those facts. Although the latter jobs are the most interesting and best paying, they are also the hardest to get. It is much easier to start your career in the reportorial role.

➤ *Guard your individuality—and your health.* For some aides, there may come a time when the work is so interesting that they can't get enough of it—but it is killing them. They have to realize that when that happens, it is time to call it quits, maybe even only after a year or two. Politicians instinctively look for one overriding trait in aides: concern for boss more than self. They know that the aide who is constantly thinking about his or her own gain is not as likely to come through in the crunch. For example, some politicians want aides who will be at their beck and call literally at all hours of the day and night regardless of whether they have families or other responsibilities. In essence, they are looking for subservience—aides who will surrender their personalities, their individualities, their pride, their time, and their interests—aides they can dominate. They entice these aides with interesting work and a chance to be part of history—and with a constant reminder that the aides owe everything to the boss. These kinds of bosses can actually be very charismatic and exciting to work for. But the toll on your body and your psyche can mount. If you can structure your life so you can eat right, exercise, and get enough sleep—keep your body in tip-top shape—you prolong the time you can deal with all of this. But if you are also making impossible demands on your body—chronically getting too little sleep and exercise, smoking and drinking a lot—you may be headed for a blowup.

Best Preparation for Political Jobs

Thirty years ago, I asked a number of people what they thought the best preparation was for working in politics. I remember two of the replies in particular. One was from the noted historian Henry Steele Commager. I thought maybe he'd say history, economics, government, or something like that. What he said instead was character, anything that built character. His theory, after spending a lifetime studying and writing about American history, was that a person's background or profession didn't matter as long as it contributed to building character.

The other comment came from an Ivy League law school professor. I thought he'd probably extol the law as good preparation. But he answered that the best preparation for politics was learning how to get elected.

I've often thought about those two comments. Taken one way, they could be miles apart—the rogue who does anything to get elected but who is then utterly corrupt in office versus the moral giant who constantly flirts with public opprobrium in order to do the right thing and loses elections as a result. But taken another way, they could be two sides of the same coin: you have to be (or at least appear to be) of good character to get elected. The following sections will explore this dilemma, but at this point, suffice it to say that I think you need both good character and a knowledge of how to get elected.

I realize, too, that when people ask, "What is the best preparation for politics?" what they really mean is, "What is good preparation for politics, which also prepares me for earning a living?" There are many things that can prepare you for both, but there is only one that is a "required course" for someone interested in politics: campaigns.

CAMPAIGNS

Most people start their political careers by serving in campaigns. I think this makes sense regardless of what aspect of politics you specialize in later or what your profession ultimately will be. If you're going to work on a politician's staff, or as a policy advocate or lobbyist attempting to influence a politician, knowing the election process is invaluable. The next election usually drives a politician's actions, from making sure he or she votes correctly to providing great (and visible) constituency service to raising lots of money.

Learning how to get elected is generally not something you learn in school (although you can learn the mechanics of it through training sessions conducted by the two national parties). The usual route to learning about campaigns is by working in them, ideally by running one. Campaigning is usually not taught well in a college course, and you probably won't meet in the college course the people you need to know later in politics.

Learning how to get elected means finding time to work in campaigns and picking up contacts and ideas through on-the-job training. The earlier you start this process, probably as a volunteer, the better—for three reasons. First, the earlier you start, the more thorough your knowledge. Because the apprenticeship approach is a bit inefficient, it takes a while to learn everything you need to know. Second, the earlier you start, the more people you meet who can help you later, either by hiring you or working with you. And last, as in sports, the earlier you learn a skill, the more time you have to practice it and thus make it instinctive. As you rise through the ranks, time pressures will require you to make decisions based on instinct—and you want them to be right.

Just being in a campaign isn't enough. You have to distinguish yourself by doing well. Campaigns are full of people out for a lark, groupies just looking for something to do. You have to stand out, by becoming an indispensable person. When you are young and just starting out, that simply means being around a lot and willing to help with any menial job, being known as a reliable, loyal, dependable worker—a go-to person. When you are older, though, it has to be by the quality of your advice on critical matters.

How do you get into a campaign? If it's your first one, and you have no one to pull strings for you, you can begin as a volunteer. You start out with the grunt work—"lick 'em and stick 'em" (stuffing envelopes), handing out "lit" (campaign brochures) on street corners or door to door, phone canvassing, and putting up yard signs. And you do a great job at it. At the end of the normal workday, the real opportunities arise. That's when most of the others have gone home and when you are more likely to catch the eye of the people who are higher up in the campaign and get a chance to do something for them and work your way up the ladder. In later campaigns, you can enter at higher levels because you will have friends who will recommend you or hire you.

If you really want to work in politics, you may have to decide whether to temporarily drop out of school to be in a campaign. It's that big of an opportunity. However, although campaigns teach you how to get elected, they lead directly to a profession for only a few people, the campaign consultants who make a career of getting candidates elected to office. These people, perhaps after having worked in different political jobs, find campaigning the most interesting and exciting of all. They consider the policy area to be boring and predictable compared with the swashbuckling nature of running campaigns. But more people look at campaigning as a means to an end, something they're willing to do only once, to get a job with the politician after the election.

SCHOOL

What do you do once you get into office? Politics is full of demagogues and rascals who know how to get elected. But then what do they do? What's the best preparation for governing? And what happens if you don't want to campaign for the rest of your life?

That's where college and graduate education come in. Note in the case studies in Chapter 8 that almost all the subjects have college degrees, and more than half have graduate degrees. Besides readying you for a profession, these degrees can be valuable training for working in politics for several reasons. If you approach it properly, school teaches you how to learn quickly and to think analytically instead of emotionally. It teaches you to see a problem's full complexity and not just the superficialities of it. But it also teaches you to get to the root of the matter and not get distracted by the details.

As I noted previously, government or political science courses do not teach you the mechanics of politics. But they do teach you some valuable background information and techniques, such as what our governmental institutions are, how they are supposed to interact, on paper at least, and how one can frequently use the analytical techniques of social scientists to examine what these institutions do. Prestigious universities support political scientists who document an increasing number of the connections between politics and other disciplines, as well as the interactions between political actors in our democracy. More and more, social scientists and political scientists are helping to explain political processes and policy outcomes. Increasingly, they can explain not only the details and ramifications of an outcome but why these things happened. It is often useful in politics to understand these findings and how to apply them.

School can also teach you many other subjects and modes of analysis that are closely related to politics and policy, such as history, economics, sociology, statistics, psychology, and the law. These are areas in which you can learn substantive subject matter that you can specialize in while working in politics and also use later. Perhaps even more important, they teach you an appreciation for specialists in those areas; in politics you need to learn how to obtain relevant information from specialists quickly and put it to use.

Should you get a law degree? It is a common question; indeed, many Americans think you have to have a law degree to be in politics. The simple answer is yes, if you like the law and want to practice law. But the answer is no if all you want to do is work in a top political job, as witnessed by the fact that most people who do that do not have law degrees. It is true, of course, that certain political jobs require a law degree. But if you do not really want to practice law—and many young people with law degrees tell me that—you may do well to think about how the money and the three years it takes to get the degree could be spent obtaining skills in an area in which you really do want to work.

If you want the law degree just out of a general sense that it will make you a lot of money, you may want to consider this: there is a big discrepancy in what lawyers get paid. It's not like medical doctors who all get paid at least a fairly high salary. A lot of lawyers do not make very much. According to a survey done by the *National Law Journal* for the year 2000, at the high end is the first-year attorney at a prestigious firm, such as the Washington office of Covington and Burling, who begins earning $125,000 a year and moves up in increments to $195,000 by the eighth year.[1] A partner in the firm earns well in excess of $500,000. But look at other lawyers' salaries. A staff attorney in state legal services made between $25,000 and $70,000, depending on the region and years of experience, with the director making $38,800 to $74,000. For public interest lawyers, starting salaries ranged from $28,000 to $49,000, with top office salaries between $35,000 and $200,000. Public defenders' salaries ranged from $30,000 to $157,000 depending on where they lived and their experience.

It used to be, up through the nineteenth and early twentieth centuries, that law was the most obvious fit for someone preparing both for a profession and for politics. Besides learning about laws, the legal profession allowed a lawyer of those days to practice public speaking, involve himself in matters that concerned everyday citizens, and thus deal with the same people he would call upon to vote for him later. But today, there are many other fields that serve as well as the law does—such as teaching (often history or economics), business, and the communications industry, particularly television and radio—and preparation for them is also good preparation for politics.

On top of those fields, there are many issue areas in which it is possible to make a career as a policy analyst in either politics or the private sector, such as arms control, energy policy, health care, and various environmental issues. In fact, for almost any public policy issue you can imagine, there is probably a Washington think tank or lobbying group that you can work for if you decide to stop working for politicians. Some of them are listed in Chapter 7. You could also teach some of these issues at a school or college if you want to move out of the Washington area.

In addition to the aforementioned academic subjects, training in public speaking also provides good preparation for politics. The ability to stand before a crowd and speak off the cuff earnestly and compellingly without distracting quirks is a highly desirable skill.

CHARACTER

Now let's get back to character and the notion that the best preparation for politics is anything that builds good character. This is very important; people desperately want their leaders to exhibit good character. But oftentimes, people don't realize that good character in public life is more complex than it is in their private dealings. When people hear the words "good character," they think of good moral or ethical qualities, such as honesty and courage and loyalty. To them, good character means standing up for what you believe in no matter what, always telling the truth, and being loyal.

"Stand up for what you believe in." This doesn't say anything about the ability to compromise, which is so important in politics, or the ability to see contentious matters from another person's point of view—to understand the art of the possible and accept that achieving something is usually better than achieving nothing. Should a politician of "good character," such as Woodrow Wilson, have sunk U.S. involvement in the League of Nations because he wasn't willing to compromise with the U.S. Senate? Is that good character? Was that in the best interest of the United States or the world?

"Always tell the truth." What do you do when the people don't want to hear the truth? Time and again, people say they want more generous government benefits (Social Security or Medicare, for example), but they don't want to pay for them with higher taxes. They are saying to the politician, in effect: If you tell us the truth, that we have to choose between one or the other, we'll vote you out of office and put in that other guy (or gal) over there who says we can have both. What's a politician and the staff supposed to do? Did Franklin Roosevelt exhibit bad character when running for reelection in 1940 when he said he would not send American boys to war and then ultimately did so?

"Loyalty." In public life, there is the problem of conflicting loyalties— loyalty to a boss versus loyalty to the boss's constituents, versus loyalty to the country, perhaps even versus loyalty to humanity. Suppose a boss asks a staffer to engage in an activity that violates a loyalty to one of these in order to be true to the others? What's the proper way out?

My point is that these situations are so complex that it is not possible to make blanket statements about the best way to deal with them. At what point is one set of principles superceded by another because it is in the "greater good"? When does complexity (say, in the tax code) that leads to fairness because it recognizes differences between groups of people become so complicated that ordinary people cannot understand the system and thus no longer have faith in it?

In sum, when we speak of building character as being the best preparation for politics, I think we are talking about building a character that is equipped to function in the public sector, not just in the private sector. That means gaining experience in organizing and leading groups of people with divergent opinions on issues that matter to them. Opportunities for this can be hard to find for young people, but running something, such as a sports team, school newspaper, or other school group, is useful—anything that puts you in the position of having to weigh competing interests.

LOOK AT THE CASE STUDIES

Although one can make a number of general remarks about what constitutes good preparation for political jobs, it is impossible to cover all of the paths available and therefore determine the best specific preparation for each and every case. However, by consulting the case studies in Chapter 8, you can begin to get a glimpse of patterns that emerge that have to do with political party affiliation, issue area, congressional or executive department, educational level, jobs people have before they get into politics, and so on. You will see there is no one way; every case is different.

Internships

In this chapter's final section, I want to present some general comments about preparing for internships. Additional information about them—such as Internet addresses—is given in later chapters. Internships are a time-honored way of getting that first position—usually unpaid—in one of the political parties, Capitol Hill, the White House, the administration, and in think tanks and lobbying groups. That young people can just walk in off the street into these jobs is a wonderful symbol of how open our government is. You can begin your search for one of these internships on the Internet by using the search engine google.com and looking under "washington intern." There you will find references to many intern programs, such as The Washington Center for Internships and Academic Seminars at www.twc.edu/internships/index.htm.

For a few top interns, internships are the crucial step to getting a paying job later. But for too many, internships become a few months of drudgery that give a false impression of what working in government is really like and that do not lead anywhere. The difference is in how useful you make yourself to the staff during the internship. It's all about being able to make their lives easier, not harder. To do this, you have to determine not to be just a tourist, waiting for someone to tell you things. You have to learn the mind-set of your bosses and anticipate their needs before they even ask you—in a sense, before you even arrive in the office.

This means working hard, both during the time you are in the office and in your free time as well: reading things, studying things, and generally learning how the place works. In large measure, what people get out of internships depends on what they put into them. Right now, not enough people are getting enough out of them. More will be said about the availability of internships in succeeding chapters, but a few important generalities need to be stressed here.

Interns often arrive in Washington inadequately prepared. It's not their fault. It's just that school and the other things they have experienced as youngsters may not have primed them for what they must do in political jobs. All too often, the result is that the staff for whom they work has to spend so much time explaining things, checking up, and redoing work after the intern is done that it is simply not worth involving the intern in the first place. The staffers conclude that it is better just to do the work themselves. If this happens, the only chores staffers are going to entrust to interns are the clerical ones, such as stuffing envelopes, photocopying, and fetching documents. To break out of this syndrome, an intern should ideally be able to do the following.

➤ *Be able to write well.* If you can write well, there are many interesting chores you can do to help staffers, such as writing letters to constituents, attending hearings and meetings and writing memos summarizing what happened, summarizing bills and amendments, and writing reports (which might be turned into term papers for school credit later). Good grammar and spelling are crucial so that little editing is required. It's also important to use newspaper style as opposed to academic style. In newspaper style, the important points are put up front, with items of lesser and lesser importance put lower and lower down in the text. Short paragraphs and the liberal use of headers and bullets break up the text, making it easier to scan. By contrast, academic style, the style taught in most schools, tends to reach a conclusion only at the end, after a long and exhaustive analysis of the evidence, often in page-long paragraphs with no headers. Academic prose tends to be loaded with ponderous, multisyllabic Latinate or Greek words instead of punchy, short Anglo-Saxon ones. The result is that it takes a long time to read something written in academic style. The best way to learn newspaper style is by studying how a good newspaper, such as the *Washington Post* or *New York Times,* is written and trying to emulate that in your writing.

➤ *Know about computers and the Internet.* It's not uncommon for young interns to know more about the capabilities of computers and the Internet than senior staffers do. This can be a real in for an intern: the ability to produce information quickly by knowing how to search for it on the Internet is an important asset. If you can do this, you may find yourself quickly interacting with the top aides in an office—and being offered a paying job later.

➤ *Be dependable.* In all likelihood, you will be tested by being given little responsibilities early in an internship and then, if you do those well, being given greater responsibilities. If you blow the early ones, you may not get better ones, so it is important to take the early ones very seriously. Keep asking yourself what is expected of you, what constitutes success. It may not always be what you are told—because no one may have had the time to tell you. If it is a writing assignment, assume it has to be ready very quickly, and make sure that the spelling and grammar are right. If it is a delivery job, do it immediately. Avoid surprises. If you're in the middle of one assignment, but someone gives you a more important second one that will make you late in completing the first one, make sure you inform the person who gave you the first one. He or she is depending on you. Always be on time; or if you are delayed, be sure to phone in. Make sure the office knows how to reach you at all times. Don't go anywhere without telling someone; the office may suddenly need you and not know where to find you.

➤ *Be cheerful.* Whatever task you are given, it is important to execute it cheerfully. The worst thing to do is to sit around whining all the time that you don't like the work. Even if you think you are only doing this with other interns, word will probably get around to the senior staffers.

➤ *Be ready to overcome a huge learning curve with little help.* It is only natural to arrive for an internship expecting to be told everything you need to know to do the job. Unfortunately, that seldom happens because your potential instructors are already overworked. So you have to research the job ahead of time and prepare yourself. First, you have to know how to find the offices that you will be asked to frequent. Getting a good floor map of the building—or making one yourself—may be in order. Second, you should keep a small notebook with you at all times, so you can jot down names, phone numbers, room numbers, and other information. It needs to be quickly retrievable. You shouldn't have to be told something more than once. If you put this information down on loose scraps of paper, you will probably lose it.

➤ *Have good common sense.* This is the forerunner to good political sense. It is unrealistic to expect a youngster to have good political sense. But if an intern doesn't even have good common sense, it will discourage a staffer from wanting to work with the intern.

➤ *Be on the lookout for more interesting assignments.* On top of being able to do well at mundane chores, you will probably need to volunteer for additional assignments that are more substantive, even if this requires you to work longer hours. Often this means suggesting how you could help. It may sound silly, but the truth is, most staffers are so busy that they can't even stop to think how an intern might be able to help them.

➤ *Look for mentors.* Try to attach yourself to a staffer who is willing to invest in you so you can be of even greater help later. Look for the staffer who is willing to spend time explaining things to you. Create a two-way street with this person; in exchange for the information, you do something to make that staffer's life easier. These people can not only become your mentors, they can become your sponsors when a paying job opportunity arises in the office.

➤ *Don't overdo the questions.* You always need to be thinking about things from the staffers' point of view. If you take up too much of their time with a lot of questions or are too pushy in asking for interesting work, they will avoid you. You have to save the questions for things you cannot figure out for yourself first.

➤ *Don't be a clutch.* If staffers think that your sole purpose for being an intern is to be a "clutch"—someone who just wants to be around those in power—it will hurt you. Certainly take advantage of such opportunities when and if they are offered to you, but don't spend all day making it obvious that this is all you care about.

Note

1. *National Law Journal,* "What Lawyers Earn 2000," www.law.com/special/professionals/nlj/earn/earns_1.html (September 11, 2002).

3

POLITICAL PARTIES

Although it is true that the main political parties have lost much of the power they once had, they still are formidable actors, much more so than most people realize. In brief, the national parties raise huge sums of money for candidates, act as a home base for many professional political organizers, provide an apparatus for political communication, run a nationwide network of state parties and state activists, and generally pay for office space, phones, and all the other paraphernalia necessary for political work.

It is also true that party nominees are no longer selected in smoke-filled rooms but by the voters in direct primaries. Nor do the parties do the volume of little favors for ordinary people that they used to, such as getting them jobs. But the fact remains that the party nomination is vital for winning most general elections. This is because voter turnout on election day is at an all-time low. Only about one-half of all eligible voters actually register, and only one-half of those actually vote. Because about one-third of the country is registered Democrat and one-third is registered Republican, and they pretty much vote the straight party ticket, these party voters carry enormous weight in an election. This is the base vote assiduously courted by the parties and inherited by the party nominee. Assuming each party is able to mobilize its base voters, elections are generally decided by campaigns that best target and persuade a relatively small number of independent or swing voters.

You have to decide which team you are going to play on: Team Democrat or Team Republican. Although idealists may like to think so, there is no "Team Independent," with anything like the infrastructure the Democrats and the Republicans have. It may be true that from time to time an independent candidate can make a difference. In 1992, for example, Ross Perot did much to dramatize the need to balance the budget, and many observers feel that without Perot's candidacy, Bill Clinton would not have won the presidency. But independents don't usually win, and they don't leave behind a growing infrastructure when they leave the stage. They may be incubators for ideas that ultimately get enacted into law, but by and large they are outsiders looking in.

A law called the Hatch Act generally restricts federal officials from doing purely political work on taxpayers' time, on government property or with facilities acquired with taxpayers' dollars—telephones, computers, fax machines, e-mails. For this reason, "Hatched" officials (those covered by the Hatch Act) often use the political parties' machines for such work, take vacation time to do it, or do it after work hours (i.e., before 9:00 A.M. and after 5:00 P.M.). That's why you'll see representatives or senators and their aides traipsing from their congressional offices to the nearby Republican National Committee (RNC) and Democratic National Committee (DNC) offices or White House officials using the political faxes and computers housed in the White House Office of Political Affairs and legally paid for by one of the political parties.

What the Parties Stand For

The following is only a general description of the issues that the Republican and Democratic parties currently espouse. There can, of course, be regional variations, with Democrats in the south, for example, seeming closer to moderate Republicans in the north than to northern Democrats.

REPUBLICANS

The Republican Party was born in the immediate pre–Civil War period as an antislavery party. Its first president was Abraham Lincoln, who freed the slaves and won the Civil War, thus guaranteeing Republican dominance for the rest of the century and beyond. Republicans point out that the first African Americans elected to the U.S. House and Senate were members of the Republican Party. During the post–Civil War period, the party evolved from an antislavery party to the party of big business, which was extremely active in winning the West and generally developing the country economically through the railroad, oil, and steel industries. After dominating U.S. politics from 1865 to 1932, however, Republicans were thrown on the defensive by the Great Depression and the New Deal, which proved that pure capitalism did not work anymore and that government intervention was necessary. Republicans particularly disliked President Lyndon Johnson's attempts to expand the New Deal in the 1960s with his "Great Society" agenda of social welfare programs. And they especially abhorred Johnson's strong-arm tactics to get southerners to vote for Civil Rights legislation while appeasing Republicans on military matters. Republicans gained new southern supporters from erstwhile Democrats because of opposition to Johnson on these matters. But Republicans really got a new lease on life with Ronald Reagan. They state that he came into office with an agenda to end the Cold War and that he succeeded. Under him, Republicans mounted increasingly successful attacks on the Great Society, attacks that continue to this day. They also won huge tax cuts under Reagan, although many of the cuts had to be rescinded later because, ironically, they led to large budget deficits, something else Republicans have traditionally opposed.

Today, Republicans are strong believers in limiting government. They particularly want to reduce regulatory burdens. They oppose many governmental regulations to improve the environment, asserting that they are not based on good science and impose unnecessary costs to industry, which, in turn, have to be passed on to the consumer. Republicans often think that government costs too much, creates too much red tape, and wastes their tax dollars on programs that don't work. They feel that the federal government is dominated by workers who are Democrats and who are willing to infringe on people's independence, particularly on the independence of the major companies responsible for this country's financial well-being. The one exception is the military; many Republicans feel that the government needs to spend more money on defense in order to ensure that our foreign policy cannot be challenged. Right-wing members of the party have also been vehemently against abortion, against gun control, and against what they perceive to be the general cultural decline of the United States that they feel began in the 1960s.

Republican administrations tend to concentrate on good management, bringing in people from business—usually at a big pay cut—and trying to run government like a business, or even like the military with a strong chief of staff, strict reporting hierarchy, orderly delegation of authority, and so on. The administration of President George W. Bush, a Harvard Business School graduate, is a good example of this. Ironically, however, the presidency of Ronald Reagan, the most popular Republican president in the second half of the twentieth century, was a bit different. Reagan proved what Democrats already knew, that the presidency is more than anything about inspiring people, not just about good management. He showed that if a president gets the role of "national cheerleader" right, the voters will overlook many other shortcomings. Republicans often feel that their job is primarily to cut back government programs, make them more efficient, and clean up scandal. They believe that leadership should be more about getting people to sacrifice for long-term gains rather than simply about buying their votes with government programs that come disproportionately from Republican tax dollars.

Republicans do a better job than Democrats in cultivating their team. They are more successful in finding their activists well-paying jobs in the private sector when they are out of office and thus replenishing their bank accounts. Their voters are generally more disciplined than Democratic voters, requiring less field organization in campaigns to make sure they get to the polls. Republicans almost always raise more money than the Democrats at all levels of campaigns and rely more on high-priced television ads, extensive direct-mail programs, and political telemarketers to motivate their base voters to go to the polls. In general, supporters include industrialists, military officers, white males, traditional women, family-values advocates, southerners and westerners (but not West Coasters), members of the religious right, and gun advocates.

Typical Republican issues include the following:

> Cut the role of government, especially the federal government, and give power back to the states.
> Lower taxes.
> Spend more money on the military.
> Control Social Security and Medicare costs.
> Spend less money on foreign aid to developing countries.
> Reduce waste in welfare expenditures.
> Reform education by raising standards and increasing teacher accountability, and by using vouchers to send students to private schools.
> Promote traditional family values.
> Support the pro-life agenda.
> Appoint judges who don't legislate from the bench.

DEMOCRATS

The Democratic Party is the oldest political party still in existence anywhere in the world, with roots going back to Thomas Jefferson and Andrew

Jackson. But it was associated with the South during the Civil War and thus was generally out of power for the entire second half of the nineteenth century. The Great Depression brought it back into power, and from 1932 (election of Franklin Roosevelt) to 1968 (election of Richard Nixon), Democrats won the presidency seven out of nine times. They also dominated the House of Representatives and to a lesser extent, the Senate all the way up to 1994 (emergence of Republican Speaker of the House, Newt Gingrich).

Democrats have been trying for years with decreasing success to keep together the winning New Deal coalition of union members, minorities, and academics. Sacred cows include such "safety-net" programs as Social Security and Medicare, which are eating up an increasingly large portion of the federal budget and thus concern Republicans—and everyone else. Democrats try to find new sources of money to fund these programs, arguing that they are the true measure of civilization; Republicans say cut the programs. Democrats retort that if Republican industrialists weren't so intent on cutting taxes or increasing military expenditures so they can make even more money off arms sales, there would be more money for other programs. Democrats have always portrayed themselves as the party of the little guy, seeking to add newer and newer groups to the base coalition, groups that have been left out in the past, such as immigrants, African Americans, Hispanic Americans, environmentalists, women, and gays. Republicans criticize Democrats as preying on people's weaknesses, especially in times of adversity, and enticing them with more and more programs. Democrats respond that while Republicans talk a good game, much of it is window dressing, designed to cover up their big business agenda, the widening gap between rich and poor in this country, and their alleged general lack of concern for the average American. Democrats say that a generation of bipartisan U.S. foreign policy and former Soviet leader Michail Gorbachev had more to do with ending the Cold War than Ronald Reagan did.

Because they view government as a friend, Democrats tend to be more creative than Republicans in how they use it. They also tend to be more chaotic in how they manage it. They bring in people—often very young people for whom these jobs represent pay increases—with new ideas and manage them in a looser organizational style. The quintessential Democratic candidate believes that all politics are local, that all politics are about helping your people, doing favors for people who need help against a system that has been rigged against them for racist, sexist, and other unfair reasons. Republicans call such a candidate a demagogue.

Democrats generally do not do as good a job as Republicans at taking care of their activists in between times in office. Democrats out of office often have a tougher time finding jobs that pay as much as the ones Republicans find. Candidates and workers, therefore, usually have to be more self-sufficient. Within the DNC itself, for example, Democrats suffer from outdated computers and underfinanced mail and telephone solicitation programs compared with the RNC. There are other wide gaps between Democrats and Republicans, such as in the use of technology, media campaigns, and better-financed state parties. Other gaps include the Republicans' more sophisticated use of "free media," to shape public opinion, such as Web site message boards, talk radio shows, and online news polls.

Democrats have to worry more about getting their voters to the polls than Republicans do. Television ads and mailings are not enough. Strong field organizations, which remind and assist voters to get to the polls, can make a bigger difference for a Democratic candidate than for a Republican one, maybe making up to five points or more in the final outcome—a large amount. In general, supporters include labor unions, teachers, lawyers, minorities, women, environmentalists, academics, big-city dwellers, Hollywood actors, East and West Coasters, and students—if they vote.

Typical Democratic issues include the following:

> Keep a progressive tax system.
> Expand the safety net to include more benefits and more groups. (National health insurance and prescription drug benefits are examples.)
> Protect the environment through regulation of polluters.
> Provide tax relief to those who need it—middle- and lower-income groups—and not the wealthy.
> Advance women's rights, especially a woman's right to choose.
> Spend more money on public education.
> Cut waste in big military hardware programs.
> Support labor unions.
> Support campaign finance reform.
> Invest in alternative fuel sources.

How the Parties Are Structured

People tend to think of the Republican and Democratic parties as being single entities, but in reality, they are broken down into many different organizations.

PRESIDENTIAL LEVEL

The parent organizations for the two parties are the DNC and the RNC. Although each is interested in the fate of its party in all elections across the entire country, they generally concentrate on the presidential race and have affiliated groups that concentrate on other races. Some of these groups, which also recruit and raise money for candidates and help run their campaigns, are listed in the following sections.

HOUSE LEVEL

At the level of the House of Representatives, there are the Democratic Congressional Campaign Committee (DCCC) and the National Republican Congressional Committee (NRCC).

SENATE LEVEL

The Democratic Senatorial Campaign Committee (DSCC) and the National Republican Senatorial Committee (NRSC) operate at the Senate level.

GUBERNATORIAL LEVEL

At the state gubernatorial level, there are the Democratic Governors' Association (DGA) and the Republican Governors' Association (RGA).

STATE LEGISLATIVE LEVEL

The Democratic Legislative Campaign Committee (DLCC) and the National Republican Legislators' Association (NRLA) work at the state legislative level.

What the Parties Do

The groups described in the previous section all essentially provide the same functions for their clients, primarily fund-raising, political organizing, and communications.

FUND-RAISING

The single most important task for political parties is raising money—hundreds of millions of dollars, and this money is on top of what the candidates themselves raise and spend. Most of it is used to pay for television ads. Understandably, fund-raising offers a wide range of job opportunities in Washington as well as at the state level. Moreover, recent moves to change campaign finance laws will almost certainly increase those opportunities.

Table 3.1, derived from the Center for Responsive Politics shows how much money each of the presidential, congressional, and senatorial Democratic and Republican organizations raised and spent in the 2000 campaign cycle (these figures do not include contributions to state parties).

Table 3.1   Fund-Raising by National Democratic and Republican Organizations for the Year 2000

	Democratic Party Totals	*Republican Party Totals*
Amount raised	$520,433,199	$715,701,784
Amount spent	$510,680,670	$679,776,825
Cash on hand	$17,860,066	$38,904,715
	Democratic National Committee	*Republican National Committee*
Amount raised	$260,560,928	$379,006,604
Amount spent	$257,309,982	$350,887,453
Cash on hand	$6,883,548	$28,963,574
	Democratic Congressional Campaign Committee	*National Republican Congressional Committee*
Amount raised	$105,096,499	$144,610,249
Amount spent	$107,321,499	$148,305,253
Cash on hand	$1,854,689	not available
	Democratic Senatorial Campaign Committee	*National Republican Senatorial Committee*
Amount raised	$104,206,648	$96,127,865
Amount spent	$104,843,221	$95,319,138
Cash on hand	$809,246	$2,155,957

Note: Cash on hand is more than the difference between monies raised and spent because of carryovers from previous accounting periods.
Source: Center for Responsive Politics. "Your Guide to Money in U.S. Elections," www.opensecrets.org/parties (November 11, 2002).

The table confirms what people in politics already know—that Republicans are generally better than Democrats at raising funds. In 2000, for example, the Democrats raised only 73 percent, 69 percent, and 73 percent of what the Republicans raised at the overall, presidential, and House levels, respectively. Only at the Senate level did Democrats outraise Republicans. Republicans have also been more successful than Democrats at getting their money from many small donors, rather than from fewer large ones; in 2000 the Republicans raised $204 million in small donations to the Democrats' $60 million. DNC chairman Terry McAuliffe admitted that the Republicans' small-donor list was 40 times larger than the Democrats', and the average age of Republican small donors was 48 while the Democrats' average age was 68.

Campaign finance has always been a critical part of politics, not only affecting whether candidates get elected but also affecting policy even after they are elected. It has also been a fairly arcane business with complicated laws to understand—and ways around them. The situation has favored experienced specialists. But in 2002, after a generation under previous laws, the campaign finance laws were changed, tending to level the playing field somewhat between veterans and newcomers. This is because, while everyone agrees that the new law will significantly alter how the game is played in the future, no one is sure exactly what the impact of changes will be, as new approaches are tried and court challenges threaten to keep changing the rules.

To take advantage of this opportunity, persons seeking to work in fundraising at the higher levels need to understand the laws governing candidates and parties, obtainable from and enforced by the nonpartisan Federal Election Commission (FEC). The laws are different for parties and candidates. Both cases require regular reporting to the FEC, which is highly specialized and time-consuming. Besides becoming familiar with the FEC, a good way of staying in touch with these laws as they evolve is by reading the magazine *Campaigns and Elections* (Web site: www.campaignline.com) or consulting the Center for Responsive Politics' Web site (www.opensecrets.org).

Those working at the higher levels of fund-raising also need to understand four major debates having to do with campaign financing.

➢ *Cutting down money in politics.* The great battle in campaign finance has always been that of reformers (read Democrats, who have less money) wanting to reduce the amount of money in campaigns, particularly the amount of special interest money. They want to keep money from dominating the system and corrupting elected officials dependent on it for financing their election campaigns. Or if it cannot be kept out, reformers at least want it regulated by the FEC. Opponents to these efforts (read Republicans, who have more money) argue that people should be allowed to spend their money the way they like. The last two times the campaign finance laws were changed, it was only after a big scandal. In 1978 they were changed as part of post-Watergate reforms, and the country operated under those laws for a quarter century. In 2002 the collapse of the company Enron and allegations that Enron had sought special favors in exchange for campaign donations spurred new changes in the law. Many experts believe it will take many years before the full impact of these changes is known. But generally, they believe that fund-raising is like a balloon: squeeze it in one place and it only pops out somewhere else to compensate. They feel that the new law may only change how money finds its way into campaigns, not diminish it.

➤ *Buckley v. Valeo.* In 1976 the U.S. Supreme Court in *Buckley v. Valeo* ruled that the right to spend money on political campaigns is a form of free speech and as such is protected by the U.S. Constitution. Persons opposed to campaign finance reforms almost always cite this case in making their arguments; it has become the fundamental obstacle to the reformers' efforts. In this case, the Court agreed with former U.S. Senator James Buckley (C-NY), who challenged a 1974 law that set mandatory spending limits for congressional campaigns. The Court rejected spending limits and caused subsequent courts to throw out a host of important campaign finance laws passed at the state and local level.

➤ *Attack ads.* Advocates of "clean campaigns" have become increasingly concerned about the proliferation of negative attack ads aired in the period right before an election, when the attacked candidate does not have time to respond. These ads, reformers charge, turn Americans away from politics, thus hurting our democracy, and should be banned. Proponents of these ads say that they are legitimate because the public has a right to know about the candidates who are running for office.

➤ *The influence of soft money.* There have been two kinds of money raised for campaigns: "hard money" and "soft money." Hard money refers to the money raised primarily by candidates—but also by parties—that is spent on directly urging the election of a specific candidate. It is strictly regulated, with individual donors allowed to donate no more than a certain amount per candidate. Soft money is raised only by the parties, and up until 2002, there was no limit on how much soft money someone could give to a party. During the Clinton administration, critics charged that some of the largest Democratic soft-money donors were given special access to the president, allowed to stay overnight in the Lincoln Bedroom in the White House, for example, or to attend special coffees with the president. Republicans were accused of the same "selling of access." *Time* magazine reported that in May 2001, Republicans hosted a black-tie gala honoring President George W. Bush that raised $24 million by targeting representatives of the energy industry, such as oil men who wanted to lift the oil embargoes against Iran and Libya, as well as coal, refinery, and utility executives out to ease pollution standards.

Originally, soft money was supposed to be spent only on "party-building" activities, such as issue advertising, paying party workers, constructing new buildings, or refurbishing state party infrastructure. But starting in the 1980s and accelerating in the 1990s, sharp lawyers noticed that soft money could be used to pay for television advertisements as long as those ads did not explicitly urge the election of a specific candidate—did not use phrases such as "vote for candidate X." As long as the ads stopped just short of those key phrases, they could be used to attack (or promote) candidates. So now the parties had a way to get around the intent of the 1978 reforms and spend virtually unlimited amounts on attack ads. Thus, in 1986 the Democrats received the first $1 million check in political history from Joan B. Kroc, widow of Ray Kroc, the McDonald's chairman. Big Democratic soft-money donors since then have included Haim Saban, the billionaire creator of the Teenage Mutant Ninja Turtles, and Hollywood executive Steve Bing, who gave the DNC $7 million and $5 million, respectively, in 2002. The contributions broke the previous record of $1.7 million given to the Republicans in 1996 by the Amway Corporation. The 2002 law banned such soft money, but fund-raisers immediately set to work to find a way around it.

Campaign finance reformers claim that soft money undermines our democracy by turning Americans away from politics because of the perception that politics was corrupt, that only big money won access and influence. Democrats argue that if one cares about prescription drug prices, one had better care about the big soft-money contributions that the pharmaceutical companies used to make to both political parties. Similarly, they say, if one cares about a patients' bill of rights, the environment, airline travel, the military, health care, or tobacco policy, one should care about campaign finance reform. Without it, they claim, taxpayers are victims of bad public policy bought by soft-money donors who get special favors from Congress and the White House. Opponents of efforts to ban soft money—mostly Republicans—claim that the ability to give soft money is a form of free speech and should not be abridged. Furthermore, they argue that soft-money donations have been documented through FEC disclosure requirements and that banning such money would simply drive contributors to find undisclosed ways to donate.

Reformers believe that soft money harmed the parties by making them less reliant on grassroots support—politically as well as financially. The parties became addicted to soft money, reformers claim, and spent more time cultivating wealthy special interest donors than they did on grassroots organizing. This, in turn, repelled voters from the parties. Banning soft money will be good for both parties, reformers say, because now the parties will have to return to their traditional grassroots organizing roles and become re-energized at the local levels. Party activists point out, however, that soft money has helped get workers involved in campaigns and get voters out on election day because such money can be spent on labor-intensive get-out-the-vote programs.

The 2002 Changes

The major provisions of the 2002 campaign finance law, which went into effect after the 2002 elections, include the following:

➤ Banning federal candidates and parties from raising or spending soft money.
➤ Barring corporations, unions, and some independent groups from using soft money to broadcast certain attack ads in the final 30 days of a primary or 60 days before a general election. Groups or individuals still would be able to run ads if they were paid for with hard-money donations and if the sources of the ads were disclosed.
➤ Allowing state and local parties to accept no more than $10,000 a year in soft money from a donor for uses such as voter registration and get-out-the-vote campaigns.
➤ Doubling the limit on regulated hard-money contributions, the amount an individual can give directly to federal campaigns, from $1,000 to $2,000 for a primary and a general election ($4,000 total per candidate). It also increased up to $95,000 during a two-year election cycle the amount individuals could contribute to candidates and parties.

In view of legal challenges to the 2002 changes in campaign finance laws, it is difficult to forecast the final outcome. The following were the immediate predictions from many election lawyers, fund-raising consultants, and party officials.

➤ *The two main political parties are the big losers.* If soft money stays banned, it will diminish the parties' roles, unless they can find new ways to raise money. Democrats will have to change more than Republicans (which is ironic because Democrats were the prime proponents of the reforms). Because the Democratic Party had been raising a larger percentage of its money from soft-money donations than the Republican Party, the Democrats will have to work harder to adapt to the new law. The problem is especially acute for the DSCC and the DCCC. In 2001 they raised 62 percent and 51 percent of their money in soft money, respectively, while their Republican counterparts raised 46 percent and 42 percent. The Democrats concede that concentrating on large soft-money contributions that could be used for advertising campaigns has made the party less adept at bringing in small donations. They acknowledge that they must build larger and better lists of direct-mail donors. But Democrats hope they can use direct mail to exploit their growing strength among upscale white professionals, who generally embrace the party's support of abortion rights, environmental protection, and opposition to the far right.

➤ *The new law will hurt minority turnout, thus hurting Democrats more than Republicans.* This is because get-out-the-vote drives used to be funded by soft money, which is now banned.

➤ *There will be a new generation of kingmakers.* Under the new rules, the new kingmakers will not necessarily be those with the bottomless bank accounts. It will be those who can get a lot of people to make contributions in sizable but still legal amounts—as much as $2,000 for a primary and $2,000 for a general election for candidates and $25,000 for political parties. For example, Vinod Gupta, a high-tech entrepreneur from Nebraska, who personally donated more than $1.2 million to the DNC for the 2000 elections, shifted to soliciting funds from his friends. In this way, he hoped to become even more important than when he used to just write a big check. But some big political donors are unwilling to remake themselves into fund-raisers because they don't feel comfortable asking people to donate.

➤ *Those with networks will become more important.* The most valuable players will be those with big mailing and e-mail lists, distribution systems, and grassroots, get-out-the-money networks that are up and running. For example, corporations will simply say to their executives, "We think Senator X is great," and everyone will get the message as to whom they are supposed to support with donations. President Bush is a prime beneficiary because of his Pioneers fund-raising group, the group that raised $113 million for him in the 2000 primaries. Under the old law, the Pioneers each raised $100,000 or more in $1,000 increments, the limit at that time for a single donation to a federal campaign. But under the new campaign finance law, that limit was raised to $2,000, immediately doubling the value of what the Pioneers can do. People like Ellen Malcolm will be more important. She is the president of EMILY's List, which raises large sums of money in small checks from mostly female donors and then funnels the money to Democratic female candidates who support abortion rights.

➤ *Increased use of bundling.* "Bundling" is a legal practice whereby a fund-raiser collects many checks made out to a candidate or party and, by turning them in together, gets credit as a major supporter. The bundler's role often is not found in public records. Many analysts believe that the pressure to shift to hard-money fund-raising will result in a large increase in bundling, which in turn will make it more difficult to identify who is actually raising the money. EMILY's List has been one of the best bundlers in the business.

➤ *Independent groups and wealthy activists may become more important and less accountable.* Independent groups, particularly politically active organizations with thousands of members that focus on hot-button issues, will get new power. The AFL-CIO, National Rifle Association, Sierra Club, and National Federation of Independent Business are among those most often mentioned. They will all drain off money that previously went to the political parties. For instance, in 2000 Jane Fonda donated $12.2 million to candidates, most of it to support Democrats who favored abortion rights. Fonda's money, channeled through nonprofit groups like Planned Parenthood and the National Abortion and Reproductive Rights Action League, paid for television, radio, and newspaper ads across the country. Most voters who saw the ads didn't realize who paid for them. Many analysts predict that political dollars like these will simply be diverted into channels that are undisclosed and less accountable.

➤ *Wealthy hard-money donors will become more important.* These are the relatively affluent people who traditionally have not given huge soft-money sums but are prepared to give several thousand dollars a year—conceivably as much as the $95,000 limit every two years. Under the new law, these people could donate as much as $4,000 annually to individual candidates and as much as $25,000 to the parties. This is the one constituency whose contributions increased under the 2002 law, virtually doubling the current limits.

➤ *Fund-raising techniques will probably change.* Just as certain kinds of individual donors will thrive in the new campaign finance system, so will certain fund-raising techniques and skills. The number of expensive gala dinners may diminish, for example. Fund-raisers say that these events make less sense if their high overhead costs can't be offset by large donor checks. The ban on soft money could accelerate the use of the Internet to reach large numbers of donors—a method that costs a fraction of traditional direct mail and telemarketing. Senator John McCain's (R-AZ) Internet campaign during his 2000 presidential run raised a quarter of his donations, thus proving that the technique can work, especially with independent voters and first-time donors.

> ➤ *You will have to be rich or famous to run.* The new law will make it harder for candidates without a lot of personal money or national name recognition to run in the presidential primaries because, without the name recognition, they won't be able to attract small donors. In the past, the parties relied heavily on soft money to finance challengers because most hard-money donors preferred to give to incumbents.

> ➤ *Candidates may spend even more time on fund-raising.* Because candidates will now have to raise money in smaller increments, they may have to spend even more time talking to potential contributors than in the past, which is ironic, in that reformers hoped to reduce the amount of time candidates had to spend on fund-raising so they could spend more on interacting with citizens and on governing.

> ➤ *The courts may strike down some provisions.* Opponents spanning the political spectrum from organized labor to abortion-rights opponents are challenging the new law all the way to the Supreme Court. They argue that the new restrictions on donating and advertising violate free-speech guarantees. And some federal regulators, such as FEC commissioner David Mason, declare that the law is so complicated that it may prove unenforceable. The FEC's enforcement office, already stretched thin, will now have to keep up with a law that became even more complex in 2002.

A High-Risk Occupation

Fund-raising is one of the high-risk occupations in politics. Although it is true that very successful fund-raisers and donors command great influence among politicians, it is also true that they are prime targets for scandal, or alleged scandal; the opposing party is constantly seeking to cut off its enemy's lifeblood—its money. Nevertheless, there is a cadre of professional fund-raisers who work for candidates or the parties.

Part of fund-raising is being careful whom you raise money from: you want it to be from people who are not expecting a great deal in return and certainly not from people who are engaging in illegal activities. The reason most people give big money to politicians is access: a chance to get in to see the politician and make their case. Donors may hope their money will do more than that and actually induce politicians to grant their requests for special benefits. But even more basic is simply to get a chance to make their arguments in person. Politicians are so busy that they would not ordinarily grant this kind of personal audience and would ask an aide to handle it instead. For this reason, donors are formally vetted (background and credentials are checked) to make sure that taking their money won't lead to embarrassment later.

Entry into fund-raising often comes as a volunteer, working for one of the professionals. As you demonstrate your ability to raise money and to organize and run fund-raising events, you may be offered a paying job to do it. Working as a fund-raiser puts you into close contact with both donors and candidates. Good fund-raisers are aggressive, communicate well, are not bothered by asking for money, and are well organized. At higher levels, some wealthy people get into fund-raising by tapping their rich friends—and then become ambassadors. About one-third of ambassadors are political appointees; the rest are career foreign service officers.

POLITICAL ORGANIZING

Probably the second most important thing the parties do is political organizing. At the national office, they divide the country up into regions and constituencies and then employ experienced "regional desks" and constituency "outreach" personnel to cultivate the two. These are usually political junkies who have a flair for organizing and campaigning and are not as interested in governing. They typically start out working for successful candidates or a state party and then get recommended for the national office. There, they hone their skills—and build their Rolodexes—working with state parties and on other campaigns, including presidential campaigns, and if their candidate wins, maybe transferring to the White House or the administration. From there, they might return to campaigning, via the party, or start their own consulting firms, or work for a U.S. representative, senator, or governor. Some of them even work on foreign campaigns. Over the years, some of them may work in several different areas within the party, say first at the DNC and then at the DCCC and later at the DGA.

These organizers identify strategies and tactics and write campaign plans. They work with vendors to identify their candidate's base vote and to update and maintain lists of these voters (the "voter file"). They consult with state parties. They handle politics and relationships between the party, elected officials, and candidates.

Before an election, they run voter registration drives. In the last few weeks before an election, they parachute into states to organize get-out-the-vote drives paid for and run by the party, not the candidate's campaign staff. Or they may get sent to a state months ahead of an election to set up a field organization, again paid for by the party, not the candidate. Some of them get recruited to "run" states in presidential elections for presidential candidates. All of them are constantly coordinating with workers from the state parties, many of them they probably know from the past.

If these are Democratic Party workers, they often participate in efforts of the "Coordinated Campaign," an effort to pool resources of all Democratic candidates running in a state—say, at the presidential, senatorial, congressional, and state and local levels—and thus campaign for all of them together rather than just have separate campaigns for each, the way the Republicans do.

When not actually doing these chores, the parties train new activists in how to do them. They run training courses in the various aspects of running campaigns, such as communications, fund-raising, research, field organization, management, and scheduling. Anyone can sign up for these courses.

COMMUNICATIONS

The last general function the parties perform is preparing talking points (fact sheets supporting a candidate or issue), press releases, letters to the editor, news conferences, and paid or free advertising on television and radio, as well as recruiting speakers to represent party interests at public events. The people who do this work generally come to party headquarters after having served as communications directors or press secretaries in prior campaigns or in the offices of elected officials. They usually leave to become press secretaries or communications officials in the White House, Senate, House, or governors' offices. Perhaps after a stint in government, they find their way into private industry as communications directors or government relations experts. Sometimes they set up their own consulting businesses.

Party communications officials are usually rabid attack dogs, constantly slamming the opposing party and its candidates. This is because they are trying to catch the attention of the press and the public, who are all too easily distracted by other events. They also are relentless in finding ways to get out their party's line and making sure everyone "stays on message" so that the public hears one message at a time rather than a cacophony of messages.

Getting on the Team

For many people interested in politics, working at the national party headquarters in Washington is likely to be only one stop in a long career, a kind of ticket punching, if you will. They may come to headquarters because of a presidential campaign and stay there only a year or so. A few may even start out as volunteers at the party and then get asked to remain in a paid capacity.

But the number of people on the parties' payroll waxes and wanes dramatically depending on where we are in the presidential election cycle. At the height of the cycle, during the summer and fall of a presidential election campaign, there may be several hundred people working at national headquarters and many others working out in the field paid by the party. This is the best time to get jobs. And then suddenly, right after the election, most of them are let go.

Regardless of whether a candidate wins or loses a presidential election, it is likely that most of the operatives the candidate placed at party headquarters will leave to be replaced gradually by those of the next candidate. This often means a certain loss of institutional memory, a certain starting from scratch again with each new campaign. On the other hand, the operatives from old campaigns, once they "get on the team," so to speak, are seldom thrown off the team and often resurface in future campaigns in one form or another.

The political parties take interns and volunteers. But to get the most out of these positions, you have to be proactive. Find someone within the party that you want to work for and use the formal intern program or volunteer recruitment structure simply to get in the door. If you don't do this, the party may be slow in assigning you work because their intern and volunteer programs tend to be loosely structured. But if you do it right and attach yourself to the right person within the party, it can be a tremendously rewarding and fun experience, teaching you how the party works and most of all, allowing you to make contacts that will come in handy for the rest of your political career. For examples of people whose careers have included a stint at one of the political parties, turn to Chapter 8 and look at the profiles of Catherine Bertini, Jon-Christopher Bua, Jim Dyer, Patricia de Stacy Harrison, Minyon Moore, Danny O'Brien, Ralph Reed, Ed Rollins, and Howard Wolfson.

4

CONGRESS

In the federal government, the U.S. House of Representatives is the closest to the people because all House members have to run for reelection every two years. This means that they think about reelection more often than senators or presidents do. They also usually have a closer connection to their constituents because they are elected more often and represent a more concentrated area. By law, the size of the House is limited to 435 members. If you divide that by the population of the United States, now about 286 million, you get a district size of roughly 657,000 people—too big to know everyone personally, but small enough that you need to know all the main leaders personally. If the first lesson in politics is "all politics is local," as former House Speaker Tip O'Neill once put it, then in the federal system, the House is where you learn that lesson the best.

There are approximately thirty-five thousand jobs on Capitol Hill, in a Congress costing somewhat less than $3 billion a year to operate. Those figures include not just the political jobs in the offices of individual U.S. representatives and senators and committee staffs (the ones that are of primary interest to us in this book) but also all other support staff, such as the Architect of the Capitol, U.S. Botanic Gardens, Congressional Budget Office, General Accounting Office, Government Printing Office, Library of Congress (and its Congressional Research Service), and the Office of Compliance. The total for just the House and Senate staffs alone is about thirteen thousand, broken down as follows:

House office staff	7,100
House committee staff	1,200
Senate office staff	3,600
Senate committee staff	1,100

Starting with FY 1979, representatives have been authorized to hire a maximum of 18 full-time staff, with up to 4 additional part-time, shared, or temporary staff. Exactly how many staff members a representative can afford depends on how much each person is paid and the office's annual dollar allowance. The allowance varies between $800,000 to $1.2 million, depending on the district's size geographically and population-wise (although all districts are supposed to be about the same size, there is some variation). Over the years, the proportion of a representative's staff working in district offices has grown so that it now amounts to about 50 percent. Besides staff, the allowance has to cover mailing and travel expenses.

Unlike the House, the Senate has no limit on the number of personal staff. It is governed strictly by the dollar allowance to the office. That allocation is based primarily on the size of the state's population. So a senator from California, for example, is going to get more money than a senator from Delaware and consequently will have more staff.

But before either representatives or senators can think about hiring their staff, they have to get elected.

Getting Elected

It is hard to understand the political system in the United States without understanding something about campaigns. This is because campaigns are the most logical way of passing the "loyalty test" discussed earlier in the book. Many people who work in the federal system of political jobs start out by working in campaigns. Campaigns are fast-paced, exciting, and inspiring. They are a place to forge lifelong bonds with interesting people and provide a chance to change society by electing someone good to office. In fact, a professional campaign organizer could argue that he or she is more effective in changing society by getting a series of good candidates into office than, for example, a legislative assistant is who works on bills once a candidate gets elected. Finding a good legislative assistant is probably easier than finding a good campaign organizer.

Campaigns also afford perhaps the best look at the relationship between candidates and constituents. The constituents tell the candidates what they want, and the candidates try to incorporate that into their platforms. One of the best ways to understand what makes politicians tick is to be in a campaign. In fact, once candidates get into office, they have to conduct low-intensity campaigns for the rest of their careers if they want to get reelected. Each staff member contributes directly or indirectly to that effort.

But although campaigns are very interesting and informative, they are also very hard work. Often the chores are menial and laborious and take a huge amount of time. I remember once hearing a campaign manager boasting that he won a contest about seeing who could get by on the least amount of sleep by averaging two hours a night for several weeks. Not exactly conducive to family life—or any other kind of life. Because of this, campaigning is usually the endeavor of young people. After a while, they tend to settle down into some other type of work, political or otherwise. Campaigning may be the most frequent way that people get jobs in Congress, but there are other ways, which this book explores. Still, I would say that those persons first coming to Congress without having worked in a campaign are at a disadvantage and need to learn about them.

House Races as a Model

This chapter takes a closer look at campaigns, starting with the typical House campaign as a model and then showing how Senate and presidential campaigns compare. What follows here are descriptions based on my own experiences and observations. I think, in retrospect, that my experiences in House races were helpful because they enabled me to see that the connection between candidate and voter is more intimate in the House race than in the larger statewide races. It is this sense of intimacy that one seeks to achieve in the larger races; but there one is forced to try to achieve it more through media contact than personal contact.

An even smaller race, such as a state house of representatives race, may actually be the best place to observe the special connection between candidate and voter. I can sum it up for you in one anecdote. I remember more than 30 years ago having a conversation with a rather unlikely state representative and trying to figure out how on earth he got elected. Eventually, it came out: "I knocked on every door in the district, every single door. It took me six months. I said: 'If my opponent comes here and asks for your vote, give it to him. But if he doesn't, then I hope you'll consider me.' "

That was it; he personally went to the door, talked to the voter, established a little rapport, and asked for a vote. His opponent didn't do that; he campaigned more through speeches and newspaper interviews. The essence of all campaigning is trying to establish that special rapport with the voters. The bigger the area you are running in, the more impossible it is to literally knock on every door. But you try to do it figuratively, to give the impression that you are establishing the same kind of rapport you would have established had you actually been there in person.

The type of House campaign discussed here as a model is a full-on campaign in a competitive urban or suburban area because that's where most House races are in this country. But many races are not competitive and thus would involve simpler campaigns than what I outline here. Furthermore, if the race were in a rural area, it might be a bit different (not so easy to knock on doors; you'd have to make more use of the media). And finally, campaigning as an incumbent would probably be different than campaigning as a challenger because incumbents have a number of advantages.

One of those advantages is the franking privilege, the ability to send mail for free. It cannot be political mail, and it cannot be mass mailings sent closer than 60 days to the election, but it can be newsletters or other material during the year concerning what the representative is doing in Washington (and back home) and which is bound to make a favorable impression on the voter. Second, the incumbent has a congressional staff that is probably experienced in campaigns. Although there are restrictions to prevent them from campaigning on taxpayer's time, these staffers know how constituency service acts as a legal surrogate for campaigning, and they work it hard. Third, the incumbent is well known because of being in office for a while and getting covered in the media extensively. And finally, it is easier for the incumbent to raise money. For all these reasons, the reelection rate for representatives is more than 90 percent, which means that if the campaign you are considering joining is against an incumbent, you are probably facing an uphill fight. It's much better to be running for an open seat, where there is no incumbent running.

There are other differences between House, Senate, and presidential races. Although all of them will be explored in more detail later, suffice it to say now that the larger the geographic area covered by the race—a statewide race compared with a congressional race; a presidential race compared with a statewide race—the more money it will take. It will also take more "wholesale politics" (expensive television and other media advertising) and less "retail politics" (meeting individual voters). At the implementation level within the campaign, many of the chores described here as belonging to one person in a House campaign are divided between more and more specialists the bigger the campaign gets. The message changes, too, based on such things as whether the candidate is running for a legislative or executive office and whether the candidate is a well-known incumbent or a not-so-well-known challenger.

If you are a newcomer to campaigns, this book can help you get more out of the experience. Certain campaign jobs have a direct carryover to jobs in an elected official's office after the election. For example, press aides in campaigns often become press secretaries and communications specialists in political jobs after campaigning. Issues people in campaigns often become legislative assistants or policy people in the White House or the administration. More senior officials in the administration of campaigns often become congressional chiefs of staff or top White House aides and department aides.

By understanding how this process works, you will be able to plan your career better and thus get more out of it. On the other hand, plenty of people do not attempt to plan it that closely, choosing instead to do something useful in a campaign and starting to sift through the job possibilities only after the election. Some people work in campaigns just for the excitement of it, without much thought at all about what will happen afterwards. A word of caution: be careful whom you share your thoughts about career advancement with during the campaign, lest people see you as a rival or think that you are spending too much time thinking about yourself and not enough about getting the candidate elected.

How House Campaigns Are Organized

Most House campaign jobs fall under one of two categories: core management and consultants. A larger campaign retains the same functions, but the work is spread among many more specialists, and there are more layers of staff.

THE CANDIDATE AND THE CANDIDATE'S FAMILY

The candidate, of course, has the final say on all decisions. Because he or she is the one who actually has to face the voters and serve in office later, the candidate gets to decide on matters of strategy, tactics, advertising, and issues. In practice, however, a wise candidate delegates many of these things to the senior campaign staffers, especially to the campaign manager and the consultants. By doing so, the candidate is free to fulfill two primary responsibilities: (1) raising money through direct phone solicitations and participation in fund-raising events and (2) boosting name recognition through old-fashioned retail politics.

In a campaign, as with an elected official, novices may hope to gain exposure to the boss because winning the boss's approval is the quickest way to advance. However, proximity to the candidate is usually a function of the advisor's campaign experience and political maturity. Therefore, for your first campaign it is unlikely that you will be allowed such responsibility and proximity. The ring of top aides will limit the candidate's interaction with lower-level staffers because it could lead to confusion and duplication of effort. Nevertheless, inexperienced campaigners can be assured that they will be recognized if they demonstrate the requisite attitude, commitment, and energy; and if you possess the aforementioned qualities, you can shoot up through the ranks and gain a lot of responsibility at a young age.

It is also true that certain jobs exist that do not require campaign skills yet allow you access to the candidate: driver, advance person (going early to a site that the candidate will be visiting in order to prepare for the visit), and handler of the candidate's family. However, these activities, although important, are not the core activities that are discussed in the following sections.

CORE MANAGEMENT

Several jobs come under the heading of core management, and although, as a newcomer to a campaign, you probably will not be qualified to hold any of them, working as a volunteer or entry-level assistant to the people in these roles is a distinct possibility.

Campaign Chairperson and Campaign Treasurer

The campaign chairperson and campaign treasurer are usually part-time volunteer positions. The chairperson is generally a person of stature in politics who will oversee the candidate's political relationships with key allies and donors and most likely assist in some fund-raising. The chairperson is a close associate of the candidate, in whom the candidate has complete trust. The treasurer is also a notable figure in politics but, like the campaign chairperson, is more of a figurehead who helps bring credibility to the campaign and helps in fund-raising.

Campaign Manager

As the day-to-day head of the campaign, the campaign manager has to be knowledgeable about every aspect of it. This means that the campaign manager is likely to be experienced in campaigning, intelligent, politically astute, a good administrator, and an inspirational leader who can motivate the other workers in the campaign. The campaign manager's responsibilities include the following duties: office manager at the headquarters office; scheduler for the candidate, the candidate's family, and surrogate speakers; and director of volunteers. Typically, however, the campaign manager has an assistant, a deputy, who can substitute for the campaign manager when necessary and to whom the campaign manager assigns some of the responsibilities already listed. In a statewide campaign, however, these chores would be parceled out among several people. Another part of the campaign manager's job is overseeing the consultants who are brought into the campaign. If you can get a job in a campaign as an aide to the campaign manager, you will learn a lot fast.

Field Director

The field director works with the campaign manager to develop a prioritized categorization of voter support in the district—solid supporters, leaners, undecideds, and those voting for the opponent. The field director then ensures that undecided voters receive mailings and telephone calls designed to help them change their minds. He or she organizes the GOTV (Get Out The Vote) effort at the end of the campaign, as well as the election day activities in the field. The field director works through a field network to achieve these ends.

The entire congressional district is broken down into a number of areas, each of which is further subdivided into smaller areas, with several dozen persons overseeing the effort at all levels. This network is used for planning and implementing direct mailings for political advertising, soliciting funds, phone banking, scheduling where the candidate should go, and deciding where to hold events. Chairpersons are responsible for recruiting and training volunteers, helping to plan the schedule when the candidate is campaigning in their area, accompanying the candidate, and delivering supplies. Persons at the lowest level in the hierarchy are often the precinct captains, who know their neighborhoods well, know the people who live there, what their concerns are, whether they are registered to vote, and how likely they are to vote.

Phone banking is also an important part of field operations. Phone banks have three basic functions. When you do not have precinct captains, phone banks can substitute to get information on voters' intentions and to contact voters during the GOTV stage, urging them to go to the polls and offering them rides and other assistance to get there. On election day, phone banks are used to remind supporters to get to the polls.

Phone bank supervisors give the volunteers making the calls lists of names and phone numbers and a model message to use when calling. They also make sure the callers correctly record the information received from voters on their contact sheets.

Like the precinct captains, phone bank volunteers are on the front line with the voters, only via the telephone. They need to be responsible people who will actually make the calls assigned to them and represent the candidate well.

Volunteer Coordinator

Usually working closely with the field director is the volunteer coordinator. Most House campaigns have many volunteers and depend on them for large amounts of work, ranging from folding letters and stuffing envelopes to ringing door bells to making yard signs and putting them out at night to making deliveries. They are typically managed by a volunteer coordinator, someone who compiles a database of the volunteers' names and phone numbers and who can call them when they are needed for projects. Statewide campaigns have hundreds and maybe even thousands of volunteers.

Many volunteers are only part time and have erratic schedules. They may start a project but then have to leave before it is finished. Or they may just decide not to come in today after all, even though the campaign was counting on them. If you are entering your first campaign and you don't know anybody, you will probably have to start out as a general volunteer. But if you can be a full-time volunteer, do excellent work day after day, and be someone the campaign can always depend on, you will in all likelihood catch the attention of those running the campaign and move up. Your objective should be to become a personal assistant to one of the key people in the campaign, ranging from the candidate and the candidate's family to the campaign manager, the finance director, the press secretary, the research director, or the field director. In midcampaign you may even be offered a paying job. But even if you are not, you are in a good position to meet many people who can help you later.

Finance Director

The finance director's job is to raise enough money from individual donors, corporations, and political action committees (PACs) to cover the campaign's estimated budget. PACs are committees chartered to raise, administer, disburse, and disclose funds that individuals voluntarily contribute for political purposes. There are nearly four thousand professional, corporate, union, and other PACs in this country.

The finance director raises money in two ways. The first is by arranging for the candidate to do "call time" daily for as many hours as the candidate can stand it (usually three to four hours). The second is through event fundraising, where donors attend receptions and dinners that require a preset dollar amount to attend. These events demand much work, and there is room for a lot of volunteer help. It can be a good way for a hardworking volunteer to meet the donors.

The job of finance director is not easy: a candidate challenging an incumbent will need to raise about $1 million to be considered viable. This figure can grow as high as $2 million. The finance director will raise a large chunk of this money from supporters living in the congressional district or the state. But donations will also have to come from out of state and from national organizations and PACs in Washington, D.C. To meet those demands, a congressional campaign normally has a finance director at the campaign headquarters who oversees in-district activities, that is, direct solicitations and events, and who hires a fund-raising consultant in Washington, D.C., to conduct fund-raising activity with the national sources. This fund-raising is crucial to the campaign's success—unless the candidate is willing, and able, to donate a lot of money to the campaign.

Fund-raising also means negotiating a labyrinth of laws and restrictions. At the congressional level (unlike the presidential level), there are no spending limits or public financing in campaigns, but congressional candidates are subject to the same contribution limits and disclosure requirements as presidential candidates.

Congressional candidates get money directly from three sources. First are individual donations, which by law are limited to $4,000 per individual per election cycle ($2,000 in the primary; $2,000 in the general election). Who gives this money to congressional campaigns? According to a study financed by the Joyce Foundation in 1997, it's old, rich, white men:

> ➤ 96 percent of 1996 campaign contributors were white.
> ➤ 80 percent were men.

➤ 80 percent were over age 45.

➤ 81 percent had annual incomes over $100,000.[1]

These people are not at all typical of the average voter. But because they are the donor class, politicians have to pay attention to what they want—which can be such things as tax cuts, access to government contracts, and entrées to foreign governments.

Second are contributions from PACs. PACs are limited by law to donations to congressional campaigns of no more than $5,000 per PAC. But there is no limit on the amount of money a PAC can spend helping a candidate as long as it operates independently of the candidate's campaign organization.

A special category not covered under the first two is candidate contributions. There is no limit on how much money candidates can contribute (or more often, loan) to their own campaigns—which, of course, favors rich candidates over poor ones. Campaigns are required, however, to report all contributions to the FEC, which posts them on its Web site for anyone to see (www.fec.gov).

In addition to the aforementioned categories governing money donated directly to a candidate, there are two categories of money not donated to the campaign but spent on behalf of the candidate. The first of these is money spent on the campaign by the political parties. The second category is independent expenditures. These are expenditures on behalf of a candidate that are not coordinated with the candidate. For instance, an insurance company PAC or an individual might spend money on ads supporting a candidate's stance on HMOs and urge a vote for him. There is no limit on how much money can be spent in this category.

Press Secretary

The main communications job in a congressional campaign is that of press secretary. Statewide campaigns and presidential campaigns will have a communications director to plot overall communications strategy and a press secretary to handle the press day to day. But at the congressional level, both chores are done by the press secretary. The press secretary's main job is to help the candidate get the maximum amount of free media coverage during the campaign. The press secretary accomplishes this through press releases, the scheduling of press events, and radio actualities (taped messages). The press secretary also acts as the candidate's spokesperson to the media. In some House campaigns, the campaign manager performs this function, but the larger the campaign, the more likely that there will be a separate press secretary.

Research Director

Most campaigns maintain a research operation to assist the candidate in identifying the issues in the campaign and formulating positions on them. The campaign needs issue briefs and talking points, as well as opposition research on the opponent's positions and weaknesses. The candidate needs speeches and debate preparation and rehearsal.

The research director is responsible for supervising and generating all of this. Research is an area for volunteers with analytical and writing skills. The premium is not on original thinking but on the quick synthesizing of available materials into a user-friendly format. The research director also sees to it that a clipping file on the campaign is maintained. Volunteers usually do the clipping—unless the campaign pays for a clipping service to do it.

Compliance Director

The compliance director oversees the campaign's accounting and reporting and ensures that they comply with FEC regulations. The compliance director makes certain that all campaign contributions and all expenditures are properly documented. Typically, the compliance director is an accountant who knows about campaign accounting practices.

CONSULTANTS

It is likely that a congressional campaign will have several consultants working for it.

General Consultant

Some congressional campaigns pay a general consultant to help develop the campaign's basic strategy and to help coordinate the other consultants. The general consultant's duties include deciding what issues to stress, analyzing information about the opponent (opposition research), helping to formulate the message for direct mailings, determining how to target those mailings for maximum effectiveness, determining which groups of voters to pursue, formulating the budget and cash flow schedule to finance all of the above, and generally monitoring the campaign's progress.

Fund-Raising Consultant

Fund-raising is so important that many campaigns hire a special consultant to help just with the development and supervision of a fund-raising strategy. The fund-raising consultant is knowledgeable about the most effective techniques for conducting fund-raising events and soliciting money from individuals and from PACs.

Media Consultant

Often a campaign will hire an advertising agency to create and place the paid media advertisements, such as television and radio commercials, newspaper ads, and billboards. There are many clerical aspects to this work that a volunteer can help with. The media consultant also uses a printing company to develop and print materials for the campaign, such as the pieces of literature, yard signs, pole signs, and bumper stickers. The campaign manager understands the lead times that are necessary for getting these items printed but could use help in making sure that everything goes according to schedule.

Direct-Mail Consultant

Quite possibly, a campaign will hire yet another consultant, the direct-mail consultant, to determine where to target direct mailings for the campaign and how to process them. Again, it is the campaign manager's job to work with the consultant and to take into account the long lead times necessary for producing these materials and getting them out, but underlings can help with all the details.

Automated-Phone Consultant

Campaigns are increasingly using automated phone messages to reach voters and hiring special companies to do it.

Pollster

Polling is vital to developing an effective campaign strategy that targets the right voters. But polling is expensive, so a House campaign will have fewer polls than will a statewide race. The pollster helps develop and then conducts polls in the field, which result in a detailed set of data used to develop a campaign message. But someone on the campaign staff has to be experienced enough to be able to study these results and realize what they mean. This is usually the pollster, the campaign manager, and the media consultant.

Voter-File Manager

State parties maintain sophisticated voter files that they provide to campaigns. Voter files are up-to-date databases of all registered voters that in most cases have additional information about addresses and when a voter actually voted in the last several years. This information is central to the retail voter contact program that the field director conducts. The voter-file manager is the person who manipulates the file to provide walk and call lists for canvassers and phone banks, produces labels for in-house mailings, and maintains volunteer lists with e-mail addresses and fax numbers.

PARTY ATTENTION

If the national political party (in this case, the DCCC or the NRCC) decides that its candidate has a good chance to win a race, the party will prioritize it as a "targeted race," which means that the party will put resources into the race. Besides cash, the party can supply operatives who are expert in many different aspects of running a campaign. In fact, one way for someone to get involved in a campaign is to start out in a party training seminar. After you successfully complete the training, you are referred to work in a particular campaign. You can specialize in almost any aspect of running a campaign in these seminars.

District Office

Assuming that the candidate has won the election, congressional offices now have to be set up. When most people think about their member of Congress, they think about an office in Washington. In reality, though, most U.S. representatives also have one or more offices in the district they represent, called district offices (DOs). In the long run, these offices may be more important to their reelection than anything they do in Washington. These offices are often located in a federal building because the rent is free there, even though that means giving up the visibility that a storefront office would have. Often the key to constant, easy reelection is maintaining a top-notch district office and using it continuously to help constituents with problems and generally smother the district with attention. If, in sum, the House is closest to the people, then the district office is the closest of all. Therefore, it is a good place for a young person to get started in politics and learn that politics is about local people's needs and concerns. It is difficult to overestimate the importance of constituents in the mind of an elected official. This is perhaps the most basic truth of dealing with Congress, either as an insider working there or as an outsider working in congressional relations or lobbying.

People experience all sorts of problems with the federal government in their daily lives, and they bring these problems to their representative. Often the representative chooses to have district office staff handle them because they are in closer physical proximity to the constituents. But some representatives have these requests sent to Washington to be worked on there.

Social Security problems are the most frequent. These usually involve senior citizens not receiving their retirement benefits on time or having difficulty applying for Social Security disability. Medicare is also big, either applying for it or getting it to pay all of the bills. Military and veterans' problems are also big—for example, people either trying to get into the military (overturn a flunked physical) or out of it (get a hardship discharge) or trying to upgrade a bad discharge. Immigration problems are probably next and usually involve trying to get a relative admitted to the United States or obtain a work permit for someone already here. IRS problems crop up, too.

And there are many other problems. Maybe a local government needs help applying for a federal grant, or a group of environmentalists is concerned about protecting a wilderness area. Questions having to do with federally subsidized housing programs arise. Or maybe people in a rural district are worried about the government trying to shut down their local hospital because its bed-occupancy rate is too low. Sometimes these problems are rather unusual: the professor who is missing in Africa, and the State Department finds that he was eaten by alligators; or the person drawn into a cult whom the parents want back; or someone wants a job; or someone needs a recommendation for something else.

If the workers in the congressional office are smart, they will take these problems very seriously and work hard to solve them. This is called "case work," and the congressional office will normally handle only the requests from people in their district and the ones concerning the federal government. They usually refer all others to the proper U.S. representative ("congressional courtesy") or state representative. But sometimes, the congressional offices will work jointly with other congressional offices or even state officials to solve the problem.

In addition to the casework, most DOs handle many other chores, generally keeping the representative's name before the public. These tasks could include staff attending meetings, giving speeches on the representative's behalf, or accompanying the representative to events, usually on weekends.

Congressional lore is full of stories of offices that go the extra mile for constituents. For instance, Congressman Jim Barcia (D-MI), once got the Treasury Department to issue a replacement bill when a constituent had a worn-out $50 bill that banks wouldn't accept. Senators have similar offices back home in their states. Senator Jesse Helms (R-NC) arranged for constituents to meet the vice president, the king of Jordan, and the pope. He also arranged for military flyovers at funerals and aided overseas travelers stuck in airports with expired passports.

Representatives or senators who fail to respond adequately to constituent requests can pay a severe price at the polls. Take the case of former senator Spencer Abraham (R-MI). A woman got so mad at his failure to respond to requests for help with her health maintenance organization (HMO) that she appeared in a campaign ad against him. She asserted that she called Abraham's office repeatedly for help in getting an HMO to pay for surgery for a rare metabolic disorder for her daughter, who later died of it. "We called his office so many times," the woman said in the ad. "If I were from a big company that could make a large donation, they probably would have returned my call." Abraham denied the charge but acknowledged the ad probably played a role in his narrow loss—which helped create a 50-50 Republican/Democrat split in the U.S. Senate.

In short, staff who work in the DO become highly knowledgeable about both the community and how the federal government affects everyday people. The jobs in a DO usually consist of the following.

DISTRICT DIRECTOR

The district director (called the state director in a Senate office) is usually a senior person who knows the congressional district or senator's state extremely well, having been active politically there for some time, but who is not interested in moving to Washington. The director keeps close tabs on the district or the state and represents the boss at meetings in the district when the boss cannot be there. Anything that the other people in the district office (or offices, if there is more than one district office) cannot handle is brought to the director.

CASEWORKERS

Each office typically has two or more caseworkers who specialize in helping constituents with requests. For example, one may specialize in Social Security and Medicare requests; another may specialize in immigration or military matters. Although the caseworkers are sometimes in the Washington office, this is not the norm. Good caseworkers represent their clients like tenacious lawyers, never judging the case beforehand, making the client's case to the federal agency involved. The key is getting an answer back to the constituent quickly—in a day or two—at least with an interim report. Federal agencies have offices that are specifically set up to field these congressional requests, and gradually the DO staff gets to know them. It is a lesson in how to serve, and compared with many other aspects of government, you see the result of what you do rather quickly.

RECEPTIONIST

Each office generally has a receptionist who answers the phone and is the initial point of contact for people visiting the office. It may be that one of the caseworkers also performs these duties.

INTERNS

DOs can have interns, although they are not as numerous as interns in the Washington office. Usually, the work consists of assisting with special projects, such as helping to organize and staff events in the district, and is not related to the legislative process. Serving as an intern in a DO can be a good way of getting a close look at constituency demands.

People get paying jobs in DOs usually because they are interested in government and politics only as they relate to resolving local issues, rather than in playing the "Washington game" (quite unlike Washington staffers). They usually don't want to move to Washington and are quite content to stay in their community. Some politically ambitious people want to work in a DO in order to establish links with the community that will help them in running for office later (although if this leads to a divided loyalty, it can become a problem for the boss). Others feel that the local connection will facilitate going into the private sector or will help them become better, more influential staffers for the same boss or other bosses later. Occasionally, they transfer to Washington, either with the same boss or another one. They usually get their jobs by being community activists, working as volunteers or paid staff on House or Senate campaigns and distinguishing themselves there, by being related to a donor, or by being referred by another trusted politician.

Washington Office

The Washington office is usually considered the main office because the representative is there during the week and the chief of staff is permanently located there. Besides the chief of staff, the Washington office typically includes a legislative director and one or two other legislative assistants (LAs), one or two legislative correspondents, a scheduler, a press secretary, an office manager, and various interns. Senate offices have a similar structure but more staffers.

CHIEF OF STAFF

The top job in a House or Senate office is now usually called "chief of staff." It used to be called "administrative assistant" (AA), but that term is being phased out. The chief of staff's job is to oversee not only the Washington office but the DO(s) as well. The chief of staff is the representative's or senator's most trusted assistant, usually because of a long association with the politician, possibly by starting off low on the ladder and gradually working through the ranks or by previously being a chief of staff in another office and getting referred. The chief of staff gets involved in everything but often works through others to do it. For example, on matters having to do with the administration of the office, like ordering equipment or getting furniture, the chief of staff would work through the office manager.

In legislative matters, the chief of staff works primarily with the legislative director (often referred to by the acronym LD) and with the individual LAs, who often specialize in one of the boss's committee or subcommittee assignments. The scheduler would keep the chief of staff informed about all the scheduling requests as well as the boss's final schedule.

Whereas it is likely that the chief of staff and the scheduler will come from the boss's congressional district, many of the other Washington office staff may not. This sometimes means that the DO and the Washington office do not have a good appreciation of what each other does. Because the chief of staff has to hold it all together, this is usually the highest-paying staff job in the office. The following people from the case studies in this book have been House or Senate chiefs of staff (or AAs) at some point in their careers: Richard Armitage, David Hoppe, Roger Majak, Bonnie Newman, Danny O'Brien, and Pete Rouse.

LEGISLATIVE ASSISTANTS

LAs concentrate on the substance of the legislative process—following legislation and helping their bosses to propose it (often in the form of amendments). They research issues and help draft bills and amendments. They attend committee hearings, draft statements for the Congressional Record, ghostwrite Op-Ed pieces for the representative or senator, work with LAs in other congressional offices to get their bosses to sign on to "Dear Colleague" letters (letters to other members asking for support for bills or amendments that have been introduced or will be introduced), and perform numerous other chores.

Many people, especially those with an academic bent, prefer the LA job to all others in a congressional office even though it usually does not pay as much as the chief of staff's job. This is because it offers substantive work in policy areas and requires less of the constituent-related or reelection work, such as answering the mail or raising money. The legislative director is usually the senior LA, in charge of the other LAs, and thus gets paid more than they do. The legislative director is the top issues person on the staff. The chief is often focused on the politics, whereas the legislative director is focused on the policy. If you are senior-level (by Hill standards) staff material, such as an attorney or someone with a lot of issues experience, but little political experience, this would be a good job to focus on. The legislative director typically not only specializes in certain issues but also oversees the entire legislative process for the office. LAs usually specialize in only a limited area, such as the congressperson's committee assignment area. The following people from the case studies have been LAs: Jim Dyer, Roger Majak, Leon Panetta, Pete Rouse, and Ted Van Der Meid.

The ideal is to work as an LA for a senior representative or senator from the majority party on issues having to do with the boss's committee assignments. This is because it increases the chances that your efforts are going to lead somewhere. Conversely, the least-desirable position is usually working for a junior member of the minority party in an area having nothing to do with his or her committee assignments. Yes, you do have one vote on all bills and amendments, and you will get to follow the legislative process, but you probably will not have much chance to influence that process. You may spend a lot of time researching issues and crafting good bills or amendments, only to see them go nowhere.

A word of advice: politicians and their LAs are usually not the origina-tors of ideas but synthesizers of other people's ideas. They advocate ideas when the timing is right. They may know a lot more about the politics of an idea than the idea itself. Thus, if you're interested in original thinking, poli-tics may not be the place for you. Perhaps a think tank would be. On the other hand, if you are interested in applying ideas to practical situations, politics may be the perfect place for you.

LEGISLATIVE CORRESPONDENT

The legislative correspondent's job is to respond to constituent requests that specifically concern the representative's position on a certain issue. Usually the office has a computer file of preapproved language on the most common questions, which the legislative correspondent uses to produce an answer quickly. But sometimes the LAs are called upon to generate letters when they are closer to the issue in question.

PRESS SECRETARY/COMMUNICATIONS DIRECTOR

One could argue that the most important aspect of a politician's job is com-munications. As former Maryland governor William Donald Schaeffer once told me, "It doesn't count unless you tell someone." Communicating is the way representatives or senators (or any other elected official, for that matter) inform their constituents about what they are doing, especially on controver-sial issues, and thus secure constituent approval for their actions. Routinely getting their name in the news is important for keeping the public aware of their existence so the public won't forget them at election time. For all these reasons, a representative is likely to have on staff someone who specializes in dealing with the media, perhaps someone who worked for a newspaper for a while before taking the congressional job or someone who had been in press relations in another office. In smaller offices, such as a congressional office, this person is called the press secretary. In larger offices (like Senate offices), the position may be called communications director, and there will be several other people also working in communications. In still larger offices (an exec-utive branch department or the White House), there might be a communica-tions director with a staff that specializes in formulating communications strategies and a separate press secretary with a staff that answers questions from the press and briefs the press at press conferences.

In a House office, the press secretary writes press releases reporting on something the boss has accomplished. Smaller newspapers may print these press releases more or less verbatim, whereas larger ones will view the press release as an announcement that something newsworthy has happened and then dispatch one of their reporters to do their own story. The press secretary may also write several newsletters a year explaining what the representative has been doing for the last few months (although these are being replaced more and more by single-issue direct-mail pieces). These will be mass mailed to constituents back home. The press secretary also answers questions from reporters, providing them with catchy sound bites that help round out their stories. The press secretary also dreams up press events, news conferences, and photo ops for the boss. These may occur in Washington or back in the district. After someone has worked as a press secretary in a congressional office, he or she may become press secretary to a higher-ranking dignitary in or out of government or later a communications strategist for a well-paying organization or business. Examples in the case studies of persons who served as press aides on the Hill include Jim Dyer and Howard Wolfson.

SCHEDULER

The scheduler makes up the representative's written schedule, often for months in advance. The scheduler gets all mail with requests for the boss to attend events, such as speaking engagements and fund-raisers, in Washington and back home. He or she often consults with the chief of staff to decide which ones should be accepted and which ones should be turned down. The scheduler typically knows the district well, possibly from having been the scheduler during the campaign, and often is a good source of political advice.

OFFICE MANAGER

The office manager assists the chief of staff with the nonpolitical and nonlegislative work of running the office, such as making sure both that everyone in the office gets paid and that mass mailings are organized.

INTERNS

Interns—usually college students—are used to help with any of the aforementioned tasks, although they usually complain that they get very little substantive work (chores associated with the LAs, for example) and mostly get administrative chores associated with the office manager (photocopying, stuffing envelopes).

WORKING WITH CONSTITUENTS

In addition to the work already discussed, Washington offices get casework that is similar to what the DOs get but that for various reasons is better handled in Washington. These requests may originate in the DO or from contacts that other staffers, such as the chief of staff and LAs, may have with constituents.

Perhaps someone back home is interested in the representative's position on a legislative matter. The chief of staff might have an LA call that person to discuss it. Or perhaps some constituents want to visit Washington. Congressman Zach Wamp (R-TN), for example, feels they deserve a first-rate tour of the Capitol, so he often conducts it himself. He estimates he has given an average of 60 tours a year for the time he's been in Congress. Most offices have to organize hundreds of these tours each year, which is a major scheduling challenge. Another common request is for American flags that have flown over the Capitol. There are House employees whose main job it is to continuously run flags up and down over the Capitol to meet the demand.

Representatives usually expect all their staff to take these requests extremely seriously. Congressman Dave Camp (R-MI) takes it so seriously that he personally signs every letter to his constituents and includes a handwritten note at the end if he recognizes the name. He'll stay late at night after the legislative day has ended or take the letters home to Michigan and sign them as he's riding around to meetings and events. He figures he's signed more than three hundred thousand letters during 10 years in office. But most offices either use autopens with the boss's name or simply have a staff member sign the boss's name to the correspondence.

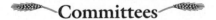

Committees

Each representative is assigned to committees that are further subdivided into subcommittees. The committees roughly correspond to one or more of the executive branch departments. For example, the House and Senate Agriculture Committee corresponds to the Department of Agriculture. In these committees and subcommittees, it is possible to specialize in a certain legislative area. Representatives appeal to their House leaders—the Speaker of the House or the minority leader—to be assigned to coveted (or "exclusive," as they are called) committees. The exclusive committees are Ways and Means and Appropriations—because they control huge sums of money—and Rules, because it determines what legislation reaches the House floor for debate. The leadership parcels out these plums generally based on seniority but sometimes in return for special service, such as agreeing to chair a DNC or RNC committee in order to raise money for other House members. Normally, however, a representative has to serve a long apprenticeship on lesser committees before being eligible for an appointment to an exclusive committee.

Which committees or subcommittees a representative is on may well determine whether you want to work there. A tried-and-true path for a staffer is to match committee assignments with issue areas that the staffer has interest and expertise in, on the assumption that the staffer will be working in this area for many years to come and thus that the contacts and information learned on the Hill will be useful as the staffer's career progresses.

Although a representative may choose a committee assignment based primarily on interest in the issue area, a more likely consideration is how it will increase the ability to help constituents back home and thus increase the prospects for reelection. For example, a congressperson who represents an agricultural district probably will want to be on the Agriculture Committee. Similarly, a congressperson whose district has a lot of veterans may want to be on the Veterans' Affairs Committee. Being on the Appropriations Committee, the committee that decides how much money goes to government programs, makes it easier to win benefits for a congressperson's own congressional district. A representative on Appropriations also has more clout with other representatives because he or she is in a position to affect their districts. These considerations affect you at the staff level as well. Other representatives have to come to your boss for favors. Depending on how special these favors are, they might start out as a discussion between representatives and then go to the chiefs of staff before being parceled out within the office, or they may start at the staff level before being brought to the representative's attention.

Working for a subcommittee or full-committee chairperson is going to put you in a position to get more done than if you were working for someone who is not. This is because the committee chairperson's powers include such things as deciding what the committee's legislative agenda will be, deciding which subjects to call hearings on, delaying a committee vote or flatly refusing to call one, choosing which witnesses will speak, hiring and supervising key committee staffers, and having subpoena power that allows the committee to scrutinize administration policies.

These powers mean that the majority can keep the minority totally out of the loop if it wants to. If you are in the minority party, working for the ranking member (the most senior member of the minority party) is best. Worst of all would be working for a junior member of the minority party.

Committee assignments also affect the type of lobbyists a representative will attract and thus whom you as staff will be spending time with—both during your stint in Congress and possibly thereafter in another career. For every issue in Washington, there is a think tank or association of lobbyists on that issue, pro and con. The more senior a representative is on a committee, the more time and money lobbyists will spend cultivating the representative and the staff, usually the chief of staff and the LAs.

Lobbyists are usually valuable resources, and congressional staffers inevitably get a lot of information from them. Lobbyists typically know their issue area extremely well and know what is the quickest, most useful format in which to supply the information. Often they know these things because they were once congressional staffers themselves. A good lobbyist will never lie to a representative or to a representative's staff because that can only be done once. The lobbyist wants to have an ongoing relationship with the representative. And trust is the key to this. So, when asked directly, the lobbyist will probably answer your question truthfully—but will probably also not volunteer to answer unasked questions if that could be self-defeating. Lobbyists can offer many other benefits, too, such as warning about problems that the office might not hear about otherwise. Lobbyists, or at least their associations, are also in a position to give generously to a representative's reelection campaign—or to the representative's opponent—which is a sobering thought.

AUTHORIZATIONS AND APPROPRIATIONS

Generally, whenever Congress creates and funds a new program, it does so in a two-step process, both of which can be sources of jobs for you. First, an authorizing committee (starting out at subcommittee level, then ratified at full-committee level) writes a bill setting up the program and establishing its parameters. This bill has to pass both the House and the Senate, and the president has to sign it into law. Then, to actually fund the program, appropriations committees (first at subcommittee level, then at full-committee level) in both houses have to write a bill establishing in detail exactly how much money is going to be spent on the various aspects of the program. And again, the president has to sign that into law. So if you are interested in an issue, as a staff person you could work on it through either the authorization process or the appropriations process.

For example, if Congress desires to create a new weapons program for the Department of Defense, a bill authorizing it would be written in the Military Procurement Subcommittee of the House Armed Services Committee. Then, it would be ratified in the full House Armed Service Committee. At that point, the bill would be sent over to the Senate, and the process would start again, first in a subcommittee of the Senate Armed Services Committee and then in full committee. Then, the House and Senate would meet in conference to iron out differences in their bills. Once agreement was reached on a final bill, it would be sent to the president for his signature. At this juncture, the program would be authorized; but with no money appropriated for it, it could not operate.

To get the money, the process starts all over again, now at the appropriations committee level. Bills have to be written in both House and the Senate Appropriations Subcommittees on Defense or Military Construction and ratified by their full committees. Then, differences have to be reconciled in conference and the final appropriations bill sent to the president for his approval.

COMMITTEE STAFFS

Committees and subcommittees at both the authorization and appropriations levels have their own staffs, and these jobs are often the most coveted among Hill staffs. Committee staff routinely write the bills that come before Congress, organize hearings, and generally function as Congress's experts on policy areas within their jurisdiction. Besides allowing you to specialize deeply in one narrow area, these jobs also have a certain amount of job security, they pay more, and it can be easier to translate them into even higher paying jobs after leaving Congress.

Getting these jobs is tough, though. Generally, you have to have deep substantive knowledge in a certain policy area. This knowledge probably comes from working professionally in the area, either as a member of the civil service in one of the executive departments or in some equally professional setting, such as the Government Accounting Office or the Congressional Research Service of the Library of Congress (which maintains staffs of experts on any issue you can think of who spend time researching them for members' offices or committees). For example, to get a job on the House Appropriations Committee's Subcommittee on Defense, you might have had to work first in the budget shop at the Department of the Army. Often the hiring is done on a "staff-to-staff" basis; that is, the directors of the committee staff hire newcomers without much involvement from the members on the committee, unlike the usual procedure when hiring someone in a member's personal office.

Other people get onto committee staffs out of law school through the recommendation of a law professor who knows the committee staff director and who is impressed with the candidate's abilities in an area of interest to the committee. The candidate may arrive on a paid fellowship or some other short-term basis but then be asked to join the committee staff permanently because of superior performance.

Still others land committee staff jobs through first working on the staff of a representative or senator. This used to be a less-common path, particularly in the House, but it has become more common in recent years. Perhaps the aide started out as an LA for the member but when the member became a subcommittee chairman, the aide was asked to go on the subcommittee staff or even be the subcommittee staff director.

Committee staffers are usually paid more than people on personal staffs and are usually older. Most committees usually have a majority staff and a minority staff. This means that while staffers' jobs are secure as long as there is no change in who controls the majority, some of the old majority staff are probably going to lose their jobs if a new party takes over because the majority staff is always larger than the minority staff. After they leave the Hill, because of their knowledge of the process and their personal contacts, committee staffers can often obtain lucrative jobs with lobbyists or law firms. This is especially true if they have been committee staff directors. Others set up their own businesses, often having something to do with the federal government.

There are four different kinds of committees: standing committees (also called permanent committees), select committees, joint committees, and ad hoc committees. Standing House committees, such as Ways and Means, have 30 "statutory" (provided by law) staff positions and a specific amount of money to pay for them. In addition, these committees hire investigative staff. There is a looser limit on the number of these positions. Most committees are divided further into subcommittees that specialize even more and hire their own staff.

Select committees, such as the Senate Aging Committee, are created to handle an issue area that cuts across many topics. Ad hoc committees are temporary committees created to address a timely issue and then disband. Joint committees, such as the prestigious Joint Committee on Taxation, serve both the House and the Senate.

The following people from the Chapter 8 case studies served on House or Senate committee staffs: Jim Dyer, Roger Majak, Janice Mays, Michael Myers, Sean O'Keefe, Scott Palmer, John Podesta, and Ted Van Der Meid.

Leadership Staff

In the House of Representatives, both the majority party and the minority party have leaders who retain specialized staff to help them with their leadership roles. On the majority side, there is the Speaker of the House, the majority leader, and the whip. On the minority side, there is the minority leader and the whip.

The Senate equivalents are the majority leader and minority leader and whips on both sides. The Republicans in both the House and the Senate also have a Republican Conference and a Republican Policy Committee. The Democrats have the same setup in both houses. All of these offices have their own staff. In addition to these traditional leadership positions, there is an "extended leadership family," ranging from chief deputy whips to leadership chairs. Thus, you could work for a member "in the leadership" simply by working in the office of one of the "extended family," and your boss's views would be sought on almost every issue.

Although these leaders have far-reaching powers because they are elected in a party caucus every two years, they cannot expect to operate in a military-style hierarchy that simply orders people around. Here are the highlights of what they and their staffs do.

➤ *Act as spokesperson on the floor.* The House Speaker and House minority leader and the Senate majority and minority leaders are the spokespersons on the floor for their two political parties. They negotiate all procedural questions. They use their powers of persuasion to carry out the party's legislative program. They round up the votes to pass the program, in part by offering assistance in meeting individual needs in exchange for support of the party program. Especially if the president is of their party, the leaders will feel considerable obligation to accommodate the legislative objectives of the president's administration and will try especially hard to pass them in legislative form.

➤ *Disseminate information.* Representatives and senators often consult the leadership about such things as when to participate in debate, committee assignments, the status of pending legislation, the confirmation of nominees, and desired administrative action by the executive branch.

➤ *Insure party discipline.* The leadership works with representatives or senators of their party in order to secure cooperation and unity in carrying out the party's legislative program, the majority leader remains in constant touch with the chairpersons of the various standing committees regarding the progress of legislation. The leadership staff regularly meets with representatives and senators to resolve issues that might arise over pending or proposed legislation.

➤ *Monitor floor activity.* The majority leadership has staff people continuously on the House or Senate floor during each session to see that the party's program is carried out. The minority leadership also has someone on the floor to protect its interests.

The following people from the case studies worked on leadership staffs: David Hoppe, Scott Palmer, Pete Rouse, and Ted Van Der Meid.

Senate Differences

Many of the Senate dynamics are the same as in the House. Both are legislative bodies that deal with the same federal issues. Senators have district offices that handle the same tasks as representatives do. In Washington the structure of the offices is similar, although senators' offices are larger, and they have more caseworkers and LAs. There are, however, many noteworthy differences, starting with campaigns.

GETTING ELECTED

It is important to understand the dynamics of running statewide if you are interested in politics because most high offices—senate seats and state houses—are won through statewide campaigns. One can even view a presidential campaign as a series of state campaigns run under a banner because, under the electoral college system, to win the presidency, the candidate has to win a certain number of states, not just the popular vote total.

Senate campaigns are quite different from House campaigns, focusing more on "wholesale" politics (television ads) than "retail politics" (knocking on doors, holding town hall meetings, etc.). This is because senate campaigns cover a much greater geographical area, and the best way to reach the voters is through mass media. For this reason, it can cost up to $20 million or more to run a Senate race.

Conceptually, many of the steps in organizing a Senate campaign are similar to those of organizing a House campaign. Many of the jobs and the players are the same, too. But there are big differences, as the following list indicates.

➤ *More people are involved.* In a Senate campaign, there is usually a higher degree of specialization and less combining of jobs; consequently, there are more people. This means more layers of control. For instance, a Senate campaign may have a political director, more field organizers than in a House race, a larger fund-raising staff, and more advance personnel.

➤ *Statewide candidates are usually well known.* Quite often people who run for the U.S. Senate are already well known because they already hold office or are celebrities of some kind. This means that they have a voting record that can be touted (or attacked). It also means that they start with a large base of support (their "base vote") and seek to build on that.

➢ *Size means change in the ratio of field operation to media operation.* The size of the state by population or geography will significantly affect the budget, strategy, and nature of how the candidates use their time. Once a senatorial campaign has to cover an area more than a certain size—say, maybe a dozen congressional districts—it is very difficult to have a field operations program similar to the one in the model House campaign, except perhaps in the candidate's base area. Beyond that, the candidate has to depend on endorsements from other candidates and local party committees and sharing resources with them. The campaign becomes more wholesale in that it relies on the media more than a House campaign would. And instead of being able to have campaign representatives (like precinct captains) find out how voters are leaning by personally meeting with them or talking to them on the telephone, the best, quickest, most reliable way is a good poll.

➢ *Use of the candidate's time differs.* Building favorable name recognition is much harder in a statewide race than in a House race because Senate candidates cannot personally meet as large a percentage of their electorate as House candidates can. So Senate candidates have to rely primarily on the media, especially expensive television ads. They can appear in public settings, but such settings have to be big—plant gates, community shopping centers, major county fairs—and not people's homes. Because a Senate candidate will have more media contact and less personal contact with the voters, it takes longer to build favorable name recognition.

➢ *The level of fund-raising is higher.* The fund-raising part of a Senate campaign is similar in concept to that in a House campaign, except that the number of contacts is many orders of magnitude larger. Senate campaigns are subject to the same fund-raising laws as House campaigns, but they may have to raise $5, $10, $15, or $20 million or more. In a statewide campaign, there would be more levels of administrative control, such as regional finance directors reporting to a senior finance director.

➢ *There are more consultants.* The larger the state, the more unlikely it is that you will find any one consultant company that can do all the work alone. This means that the Senate campaign will probably have to find different companies to be the fund-raising consultant, the media consultant, and the direct-mail consultant. The general consultant usually hires these.

OTHER DIFFERENCES

In addition to the differences between House and Senate races, there are differences between how House and Senate offices function, including the following.

➤ Senators only have to run for office every six years, not every two, the way representatives do, so they are not subject to the same quick retaliation from the voters that House members are.

➤ Senators have to spend even more time raising money because their races cost a lot more than House members' do.

➤ The Senate is a more collegial body than the House and less partisan, which often makes it a more enjoyable place to work. The House is more about moving large numbers of people—218 (a majority)—in a certain direction, whereas the Senate is more about moving individual personalities.

➤ Senate staffers usually get paid more than their House counterparts (although, interestingly, senators get paid the same amount as representatives).

➤ Senators usually have more clout than their House equivalents and are more often regarded as national figures, even potential presidential candidates. That can facilitate a Senate staffer's life in a number of ways, ranging from getting the attention of a federal bureaucrat to getting a recommendation for another job.

➤ Whereas the House generally has primacy in money matters, the Senate has primacy in foreign affairs. For example, only the Senate has to ratify treaties.

➤ The Senate has exclusive jurisdiction over the confirmation of the president's appointments to federal jobs.

➤ The Senate is often an "appeals body." The House often (but not always) goes first in the legislative process and passes its bill first. The Senate then often reviews the House's work, accepting most of it, and focuses only on a few specific items of interest in producing its version of the bill. Lobbyists not happy with the House bill bring their case to the Senate, and the Senate often adds items not in the House bill or increases the dollar figures in the House bill. The result in the House-Senate conference on the bill is often more than was in the original House bill—but less than was in the Senate bill.

➤ The Senate has procedures that are different from those in the House, which can often be used to slow down actions of Congress. For example, any individual senator can put a hold on an item, which, although usually not killing it by itself, can slow it down. This makes negotiating within the Senate very different from negotiating within the House. The Senate filibuster (long speeches that cannot be stopped) is another tool for slowing things down.

➤ Staff plays an even greater role in the Senate. Given that the Senate has the same number of committees as the House, but only one-quarter the number of members, one can see that senators are spread pretty thin, serving on many more subcommittees than House members do. Therefore, senators have to rely on staff more than House members do.

➤ In the Senate, it is easier to move from service on a senator's personal staff to service on a committee staff or subcommittee staff than it is in the House.

➤ The proportion of Senate staff working in DOs is about 30 percent, compared with about 50 percent for the House.

Hill Pay

There is a big difference between what people get paid on the Hill. According to the Congressional Management Foundation, which keeps data on House and Senate staff salaries, as of the fall of 2000, $40,200 was the average salary for a college-educated aide serving on the personal staff of a senator or a representative.[2] The foundation found the average House chief of staff earned $97,600; legislative director, $61,100; and press secretary, $45,300. The youngest receive considerably less: $23,800 a year for the average 25-year-old staff assistant on the job about a year. Senate pay tends to be higher. The following are samples of the highest-paid staff in the Senate and House:

Senate

➤ $127,000–$142,415: Senate committee staff director
➤ $140,599: Senate personal staff, legislative director
➤ $122,500–$140,599: Senate personal staff, chief of staff
➤ $110,000: Senate state director

House

➤ $125,000–$136,758: House personal staff, chief of staff
➤ $100,000–$106,000: House legislative director

Looking for a House or Senate Job

The better the job, the more it's like getting into a club; they ask you, you don't ask them. This is because they want to be very certain of your abilities and loyalty before they hire you. That means either observing you for a long time first or having you referred to them by someone they really trust—or both. Just being intelligent and hard working is not enough. You also have to be politically astute and able to work under tight deadlines and a lot of pressure. There is a lot of competition for Hill jobs, so the offices can afford to be picky. Therefore, any long-term strategy for advancement on the Hill should involve working with many important members and their staffs so that they have a chance to observe, and presumably be impressed by, your abilities.

But that is down the road. First, you have to crack the club. As I have already noted, I personally think that the best way to land a job with a member is to work in a campaign. This is an excellent way for the member's aides to observe you under pressure and therefore for you to earn the member's trust. But this presupposes that you have planned this out way ahead of time: know who you want to work for and get a job in that campaign.

Many people get jobs without campaigning, however. The following are some strategies for doing that. Essentially, you need to create a "job-search network." The secret is setting up a wide enough network and then giving it time to work. Jobs open up all the time on the Hill, but most people don't hear about them. Your task is to create as wide a network as possible and then stay in touch with the people in it. Eventually, someone will hear of something. You never know about the Hill. You may go months without hearing anything and then all of a sudden not only is there a job but they want you to start tomorrow. Leave plenty of time (many months) for all this to happen. If you do, you will likely find a job. Here are some steps to take in getting a Hill job:

➤ *Determine what kind of member you'd like to work for.* Remember, the easiest way to progress up the ladder is to pick a really good representative or senator who is going places and then hitch your star to his or hers. As the member rises, so do you, not only in the Capitol Hill pecking order but also within the member's office. Switching from member to member is harder (but doable). Therefore, before you commit to a member, you need to decide not only whether you can get along with the member but whether you genuinely respect him or her. You need to decide such things as whether you are a Republican or a Democrat and what issues you are interested in. You can research the members, their districts, and their voting records in books such as the *Almanac of American Politics.* Become familiar with the committee jurisdictions and which members are on which committees. Committee assignment is very often a key reason you might choose to work for a particular member. Once you narrow your choices down to a few members, start to learn what you can about their offices and what they are like to work for. Do they have high staff turnover? That's a bad sign. To follow what's happening on Capitol Hill generally, you can read *Congressional Quarterly*, *Roll Call*, and *The Hill*, which in many ways are the industry newspapers.

➤ *Go see the staff of your own representative and senators.* Once you have an idea of what you would like to do, go see the chiefs of staff in the offices of your own representative and senators. Tell them that you are looking for a job, and give them a resume. Sell yourself aggressively in terms of what you can do to help with some aspect of the work. It's important that you make a good impression on the chiefs of staff so that they remember you, are impressed with you, and are motivated to help you. Here's where you start getting your "rap" down. If they like you, they'll help you improve it, help you accentuate skills you may not have realized were so important. You may even luck out and find that they have an opening and want to give it to a constituent. But more realistically, you want the chiefs of staff simply to keep their eyes and ears open for you and to give you the names of other people you can see and add to your network—people in other offices, LAs, committee staffers, that sort of thing. Chiefs of staff like to be able to do favors for other offices, such as being able to make a successful referral, so they often keep a stack of resumes in their desks.

Then, go see the people the chiefs of staff suggested and just keep adding people to your network and repeating the process. Check in with the people already in the network from time to time to keep the contacts fresh. Probably the better you get to know them, the more help they will give you.

➤ *Consult the job referral offices on the Hill.* The Senate Placement Office's phone number is (202) 224–9167; it does not maintain a Web site. Historically the first placement office in either the Senate or the House, it originally dealt only with clerical and support positions. Today, however, it has expanded and deals with a wide range of positions, including many of the jobs mentioned in this book. You can learn about some of the job openings in the Senate by calling the recording at (202) 228-JOBS or obtaining the printed version that comes out each Tuesday. But many of the best openings are not published. The Senate Placement Office is a referral service only. Applicants should be available to work within two weeks. The posted openings indicate the proper approach to apply, which varies per job. To be considered for all positions, candidates should visit the Senate Placement Office to complete an application and submit a resume. A counselor will conduct a screening interview with a candidate right then. A counselor will forward appropriate applications and resumes to the various Senate offices based on a match. Senate staffers contact candidates directly if there is an interest.

On the House side, there is the Office of Human Resources that maintains a Web site (house.gov/cao-hr/) that lists vacancies only in the support area—not political jobs. But the site also refers to a House of Representatives job line, (202) 225–2450, which does list vacancies in political jobs. Press option 4, then option 2, then option 3, "Member and Committee Vacancies," to hear descriptions of vacancies in the House—and even some in the Senate. The newspapers *Roll Call* (www.rcjobs.com) and *The Hill* (www.thehill.com/classifieds/employment) also publish listings of Hill jobs. For another site that lists jobs, visit www.hillzoo.com.

➤ *Get an internship or fellowship.* A fellowship is a paying internship. Interning is an excellent way for a young person to start out in a Hill office, and it can be a good springboard to a paying job for two reasons. First, if you are physically in a Hill office every day, your "rabbi," or perhaps the chief of staff or the intern coordinator, is constantly reminded that you are still looking for a paying job. Once you go off the Hill, you have to make a big effort to get people to focus on the fact that you still haven't found anything. The second reason interning is good is that it gives you a chance to show your stuff to the office so that they may want to hire you later. But remember, if you want to convert the internship into a paying job, you have to really stand out because these offices see a lot of interns. Standing out means being available to do a lot of drudge work at first. Ideally, you want to become close to the chief of staff in the office, for he or she is the one who will be doing any hiring later. For example, if you have normal duties during the day that do not put you in contact with the chief of staff, you may want to look for ways to help him or her after work hours, such as volunteering to help take care of mass mailings and things of that sort.

You can find lists of internships on the Internet through the search engine www.google.com. Look under "washington internships," "washington fellowships," "capitol hill internships," "capitol hill fellowships," and so on. If you would like to look into an internship in the Congressional Research Service, a part of the Library of Congress devoted specifically to doing research for Congress, you can consult lcweb.loc.gov/resdev/browse/i.html. Look under the heading "Internships and Fellowships."

➤ *Have an electronic version of your resume ready to send at the drop of a hat.* On the Hill, when people are looking for a new person, they often will just send out an e-mail soliciting resumes to friends, and the friends will e-mail the resumes they have. So job seekers need to be ready to follow up with e-mails quickly after meeting with someone or having an informational interview.

Women Working on the Hill

The bad news is that the percentage of women working in the highest staff jobs on Capitol Hill is substantially less than the percentage of men. The good news is that the women's percentage is steadily growing. According to a 2001 study by the Congressional Management Foundation, 25 percent of Senate chiefs of staff were women, and 75 percent men.[3] In the House, for the year 2000 it was 32 percent women and 68 percent men.[4] (These figures, incidentally, are substantially better than the percentage of women actually serving as representatives or senators, currently 17 percent and 13 percent, respectively.) In 1990, the congressional management foundation reports, 76 percent of the employees in low-level support jobs were women, and 24 percent were men. But by 2000 those numbers had shifted to 67 percent women and 33 percent men.

Where Hill Jobs Lead

It is possible that after a Hill job you might decide on a career completely unrelated to Congress. But it is more likely that you will combine other skills with your knowledge of the Hill and your acquaintance with people who still work there. Probably you will be engaged in something akin to lobbying—if not directly trying to influence Congress on behalf of a client, then at least explaining to the client how to navigate the labyrinth that is Capitol Hill. People from the case studies who fit into this pattern include Richard Armitage, Roger Majak, J. Bonnie Newman, Leon Panetta, Howard Wolfson, and Sean O'Keefe.

For example, you may have a law degree or some other advanced degree and now work in private practice after your stint on the Hill. Your value to your firm is enhanced by the fact that you could help with business before Congress. You could help design a communications program for your company that resonates on Capitol Hill because you have figured out how to get your message into the districts of some key members and then have it reverberate back at the members through their most revered source of all, their constituents. Or you may simply be able to show a key committee staffer more information on a matter and convince him or her that your firm's position is the one the committee ought to adopt.

The same is true if you go to work for an executive department within the administration or even the White House. While working in Congress, you will probably add to your expertise in an issue area, and after the election, your boss, a senator or representative, could very likely become a new rabbi and recommend you to people in the administration and they hire you. In your new job, your knowledge of how to get things through Congress would probably be very useful. And after that job, with both a knowledge of how the administration and the Congress work on your issue area, you would be that much more valuable to a client in the private sector. John Podesta from the case studies is a good example of someone who followed this pattern.

Some people stay in Congress more or less for a whole career, working their way up the ladder. Maybe they started out as a Senate LA 20 years ago, but now they work on the Senate Finance Committee and helped write the law on Social Security or the corporate income tax structure. Or maybe they work for the leaders of the House or Senate. They are, in short, major players in this country's history. Examples from the case studies include David Hoppe, Janice Mays, Michael Myers, Scott Palmer, Pete Rouse, and Ted Van Der Meid.

Notes

1. Joyce Foundation, "Survey of Large Campaign Contributors Finds Opposition to System That Provides Them Access," www.joycefdn.org/news/9806_pr_campaigndonors.html (September 17, 2002).
2. Congressional Management Foundation, "2000 House and Senate Employment Studies," www.cmfweb.org/temp/display.cfn?id=194 (September 17, 2002).
3. Congressional Management Foundation, *2001 Senate Staff Employment Study* (Wasington, D.C.: Congressional Management Foundation, 2001), 15.
4. Congressional Management Foundation, *2000 House Staff Employment Study* (Wasington, D.C.: Congressional Management Foundation, 2000), 15.

5

❦

THE WHITE HOUSE

People working in the White House are a mixture of those who have worked on the campaign and are accomplished organizers and those who are experts from other arenas, including previous White Houses. Particularly at the highest levels—chief of staff, the deputy chiefs of staff, and other office heads—it is important for a new president to have people who know how the White House works and who have had a lot of experience with how political, media, and governmental Washington works.

By and large, these are very demanding jobs where it's possible to mess up big time. Therefore applicants are scrutinized closely. Being bright is not enough; you have to be quick on your feet and tireless because the pace and nature of events can be crushing. Furthermore, White House staffers often have to be "entrepreneurial," in that, while they have a general mission—make the president look good—they often have to do much of the work themselves: devise the concept, implement it, write it up, and promote it all by themselves. Often, because the president wants to impress the public that his office can run with fewer staffers than his predecessor's did, there isn't very much staff assistance.

Most people who get White House jobs (or political appointments in the administration) have had to go through a presidential campaign at one time or another, so this chapter begins with that process. As you will see, such a campaign is long and involved, with many subspecialties that can allow you to hone skills that will be useful in specific White House jobs later. Others transfer to the White House from the Hill because they have political experience and personal contacts useful to the president and because they come highly recommended by someone the president trusts, probably because that person helped the president get elected. Still others are detailed temporarily from other departments or agencies within the government (*detailees*). Others come to the White House because they represent constituencies in which the president is particularly interested.

A lot of college students get their first job in the White House as White House interns. You can consult the program's Web site for more information: www.whitehouse.gov/government/wh-intern.html. White House internships are competitive, but if you can get one, and you are willing to work hard to make the most of it, you can have an extremely valuable experience and possibly land a paying job in the White House after the internship is over. Interns typically get assigned to one of the White House offices discussed later in this chapter and work there for about 90 days. If you want a paying job to come out of it, the key is to stand out. This will require your being willing to work long hours enthusiastically, being extremely reliable, and catching on with little formal training. The information in this book, however, can constitute much of that training.

For a few older, extremely qualified persons, there is also the prestigious White House Fellows program. After a highly competitive selection process, 11–19 men and women are chosen to serve for a year as special assistants to a cabinet member or senior presidential advisor and also participate in an education program designed to nurture their development as leaders. The Web site for this program is at www.whitehousefellows.gov/about/index.html.

Getting Elected

Presidential campaigns are massive affairs that effectively run over several years, cost hundreds of millions of dollars, and employ thousands of workers. They are also the major entry point for thousands of people into the White House and administration job market after the election. People are generally familiar with the latter stages of public campaigning: the fall rallies, debates, television ads, and so on. But they are probably not familiar with the long buildup to the fall campaign and the staggering sums of money that are raised and spent not just by the candidate but by other organizations on the candidate's behalf.

Nature of Presidential Campaigns

Chapter 4 looked at the key jobs in the model House campaign, such as the candidate, campaign manager, field director, finance director, press secretary, and research director. It also discussed how those functions persist into the statewide senatorial campaign, although on a much larger scale because of the change in geographical size of the election area.

As that chapter noted, Senate campaigns differ in many respects to the House campaigns. Senate campaigns mean more people and thus more layers of hierarchy. Most statewide candidates are widely known before the race starts, and the change in geographic size means that relatively less resources are put into the field operation and more are put into media operations. In addition, there may be such a lack of volunteers in a statewide race that the campaign has to pay vendors to do by phone what the volunteers would do in person. Voters connect with the Senate candidate through television ads rather than personal contact. The rules of fund-raising are similar to that in House races, but the dollars go way up. Finally, statewide races require more consultants who come from different firms, and operations are more computerized in the statewide race.

In the presidential race, these trends are taken even further. Although the functional categories in a presidential race are still the same as in the House or Senate campaign, the change in scale is so vast and involves so many more subspecialties and people that the result is a totally different kind of race. In addition to these tremendous changes in scale, there are several new elements added to a presidential race, including the following.

➤ *Electoral college.* In the general election, a presidential campaign is akin to 50 Senate campaigns all overseen from a central headquarters, even though each state has its own strategy for winning that is carried out by statewide managers located in one or several state headquarters. This is because the presidency is won not by winning the popular vote as in a House or Senate race but by winning states in the Electoral College. It's winner take all; winning the state by half a point is as good as winning it by 10 points. This means that the central headquarters needs to concentrate resources—money, candidate's time—on the swing states, the ones that could go either way, while doing just enough to hold on to the candidate's base states and not doing much of anything in the opponent's base states.

For example, base states for Democrats have recently included California, Connecticut, District of Columbia, Illinois, Massachusetts, and Rhode Island.

Base states for Republicans have recently included Alabama, Arizona, Colorado, Georgia, Kansas, Mississippi, Montana, Nebraska, North Dakota, Idaho, Ohio, Oklahoma, South Carolina, Texas, South Dakota, Utah, Virginia, and Wyoming, Swing states have recently included Florida, Michigan, New Mexico, Oregon, Wisconsin, Pennsylvania, Tennessee, and Washington.

➤ *Different fund-raising rules.* In a presidential campaign, unlike a House or Senate campaign, candidates can qualify for federal matching funds in exchange for agreeing to abide by strict restrictions on how much other money they raise and how they spend all monies in their campaigns. This seriously complicates both fund-raising and how campaigns spend money. To receive these matching funds, particularly in the primaries, the campaign has to spend considerable time filling out the forms required by the FEC to determine a candidate's eligibility for public funding and to monitor the candidate's spending. In addition to contracting some accounting tasks to outside operations, the campaign will have its own staff members specializing in specific areas of compliance, such as certification of donations and preparation of applications for matching funds. Obviously, a large fund-raising staff is needed at the national headquarters. During both the primary and general elections, the campaign has to dedicate large amounts of time to monitoring the campaign's spending nationwide to be certain it stays within the FEC expenditure limits.

➤ *Even more media.* The problems of scale seen in going from a House race to a Senate race are so much greater in the presidential race that the relation between money spent on grassroots field operations and money spent on television ads is even more skewed toward large, expensive media buys. The candidate cannot be in each state very often, so the campaign compensates by maximizing the impact the visits have that the candidate can make and building a connection with voters through various other means. These include paid, nationwide television commercials, media interviews, and "earned" media coverage (news coverage, as opposed to paid ads) of the campaign. It also includes surrogate speakers, direct mail through state parties, automated phone calls, and endorsements in the individual states. At the same time, each state is running a field operation similar to what it would do in a Senate campaign, with increasing use of direct mail, paid voter preference identification calls, and automated messages phoned to tens of thousands of voters.

A couple of decades ago, traditional campaigning emphasized large grassroots volunteer and field operations that created excitement with lawn signs, bumper stickers, buttons, and literature. These methods were gradually replaced by more and more spending on media and media experts in presidential campaigns. In recent years, however, there has been a trend toward developing more grassroots efforts to get back to the "knock-on-every-door" philosophy of high-quality personal contact more common in state representatives' races.

For example, in 1996 organized labor, a traditional Democratic ally, spent a lot of money on television ads aimed at vulnerable freshman Republican representatives. But this approach didn't really work, so the unions reallocated funds from media-driven ad campaigns toward grassroots organizing, voter awareness, and get-out-the-vote efforts. The same thing was done with get-out-the-vote efforts aimed at African-American voters. Both proved effective in 1998, showing that emphasis on grassroots, person-to-person contact can have a decisive affect in generally low-turnout elections.

➤ *Secret Service protection.* Unlike any other candidates, presidential candidates receive Secret Service protection, which complicates the logistics of anything the candidate does in appearing before the public.

➤ *Travel by plane.* A presidential candidate is going to travel almost everywhere by airplane, bringing some campaign staff, the Secret Service, and even representatives of the media in his entourage. This makes for sophisticated logistics and tight schedules.

The following sections describe what you can expect if you work on a presidential campaign.

PHASE ONE: SETTING UP A POLITICAL ACTION COMMITTEE

Starting three or more years before the presidential election, a would-be candidate may start a PAC to raise money for candidates running for other offices two years before the presidential race. A staff is needed for this, and it is the first opportunity to get involved with the candidate. The idea is that beneficiaries of the PAC will return the favor later by helping the candidate win the party's presidential nomination. Besides creating "chits" to draw on later, the candidate is also building and testing a fund-raising operation. At the end of 1998, for example, Vice President Gore's PAC, "Leadership '98," raised about $4.3 million. After the PAC has completed its work, it is closed down to make way for the national campaign.

PHASE TWO: SETTING UP A NATIONAL HEADQUARTERS

Although a presidential candidate may start a national campaign headquarters as much as a year and a half before the November election and appoint a campaign chairperson then, the size of the staff will start out quite small and fluctuate depending on the availability of funds and the level of activity. During the height of the general election campaign, the paid national headquarters staff will probably number several hundred and will be assisted by numerous local volunteers. Each of the swing states and base states will also probably have 50 or more paid personnel at a central state headquarters about four months out from election day, a number that will grow considerably as election day approaches. These paid staffers will be assisted by hundreds of volunteers. There will also be paid and unpaid people in many area offices around each of these states.

In addition to orchestrating the campaign at the national level, the headquarters staff also is responsible for directing and funding the activities of the network of state and local salaried workers and volunteers. After the election, only a few members of the finance and legal staffs will remain on the payroll until they file the final reports with the FEC, as much as a year or more after the election.

The national headquarters' size and activities will expand and contract to meet needs and control costs. Major activities of the organization during the primary campaign period include raising enough money to qualify for public matching funds and building a national network of state and local campaign organizations. Another activity is developing and implementing a strategic plan to win as many key primaries (and thus delegates) as possible, before the party's convention in the summer.

PHASE THREE: RAISING MONEY FOR THE PRIMARIES

Starting in the spring, one-and-a-half years before the presidential election, the candidate needs to start raising more than $20 million by the fall in order to participate effectively in the following year's spring presidential primaries. The candidate's party cannot help with this; it has to remain neutral until the candidate officially gets the party nomination in the summer of the election year. Thus, the candidate has to organize and execute dozens of fund-raisers (dinners, receptions, other events) to which people with means are invited and to seek contributions through direct solicitations. The old PAC is disbanded and a new fund-raising organization is created. More staff is recruited, paid and unpaid. If the candidate cannot raise an impressive amount of money during this phase, the press may not take the campaign seriously, which can lead to difficulties in raising more money and securing endorsements.

Fund-raisers carefully vet donors to maximize the amounts of money from people who do not want very much in return—personal friends of the candidate, enemies of the opponent, people who just want an autographed photo with the candidate, party activists, and others who agree with the candidate's position on the issues. In turn, fund-raisers seek to minimize or eliminate entirely the amounts raised from people who could be perceived as wanting a great deal in return—tax breaks or other special consideration in business pending before the U.S. government—or who represent interests that are in conflict with the candidate's agenda.

Presidential Fund-Raising Laws

At this juncture, it will help to review the laws relating to presidential fund-raising because much of the art of fund-raising is negotiating this obstacle course. The current system is the result of reforms that were enacted in 2002. In a nutshell, presidential campaigns are covered by the same contribution limits and disclosure requirements as congressional candidates (see chapter 4). But unlike congressional races, presidential candidates also receive public funds (federal matching funds) if they agree to voluntary spending limits. The first round of these funds is for the primaries; the second is for the general election. This system is funded by the voluntary tax check-off on federal income tax forms.

In 2000 Vice President Gore agreed to the matching funds plan for the primaries and therefore was capped at raising about $34 million and spending about $43 million in the primaries. But the financial apparatus of his opponent, Governor Bush, run by a network of two hundred business friends known as the "Pioneers," was able to raise such a huge war chest—about $113 million—that Bush decided to forgo federal matching funds and therefore had no limits on what he could raise and spend in the primaries.

For the general election, however, both candidates agreed to accept $67 million in federal funds in exchange for not raising or spending any other monies. But much more money than that was spent on their behalf using the same methods as those that exist for House and Senate candidates—party expenditures, soft money contributions (now illegal), and independent expenditures.

Most of this money went to television advertising. According to Luke McLoughlin, coauthor of *Buying Time 2000: Television Advertising in the 2000 Federal Elections* (2001), candidates, parties, and groups spent in excess of $112 million in television advertising for Governor Bush and just over $92 million for Vice President Gore in the 2000 election cycle. The figures for just the general election were more than $89 million for Bush and more than $76 million for Gore. These figures actually understate the amount because they do not include the premium charged to buying time during very busy periods, estimated to be in the range of 10 to 20 percent. The roughly $13 million difference in television ad buys meant that Bush, the Republican Party, and pro-Bush groups aired about seven thousand more ads than Gore, the Democratic Party, and pro-Gore groups.

PHASE FOUR: FEWER FUND-RAISERS, MORE CAMPAIGN WORKERS

After the candidate has raised enough money to pursue the nomination—probably during the winter before the presidential election—many of the fund-raisers leave the candidate's campaign and move to the DNC or the RNC to raise money for the parties. The parties, in turn, spend that money on electing their candidate to the presidency after the candidate wins the party nomination. But they have to abide by the law in exactly how they can raise and spend the money.

In addition, after the candidate has finished raising money for the primaries and starts to help the national party raise money, more staff is hired, including researchers, political organizers, and communications experts. These are both paid and volunteer positions. The paid positions generally go to people who have had prior experience in this work, and the unpaid positions to those who haven't. But there are plenty of exceptions, usually based on who you know and what your skill level is. During the spring, starting in Iowa and New Hampshire, primary elections take place in almost every state in the Union. In addition to the headquarters staff at the national campaign office—another source of jobs—there are the campaign offices in each of the primary states.

For those who have absolutely no idea how to join a campaign, they can simply walk in the door of the headquarters in one of these primary states and sign up. The campaigns will probably be happy to see you and put you right to work. At first, you will probably do a variety of mundane chores, such as stuffing envelopes, making rally signs, delivering boxes of campaign brochures, picking up people, participating in rallies, and knocking on doors. But if you do them well and are always available and reliable (day and night), you'll move up fast. If you want, you can move from state to state during the primaries or just work on the one in your home state. After each primary is over, the paid staff is quickly laid off to save money. The best workers move on to other states and get paying jobs there. Others call it quits after working several months on one primary and don't do anything more until the general election in the fall. As the primary season ends and the political and financial workload decreases temporarily, the headquarters staff will be dramatically downsized in order to keep costs within mandated expenditure limits.

PHASE FIVE: LULL IN THE CAMPAIGN

There can be a long gap—maybe three or four months—between the time it is effectively known that the candidate has wrapped up the nomination in the spring and when the candidate gets the matching funds for the general election. This is because the nomination isn't officially made until late summer at the party convention, and the candidate cannot legally receive the money until then. It may be that a candidate is out of money during this period, having spent everything on obtaining the nomination, and thus that the campaign is not as visible as the opponent's. It may also be the worst time in the cycle for you to get a paying job with the campaign, but it may also be when volunteers are even more valuable.

PHASE SIX: THE CONVENTIONS

In the presidential primary season, generally speaking, winning a state primary means that the candidate wins delegates pledged to vote for him or her on the first ballot of the party convention that summer. The exact formula varies from state to state and from party to party. But with most states having a presidential primary these days, it is possible to know with certainty who has effectively won the Democratic and Republican nominations at the end of the primary season, and increasingly, one knows only partway through it. The convention merely officially ratifies this decision. Still, although the conventions are no longer the dramatic events they used to be when the nominations were actually decided there, they are still the most important quadrennial party rallies, and people interested in politics generally try to wangle a way to participate in them. Many people do this as volunteers, agreeing to help the party with running the convention in exchange for just being able to get an admissions pass. At a convention, there are usually about 230 to 250 paid staff and more than a thousand volunteer staff.

PHASE SEVEN: MATCHING FUNDS KICK IN, GENERAL ELECTION

After the candidate has won the nomination, the one-on-one presidential race starts officially at the convention in August (about three months before election day) and kicks into gear a month or so later, after Labor Day. After the candidate officially receives the matching funds, the campaign hires even more workers for the final two-month push. The campaign quickly expands again, reopening state operations in all targeted states and developing and implementing a strategic plan for the general election campaign. Again, some workers are based in the national campaign headquarters, but most are based in the state campaign offices. After obtaining the nomination, the candidate will also receive help from his or her political party, both in terms of workers and of money spent on the candidate's behalf, but not given to the candidate directly. Some staff will transfer from the candidate's campaign to the party and vice versa. All throughout the long campaign process, starting with the PAC years before the presidential campaign, there are opportunities for you to break into politics by meeting people and impressing them with your skills. Gradually, you get to know many of the players on your team. You learn to be sensitive to ongoing "turf wars" and to avoid them. Every political campaign is a stew of egos and ambitions, temporarily and uneasily held together to achieve a common goal. Sometimes you will see such crazy backbiting and infighting that you'll think your side could never win. But it can.

The Transition Team and the Inaugural Committee

Even though a candidate wins the presidency in November, the president doesn't take office until January 20—about two-and-a-half months later. If it is a new president, there will be a presidential transition period during which the president-elect starts to recruit staff and decides how to run the new presidency. The Presidential Transition Team that runs this process provides another opportunity for breaking into the job network, perhaps by cementing contacts built during the campaign or by having expertise on an issue that is needed right then. Many people do this as volunteers, assisting in putting together briefing books and other materials to help determine how the government will be run and who should be recruited to fill the jobs, particularly the seven hundred or so "subcabinet" positions that have to be confirmed by the Senate.

The team selected to help with transition typically includes a mix of lawyers and professionals in the executive search field, as well as people who have had experience in government and not just the private sector. There are usually about five hundred people on the transition team. They consult with the candidates for the subcabinet jobs, members of Congress who may sit on a committee having jurisdiction over the department, presidential staff, agency heads, and informed outsiders to make up short lists of three to five people for each job that are then taken to the president. The names that usually get on these lists are not just people with impressive resumes but people who have experience in getting results similar to those the administration is looking for now. Only after these folks get their jobs are the thousands of other political appointments made, the ones that do not require Senate confirmation.

Also taking place during this transition period are preparations for the presidential inauguration. The inaugural is run by a separate Presidential Inaugural Committee (PIC), which is assisted by a Joint Congressional Committee on Inaugural Ceremonies (JCCIC) and an Armed Forces Inaugural Committee (AFIC). The JCCIC handles the inaugural activities at the Capitol, including the swearing-in ceremony and the traditional luncheon honoring the president and vice president. The military personnel of the AFIC handles planning, operations, communications, logistics, and personnel support for the PIC. There are between 250 and 300 paid positions on the PIC, although most of these go to campaigners as a sort of reward—and another paycheck after they've been cut off the campaign payroll. The inaugural is one big party, or rather hundreds of parties and events, all of which have to be organized. The PIC determines who will be invited to participate in the inaugural events, such as the parade and the parties. The PIC also determines where the balls will be held, what kind of balls they will be, and what kind of special events there will be. Fortunately, much of the inaugural is generic and the eight hundred or so professionals from the AFIC who have done many inaugurals before provide ample assistance to the less-experienced "politicals" at the PIC.

Layout of the White House

Before turning to the various jobs in the White House, there needs to be a little orientation to the geography of the place. When one hears the term *White House,* one automatically thinks of the elegant white building in which presidents and their families have resided since 1800. This is actually called the Residence. The White House complex is much bigger. On one side of the Residence is the East Wing, and on the other the West Wing (the "West," for short), which houses the Oval Office (the "Oval"), the president's personal working office. Running by the West Wing is a street called West Executive Avenue, and on the other side of that is the Eisenhower Executive Office Building, or EOB for short.

Built in the 1870s and 1880s, originally to house the State, Navy, and War Departments, the EOB is possibly the most unusual place to work in Washington. It has wide corridors with floors of black and white marble squares, resembling a gigantic chessboard. It also has high ceilings, ornate decorations, and unusual but colorful Victorian color schemes. Among their many duties, White House staffers are expected to give evening tours of both the EOB and the West Wing to special guests.

All these buildings are bounded by a black metal fence and patrolled by Secret Service guards, some in white shirts and black pants with a gold stripe on the leg and a few others in dark Ninja-like attire and dark baseball caps, carrying machine guns concealed in big canvas bags.

Across from the EOB, on the other side of Seventeenth Street, are several more buildings containing White House staff. Across Pennsylvania Avenue at the north end of the Residence, is Lafayette Park, which is bordered by many old restored buildings saved from demolition by Jacqueline Kennedy, containing yet again more White House staffers.

All of these areas are called the White House, and the people who work in them are called White House staffers. But because proximity to the president of the United States (POTUS) is key, and the president works in the West Wing, the most prestigious staff offices are there. These are small, however, sometimes no more than converted bathrooms, and only about two hundred people work there. Most of the rest are in the more elegant offices in the EOB. For most offices, the head person and one or two assistants are located in the West Wing and the rest of the staff is over in the EOB.

How the White House Is Organized

To understand how the White House is organized, one must first understand the difference between the White House Office and the larger Executive Office of the President (EOP), of which the White House Office is but one part. The group of staffers most commonly thought of as White House staffers make up the White House Office, which is broken down into more than two dozen smaller offices that will be examined shortly. A White House telephone directory from the Clinton administration listed 537 names under the White House Office.

The EOP is broken down into about a dozen offices (one of which is the White House Office). The White House phone book listed 1,114 names in addition to the White House Office, thus making a total of 1,651 people who could qualify for the term *White House staffer*.

Even this, however, is not the real number of people who work in the White House because it does not include interns, volunteers, detailees, or assignees loaned from other departments or agencies. Although it is difficult to break out the number of these people who work directly for the White House Office as opposed to the EOP, the White House as a whole has a pool of about a thousand volunteers (some of them full-time) and 75 to 200 interns, with the largest number of interns working during the summer.

Although detailees work in the White House, they are paid by their department or agency of origin. Normally, they cannot serve at the White House for longer than six months in any fiscal year. However, by starting their service at the end of one fiscal year and finishing it in the first half of a second, they can put together one consecutive calendar year at the White House. After that, they are supposed to return to their agency of origin for a period of time before being eligible for another stint at the White House. There are also certain limits on the type of work detailees can do. For instance, they are not allowed to do any political work. An assignee is someone detailed to the White House with no time limit. Many of the employees in the George W. Bush administration's newly formed Office of Homeland Security are assignees.

Unlike individual offices in the House of Representatives and the Senate, the White House does not have a legal ceiling on the number of employees or detailees/assignees it can have. However, with only a few exceptions, such as the aforementioned Office of Homeland Security, the ceiling has remained fairly constant over the last decade, according to the House Appropriations Subcommittee on Treasury, Postal Service and General Government, which funds the White House. So, although there is no legal ceiling, there is a de facto one that Congress tries to maintain except in unusual circumstances.

In his book *The White House Staff: Inside the West Wing and Beyond* (2000) Bradley Patterson gives the total number of what he calls the "White House Staff Community" at almost six thousand people. But it is critical to understand that most of these workers do not get "fired" if the administration is voted out of power. There is a large career institutional White House that stays from administration to administration, and there are detailees from other departments who get rotated in and out of the White House but get paid by their department of origin. They all keep their jobs regardless of who gets elected president. Generally speaking, all White House Office employees lose their jobs if their party loses the presidency. But only some of the other EOP employees do, the ones who head up certain offices. Much of the staff of these offices consists of career White House employees who stay. It is hard to make a blanket statement about just how far down this process goes in each office. The reader must simply keep in mind, when discussing the EOP, that some workers are political appointments and some are not.

White House Office

The descriptions in this section of offices within the White House Office are based on how the White House was set up in the Clinton administration. They derive from White House manuals and telephone books, Bradley Patterson's book, and my own observations and those of my colleagues.

Although other administrations have been similar, none are exactly the same. Some have added or subtracted offices from this list or combined responsibilities in different ways. (Throughout this chapter, the number of persons working in an office as indicated in the White House phone book is added as a parenthetical insertion after the title of the office. This number does not include interns, volunteers, detailees, or assignees.)

OFFICE OF THE CHIEF OF STAFF (21)

The Office of the Chief of Staff is responsible for directing, managing, and overseeing all policy development, daily operations, and staff activities for the president. The office coordinates and communicates with all departments and agencies of the administration. Essentially, it enforces decision-making procedures and makes sure no one bypasses the system. It facilitates linkages between other offices. It aims to be aware of all significant enterprises happening in the White House, although sometimes this becomes difficult with secret National Security Council (NSC) issues. The chief of staff takes the heat for denying people access to the president. Case studies of Andrew Card, Leon Panetta, and John Podesta, all chiefs of staff, are found in Chapter 8, as are case studies of Maria Echaveste and Sylvia Mathews, deputy chiefs of staff.

OVAL OFFICE OPERATIONS (9)

The Oval Office is the president's primary working office. Oval Office Operations staff are in charge of carrying out the president's daily office schedule and providing office support as needed. The office consists of a director who is a gatekeeper responsible for traffic in and out of the Oval Office, the president's personal secretary who handles the president's phone and makes the president's personal appointments, a personal aide who accompanies the president at all times, a staff assistant, and an intern. The office also organizes the president's weekly radio address.

PRESIDENTIAL SCHEDULING (12)

Probably two-thirds of the president's time tends to be engagements for which the president has little choice: NSC briefings, Legislative Affairs briefings, staff meetings, and more. The other third is more discretionary, and the Scheduling Office sets up a schedule far into the future to ensure that the president uses this time well. Several sources must approve each scheduling request. First, there are internal scheduling requests. The planning group from the Domestic Policy Council, for example, or the Office of Political Affairs, or Cabinet Affairs, or Communications, might decide on a scheduling request.

Then there are many external requests received every day. These are reviewed, and only a few of the best ones are circulated to a few key staffers. A scheduling committee meets every week to review requests from the White House staff (in written schedule-proposal format). These usually consist of invitations from the public that survived the aforementioned review, recommendations from cabinet members brought through the Cabinet Affairs office, and requests from Congress brought by Legislative Affairs. A small number of these requests make it on to the president's schedule, and the appointments secretary has to inform all the people who were turned down.

The final schedule is put on computer and listed minute by minute for weeks in advance. The Scheduling Office then sends a "set-up" memo to the Secret Service, the first lady's office, and the press secretary. After an event takes place, the presidential diarist writes it up. The name of every person who met with the president is entered, as are the subject of the meeting and every phone call associated with it, along with the unclassified papers used.

OFFICE OF PRESIDENTIAL ADVANCE (12)

The Office of Presidential Advance organizes and implements the president's and first lady's visits outside the White House complex. Advance is responsible for the design and structure of activities at each location that the president or first lady visits. For most trips, advance staff serve as the primary coordinators between the White House, the White House Military Office, the Secret Service, and the local communities to be visited. Advance prepares presidential trips, which are exceedingly complex affairs and usually take months to arrange. Every minute is accounted for.

This office uses many local volunteers. It also uses people detailed temporarily from other departments. The process of a trip begins with deciding what message is desired to be delivered. Advance then helps determine where to go. Perhaps there is an event that is already set to take place that the president could jump into. More likely, though, an entirely new event needs to be structured. Several possible locations and scenarios are weighed. This is called *preadvance*. Finally, one recommendation is made.

The Office of the Counsel to the President (see description that follows) decides what percentage of the trip is official and what percentage is political. The taxpayer pays the former, but the president's political party or some other source pays the latter.

Advance teams use checklists to make final survey visits. The advance office is in charge of crowd generation and press advance, which means setting up special areas for the press and making other arrangements for them. Huge advance teams cause problems especially for U.S. embassies in foreign countries and for foreign officials not familiar with the magnitude and complexity of a presidential trip.

If the president's schedule calls for a trip involving Air Force One, there will inevitably be a lot of jockeying both from inside and outside the White House for places on the plane for at least one leg of the trip. White House aides all suddenly volunteer to be part of presidential advance for the trip, especially if it is a foreign one. People who get jobs in the advance office have usually held similar positions in the campaign.

STAFF SECRETARY (4)

The staff secretary clears all materials for the president. This includes communications, decision memos, briefing papers for the president's briefing book, call sheets (recommended telephone calls), speeches, and correspondence. John Podesta was a staff secretary prior to becoming chief of staff. The staff secretary may circulate the materials to other White House offices, executive departments, or agencies before forwarding them to the president. The staff secretary attends meetings in order to become familiar with what is going on. Each evening, the staff secretary assembles the president's daily briefing book. It has the schedule for the next day, tabbed briefing papers, and talking points for each event. Each event is assigned a contact person. The staff secretary is the funnel for papers coming in and out of the Oval Office and is responsible for notifying those concerned about the president's decisions. The staff secretary's office also builds an archival record and oversees the Department of Correspondence and Presidential Messages.

Department of Correspondence and Presidential Messages (5)

The Department of Correspondence and Presidential Messages receives and processes all correspondence addressed to the president. The department oversees the following agencies:

> ➤ *Agency Liaison (6)*. This office assists members of the public who request help from the president or first lady in resolving a problem. It functions similarly to caseworkers in congressional offices. The office refers many requests to established contacts in federal agen-

cies or in private sector organizations, depending on the nature of the casework.

➤ *Public Access Electronic Mail Office (2)*. This office accepts and responds to all electronic mail sent to the president.

➤ *Gifts Unit (4)*. The Gifts Unit catalogs all gifts received by the first family and members of the White House staff. It, or the Office of the Counsel to the President, is available to answer questions from White House staff regarding gifts they receive for themselves or on behalf of the first family. In order to avoid even the appearance of impropriety, there are strict rules governing the gifts persons in the White House can receive.

➤ *Mail Analysis (16)*. This office analyzes, routes, and processes the 3 to 4 million pieces of mail the president receives each year. It is augmented by many volunteers, depending on the volume of the mail.

➤ *Presidential Inquiries, Greetings, Comments (3)*. Presidential Inquiries is responsible for Greetings and the Comment Line. Greetings is responsible for filling requests from the public and from congressional offices, such as a presidential letter commemorating someone's one hundredth birthday. The Comment Line takes calls from the general public who wish to convey their opinions and ideas to the president.

➤ *Presidential Letters and Messages (9)*. This office drafts and reviews all individual letters, messages, and proclamations ("procs") signed by the president.

➤ *Presidential Support (9)*. This office prepares all documents generated by the Correspondence Department for the president's signature (usually by autopen) and provides support to the Executive Clerk. Large form-letter mailings are also processed in this office.

➤ *Special Projects (2)*. Two people serve here as ombudsmen between the administration and the public on all complaints and inquiries. They also work on certain letter projects and maintain a file of personal issue stories for presidential speeches, trips, and testimony.

➤ *Student Correspondence (4)*. This office responds to all requests from children and students through high school age. Student Correspondence also produces publications for use by teachers in classrooms.

➤ *Volunteer Office (3)*. The Volunteer Office manages activities performed by volunteers in the White House complex. It recruits volunteers, secures passes and security clearance for them, assigns them to offices, and develops incentives for them (offering them free tickets in the presidential box at the Kennedy Center, for example).

➤ *Executive Clerk (5)*. The executive clerk is responsible for the preparation and disposition of all official presidential documents, such as nominations to be submitted to the Senate, commissions of appointments, executive orders, proclamations, messages to Congress, and memoranda from the president to units of the executive branch. In addition, the office serves as the official point of presidential receipt of formal documents from Congress, such as joint resolutions, enrolled bills, and Senate confirmation resolutions. The office is charged with maintaining the official White House record of presidential action on these subjects.

➤ *Records Management (24)*. This office offers guidance on the creation and maintenance of files and appropriate filing procedures.

OFFICE OF THE COUNSEL TO THE PRESIDENT (34)

The Office of the Counsel to the President consists of a battery of lawyers who advise the president and the rest of the White House on all legal issues concerning the Office of the President and the White House. The Counsel's Office is also responsible for advising on the legal aspects of policy questions, legal issues arising in connection with the president's decision to sign or veto legislation, ethical questions and financial disclosure, conflicts of interest, postemployment restrictions, and appropriate lines between official and political activities. For example, the Counsel's Office will decide what percentage of a presidential trip is political and which is official, with the DNC or RNC paying for the former. The Counsel's Office is the only channel between the White House Office and the Justice Department.

The Counsel's Office oversees the first family's legal business. It also oversees the granting of pardons, reviews speeches, and prevents businesses from trying to associate themselves with the president's name or image for commercial purposes. It cannot help a White House staffer if it knows he or she has done something illegal; the Counsel's Office is duty bound to report it to the attorney general. It oversees requests from Congress for documents. It oversees vetoes. With the Office of Presidential Personnel, it also oversees tax compliance investigations and Federal Bureau of Investigation (FBI) reports on persons to be hired. It vets judicial appointees.

OFFICE OF COMMUNICATIONS (8)

The Office of Communications decides what messages the president and the entire government should communicate from the "bully pulpit," both long term and day by day. Its recommendations often determine the events the president participates in each day and how the communications offices of the various executive departments should "amplify" each event. The Office of Communications supervises not only the White House Office of Media Relations and Television Affairs but also the speechwriters and the Office of Public Liaison. This is to ensure that the entire administration speaks with one voice, or "stays on message," as the saying goes.

The Office of Communications seeks to control the press corps. For instance, it asks reporters to go through the press secretary's office to ask questions and has to approve what White House staffers say to the press. If reporters try to circumvent this system, the office can decide to punish them by depriving them of sources and briefings. It includes a Media Relations Office, which is a White House liaison to local media. Media relations might ask the public affairs officers in the various departments and agencies, for example, to write Op-Ed pieces and plant them in small papers all over the country. Within the Office of Communications are also Communications Research and Speechwriting:

Communications Research (5)

Typically, one writer and one researcher are assigned to write a speech. The researcher prepares material on the event at which the president will be speaking: the history, background, and setting. Research also does fact checking and from time to time produces talking points on administration accomplishments. Research has its own library and full use of the Library of Congress, as well as access to personnel in the departments and agencies of the federal government.

Speechwriting (9)

The president's inaugural address and the State of the Union (SOTU) address are traditionally very important speeches. But there are many others to prepare, ranging from those for presidential trips to greetings for special groups gathering in the Rose Garden or the Executive Office Building. There are also many smaller speeches for appearances before constituency groups. Speechwriting also prepares the president's weekly radio address. The Speechwriting Office is the gateway to the president. Other people may suggest drafts, but they must go through this office to make the suggestions.

OFFICE OF THE PRESS SECRETARY (23)

The Office of the Press Secretary is the only routine on-the-record White House source for journalists assigned to cover the president. The press secretary has to be well briefed on what is going on and has to develop a good sense of the president's purposes and priorities.

Every day or so, the press secretary gives both an informal morning press briefing (called the "gaggle") covering the White House beat and a formal afternoon briefing, and also arranges other sessions for individual reporters. The press secretary advises the president and the president's colleagues as to what the press reaction will be to proposed initiatives. The press secretary also prepares the president for presidential news conferences. This entails pulling together briefing materials and guessing at several dozen questions the press might ask and then getting the answers from the appropriate departments. The Office of the Press Secretary then conducts a rehearsal to help the president master the answers and the delivery.

The Office of the Press Secretary prepares press plans for upcoming trips, deciding, for example, who in the presidential party should meet with the press. The press secretary consults with the Washington bureau chiefs of the television networks, primarily to discuss details for trips and the facilities needed by the reporters.

The press secretary leads a team of press secretaries from the cabinet departments to make sure they are all working off the same page. When one of the departments has a key announcement, it will hand it to the press secretary to make, or even to the president. When there is bad news, the department will make the announcement.

The press secretary maintains three offices: the Upper Press Office, which is on the first floor of the West Wing and gives verbal briefings to the press; the Lower Press Office, which is on the second floor of the West Wing and gives paper material to the press; and the Executive Office Building Press Office, which houses most of the staff. Chapter 8 provides the biography of Marlin Fitzwater, press secretary during the Reagan and George H. W. Bush administrations.

OFFICE OF CABINET AFFAIRS (7)

The Office of Cabinet Affairs connects with the chiefs of staff in the cabinet departments. It ensures that the cabinet secretaries will be informed as to what the president is doing and vice versa. In the latter regard, it requires weekly reports from the departments and agencies so that it can inform the president. It also requires that each departmental chief of staff send a memo each day alerting the president as to what is happening that day. The Office of Cabinet Affairs also asks cabinet secretaries to amplify important presidential initiatives or messages, such as the State of the Union address. Cabinet members are assigned media markets they are supposed to hit. They report the results to the Office of Cabinet Affairs; which in turn gives a report to the president.

OFFICE OF INTERGOVERNMENTAL AFFAIRS (8)

The Office of Intergovernmental Affairs serves as the liaison between the White House and state and local governments. For instance, it provides information on the impact federal programs would have on these governments. It receives complaints from state and local officials and advises them on how to cut through the maze of federal bureaucracy. For example, if a federal plan or policy threatened a local government, that government could appeal to this office. The Office of Intergovernmental Affairs also coordinates natural disaster relief. In addition, it represents the views of state and local elected officials in policy formulation within the administration. It works closely with organizations representing state and local elected officials, such as the National Governors' Association and the United States Conference of Mayors. No one cabinet department could handle all these kinds of problems because they often cut across lines, and a special coordinating entity is needed. Because they exercise governmental power, governors, mayors, county commissioners, state legislatures, and tribal chairmen differ from the other external agencies that communicate with the White House. Mickey Ibarra, who is profiled in the case studies, was the director of intergovernmental affairs during the Clinton administration.

OFFICE OF LEGISLATIVE AFFAIRS (20)

The Office of Legislative Affairs serves as the president's lobbyist on Capitol Hill. Its major responsibility is developing strategies for getting the president's legislative agenda enacted into law. This office also is the point of contact within the White House for representatives and senators to register their concerns and to bargain with the president. It is subdivided into House and Senate sections and also has a branch that concentrates on confirmations. Congressional mail to the president comes first to this office. When Congress is in session, a number of legislative affairs staffers spend their day on Capitol Hill, operating out of the offices of their respective parties' leadership. They take the pulse of the Hill and inform the White House as to whether a presidential initiative will pass muster on the Hill or what it will take in the form of presidential largess to make it pass muster. They visit congressional offices, take vote counts, and send the results back to their colleagues in the White House so that the president can lobby recalcitrant members. The Office of Legislative Affairs responds to congressional requests for presidential perks and favors, such as White House tours, photos with the president, seats on Air Force One, and seats in the presidential box at the Kennedy Center. It writes briefing materials about members coming to see the president and call sheets for presidential phone calls. The office leads a team of congressional relations staffers from the executive departments so they can divide up the vote counting and lobbying and get it done quickly. It keeps score on who voted how, who usually supports the president and who does not, and therefore who should get presidential patronage and who should not.

OFFICE OF POLITICAL AFFAIRS (10)

The Office of Political Affairs handles relations with the president's party (the DNC or RNC) and carries out some of the functions at one time performed by the parties. Although the president is the titular head of the party, the fact is that the party and its staff are in the day-to-day hands of the party chairperson, not the president. And sometimes the interests of the party are not exactly the same as the interests of the president. When this occurs, the president may wish a channel that is quicker and more direct; the Office of Political Affairs is that channel. But this office still works closely with the party because the party has resources that the White House lacks. For example, the party can pay for political mass mailings that the White House is not legally allowed to do. It can receive the money donated through the president's fund-raising appearances. And the parties employ staffs of people to vet donors and make sure they will not cause embarrassment to the president. In some cases, the White House seeks to widen its political support beyond the party. These efforts, of necessity, have to be coordinated at the White House, not at party headquarters.

Political travel requests for the president that emanate from the Office of Political Affairs get expedited treatment. Helping candidates is a function of this office, particularly arranging for presidential attendance at fund-raisers. Office staff, divided into "regional desks," receive these requests, vet them, help arrange the president's trip, and help arrange and vet the people who will be in the photo-receiving lines to shake hands and have their picture taken with the president. The office also produces travel briefs for the president, vice president, and first and second ladies that describe the political situation in the state the principal is visiting. The office also writes a weekly report to the president on hot political news from around the country.

The Office of Political Affairs is one of the few offices in the White House in which staff is allowed to work on purely political matters on government time. Staff cannot, however, use government resources to do this, unless it is in direct support of the president while the president is not a candidate. For example, if the president is going to make a speech on behalf of a candidate running for office, it is permissible for this staff to expend taxpayers' money researching and writing the speech for him. But if the activity is not in support of the president, then this staff must use special DNC or RNC computers, credit cards, phone lines, and fax machines for their work. Special ones are housed in the Office of Political Affairs for that purpose, paid for and installed by the parties. Minyon Moore, profiled in the case studies and past executive director of the DNC, used to be director of political affairs in the Clinton administration. Ed Rollins was a deputy director in the Reagan administration.

OFFICE OF PUBLIC LIAISON (20)

Leaders of constituency groups want the White House to promote their agenda, and the White House is always looking for members of the public to support White House initiatives. This is the reason for the Office of Public Liaison. Staffers in this office get their jobs because they have strong political and communications skills and understand the role of constituent groups in the politics of policy initiatives. Staff often have links to the constituent groups that helped get the president elected. Their primary goal is to nurture the president's and vice president's existing ties with these groups, as well as to develop relationships with new groups that have a stake in White House initiatives—legislative or otherwise. In the Office of Public Liaison, the classic dilemma may be whether the staffer is representing the president to the constituency group or representing the constituency group to the president. And if a president consistently goes against the wishes of a certain constituency group or limits communications, this creates problems for the staffer who represents it. Ideally, a two-way street is created in which the constituency groups act as a reality check and early warning device for the White House, and the White House keeps the constituency groups informed as to what it is thinking and planning.

One of the main activities of the Office of Public Liaison is to build support for the president by arranging meetings between the president, the constituency groups, and the president's chief aides at the White House. Another common task is organizing events around the country, or sometimes even abroad, to promote initiatives. Research has to be done, participants need to be vetted, briefing packets have to be prepared for the constituency groups who will attend the meetings, and memos and talking points have to be prepared for the president. These activities enable the White House to develop sound policy and deal authoritatively with Congress and the federal departments. Incentives that the president can use to build relationships with strategic constituencies include meetings at the White House, invitations to state dinners, evening West Wing tours, attending signing ceremonies or the president's Saturday radio address, use of presidential boxes at the Kennedy Center, and barbecues at Camp David. Most important, though, is access to the White House staff and the president and vice president. White House access adds to the constituent groups' credibility back home. Minyon Moore in the case studies was once the director of the Office of Public Liaison in the Clinton White House. Danny O'Brien, also in the case studies, worked there as well.

OFFICE OF PRESIDENTIAL PERSONNEL (21)

The Office of Presidential Personnel clears out carryovers from the previous administration and recruits, vets, and recommends new candidates for presidential appointments to federal departments and agencies.

This office controls roughly 5,600 patronage jobs, although this does not include White House jobs (and also does not include the approximately two hundred federal judgeships that the office also controls because I do not consider them political jobs). Roughly 20 percent of the 5,600 patronage jobs require Senate confirmation and include such jobs as deputy cabinet secretaries, general counsels, undersecretaries, assistant secretaries, ambassadors, district attorneys, and U.S. marshals. A little less than 40 percent of the patronage jobs are the Schedule C and Senior Executive Service jobs that nominally belong to the departments or agencies; but in fact, the White House controls them, too, by being able to veto the department's choice if it wants to. The rest are part-time advisory boards and commissions—some volunteer, some for pay—about 20 percent of them requiring Senate confirmation and 80 percent not.

When a new administration first takes over, the Office of Presidential Personnel uses many staffers, consisting of a combination of executive recruiters from the private sector and a couple hundred volunteers to process the thousands of applicants. Slowly, as these applicants are processed, the staff of this office shrinks to a smaller group, which stays as the permanent office staff.

To determine whether someone should win a political appointment to a job, the Office of Presidential Personnel looks at both professional qualifications for the job and what the applicant has done for the president, usually in the last election campaign. About 80 percent of the workers in President Clinton's first election campaign in 1992 were offered administration jobs. But things got a lot tighter in the second term because not many people left their jobs. In the second term, only about 40 percent got jobs.

Some of the choicest jobs go to the biggest donors, the people who donate hundreds of thousands of dollars to the political parties and help raise much more. These people typically like either part-time jobs on presidential boards and commissions, such as the Fannie Mae Board of Directors, or ambassadorships. The base pay for a board or a commission is $23,000 a year, plus $1,000 per board meeting. There are seven board meetings a year. But then there are bonuses that can boost the package to $50,000–$75,000 a year, or even more. Directors also get a big plaque to hang on their wall that states that the president appointed them to the commission, which looks good in the office. And they do not have to give up their regular job to get one of these jobs.

Ambassadorships are also big. According to White House aides, 1,700 people sought top jobs at U.S. embassies at the start of the George W. Bush administration. Two hundred made the first cut, and 49 were made ambassadors. One of the things many of these people had in common was that they raised money for George W. Bush. Eighteen of the 49 who made ambassador were "Pioneers," the special group of at least 212 (66 from Texas) Bush fundraisers who each raised at least $100,000 for the campaign, and often two or three times that or more. Some of them also donated another $100,000 to Bush's inaugural celebration. These and other job seekers orchestrate lobbying efforts by having governors and other politicians contact the White House director of presidential personnel on their behalf. Recent administrations have set aside about a third of the approximately 160 ambassadorial jobs for political appointees, with the rest going to career foreign service officers. The political appointees are interested in posts in western Europe and on some of the Caribbean islands, leaving the hardship assignments in Latin America, Africa, and Asia to the career foreign service officers. Some of the Bush Pioneers, for example, were appointed ambassadors to France, Switzerland, Spain, and Portugal, as well as to the European Union headquarters in

Brussels. Other Pioneers were made cabinet secretaries, put in senior admin-istration posts, or served on the transition team that helped select ap-pointees for the departments that oversee their industries—and thus were in a position to do their industries a lot of good. One was named to the board of the Kennedy Center for the Performing Arts. Bob Nash in the case stud-ies was director of presidential personnel in the Clinton administration.

OFFICE OF THE FIRST LADY (17)

The First Lady's Office supports the first lady in the areas of domestic and in-ternational issues and projects. It has scheduling and press relations offices, similar to those discussed already for the president, but smaller. It also con-tains a Graphics and Calligraphy Office. The office also includes the Office of the First Lady's Correspondence and the Office of the Social Secretary:

First Lady's Correspondence (3)

The Office of the First Lady's Correspondence processes all mail sent to the first lady, including all first lady scheduling requests. The office also prepares messages of greeting from the first lady for events throughout the country, edits letters from the first lady drafted by other departments, sends apprecia-tion letters to advance staff and local volunteers following all first lady trips, and staffs special projects as required.

Office of the Social Secretary (3)

Three people run the Office of the Social Secretary, augmented by many volunteers and detailees from other departments. The office organizes and executes all social functions that occur in the executive residence and on the surrounding grounds. Its responsibilities include the planning of enter-tainment, decorations, menus, distributions of invitations, guest-list mainte-nance, and sequence of each event. The office may be arranging as many as 15 to 20 events at any one time. It uses many volunteers to call invitees to events and confirm whether they are coming.

WHITE HOUSE OPERATIONS (6)

White House Operations is a branch of the Office of Management and Ad-ministration (discussed under the next section, "Executive Office of the President"), which is dedicated exclusively to serving the White House Office. It provides day-to-day administrative support to the White House Office, including the scheduling of EOB conference rooms, purchasing supplies and equipment, arranging for servicing equipment, processing approved bills, formulating annual budget plans, subscribing to magazines and newspapers, and providing travel management services, such as processing travel vouchers and authorizations. This is the only office in the White House Office that has the authority to expend funds on behalf of the White House. It oversees a number of other offices.

Intern Office (1)

One person runs the Intern Office (with the help of many interns), which coordinates all aspects of the internship program, from the application process to placing interns in the various White House offices.

Photography Office (8)

A number of official photographers accompany the president all the time and take official photos. The Photography Office maintains a library of the contact sheets from these events, edits photos for release through the press office, or to the public, and provides photos for specific publication requests.

Telephone Operators (2)

Two people run the office of legendary phone operators who can track people down all over the world.

Travel Office (6)

The Travel Office provides airline and train tickets, rental cars, and hotel accommodations for all officially approved travel. It also provides logistical support for the White House Press Corps travel in conjunction with the president's travel.

Visitors' Office (7)

The primary purpose of the Visitors' Office is to administer tours of the White House. These include tours for the public (individuals and groups), congressional and agency ticketed tours, tours in which members of Congress personally escort guests to the gate, and tours at special times for guests of the president. The office allocates special tour slots among congressional and senior White House staff offices, for example, for Christmas holiday tours; Legislative Affairs heavily influences this scheduling, though. In addition to tours, the Visitors' Office coordinates guest invitations and ticketing for arrival ceremonies for heads of state and Marine One helicopter departures for the president. The office is responsible for crowd raising for White House events.

WHITE HOUSE MILITARY OFFICE (24)

The White House Military Office (WHMO or "Whammo") serves as an administrative liaison with the Department of Defense. The Military Office exercises managerial and oversight responsibility for all Department of Defense resources that support the president in the president's role as commander in chief, chief executive officer, and head of state. All facets of military support are provided, including logistical, communications, transportation, military aides to the president, and medical support, as well as "the black box," the portable apparatus for initiating a nuclear strike. The office supervises 1,300 military personnel, headed by five career officers. The whole office is headed by a civilian. It reviews military hardship cases (casework) and supervises the following White House support units:

- Air Force One and the 89th Military Airlift Wing.
- Marine Helicopter Squadron One.
- The Staff Mess and three adjacent dining rooms in the West Wing. Two hundred White House staffers (and the cabinet) are eligible to dine there. Also, the Presidential Watch, which serves lunch in the Oval Office.
- Camp David. It is managed by the U.S. Navy, and there are four hundred personnel there when the president is present.
- White House medical unit (15 people).
- White House Emergency Planning Group (12 people). This organization keeps current options to evacuate the president in case of emergencies.
- Naval Imaging Command. They make videos of presidential activities.
- White House Garage. Fifty military chauffeurs for White House staff on official business operate out of this office.
- White House social aides.
- White House Communications Agency. This agency oversees eight hundred people. It operates the Signal Board, which con-

nects the president to all military and diplomatic nets. It also operates the Secure Voice Board, "Crown" radio (the White House's own radio network), and the NSC's classified communications center. It supplies the Secret Service with its communications systems. It supplies lights, microphones, and public address systems for the president's public appearances.

SPECIAL OFFICES

Whereas most offices stay the same in each administration, a few are dropped or added by new administrations. For example, here are three that President Clinton added that no longer exist in the Bush administration:

> ➤ *Office of Environmental Initiatives (2)*. This office was created to implement the president's initiatives regarding global warming.
> ➤ *Millennium Council (5)*. This office coordinated the activities of governmental departments to mark the advent of the new millennium.
> ➤ *President's Initiative for One America*. This office coordinated the president's efforts on race reconciliation.

Executive Office of the President

This section examines the larger Executive Office of the President, of which the White House Office is only a part. The EOP is the umbrella term used to describe all the agencies and offices that serve the president. Many of these people keep government jobs from administration to administration. Only the leaders at the top are the political appointees who have to leave when their administration leaves office. As with the White House Office, EOP offices may not be exactly the same from administration to administration. For instance, the Clinton administration added the Office of National Drug Control Policy to coordinate the administration's War on Drugs. And the Bush administration added the Office of Homeland Security to coordinate the War on Terrorism. But the basic structure is similar to that of the Clinton administration, as outlined in the following sections.

OFFICE OF THE VICE PRESIDENT (84)

The Office of the Vice President assists with the vice president's chief duties, which include the following: president of the Senate, member of the president's cabinet and acting chairperson when the president is absent, member of the NSC, ex officio member of all cabinet councils, and member of the board of regents of the Smithsonian Institution. The Office of the Vice President supports the vice president in a manner similar to the way the president is supported, but with fewer people:

- ➤ Chief of staff and administration (14)
- ➤ Scheduling and advance (9)
- ➤ Communications (12)
- ➤ Correspondence (7)
- ➤ Domestic policy (7)
- ➤ Legal counsel (4)
- ➤ Legislative affairs (4)
- ➤ National security (15)
- ➤ Assistance is also provided for the spouse of the vice president (10)

OFFICE OF MANAGEMENT AND BUDGET (390)

The primary mission of the Office of Management and Budget is to assist the president in overseeing the preparation of the federal budget and to supervise its administration in the executive branch departments. In helping to formulate the president's spending plans, this office evaluates the effectiveness of programs, policies, and procedures; assesses competing funding demands among departments; and sets funding priorities. The Office of Management and Budget ensures that departmental reports, rules testimony, and proposed legislation are consistent with the president's budget and with administration priorities.

NATIONAL SECURITY COUNCIL (163)

The NSC consists of the president, the vice president, the secretaries of defense and state, the chairperson of the Joint Chiefs of Staff, and the head of the Central Intelligence Agency (CIA). It is led by the president's assistant for national security affairs and staffed by a few political appointees and many detailees from the CIA, the State Department, and the Department of Defense. The assistant and the political appointees lose their jobs when the administration leaves office, but the detailees just go back to their departments of origin.

The NSC is a process management system that ensures that the president is presented with a full range of options. To prepare options for the

NSC's consideration, the assistant for national security affairs directs the staff to write briefing papers for NSC meetings. Following the meetings, the assistant prepares decision memos describing who is to do what. The assistant for national security affairs is also a source of independent advice to the president—which can lead to tensions with the secretary of state and the secretary of defense. The NSC also tracks information from the entire military establishment. The White House Situation Room is one way it does this. It tracks State, Defense, and CIA cables. The assistant also monitors policy execution and is a back-channel negotiator for the president, as well as a crisis manager. The NSC consists of the following offices:

- Office of the National Security Advisor (10)
- Executive Secretary (8)
- African Affairs (4)
- Asian Affairs (5)
- Central and Eastern Europe (1)
- Defense Policy and Arms Control (7)
- European Affairs (8)
- Multilateral and Humanitarian Affairs (6)
- Intelligence Programs (5)
- Inter-American Affairs (4)
- International Economic Council (3)
- Legal Advisor (5)
- Legislative Affairs (4)
- Near East and South Asian Affairs (6)
- Nonproliferation and Export Controls (5)
- Public Affairs (4)
- Russia/Ukraine/Eurasian Affairs (6)
- Strategic Planning (4)
- Transnational Threats (8)
- Administrative Office (8)
- Systems and Technical Planning (10)
- Records and Access Management (16)
- White House Situation Room (26)

PRESIDENT'S FOREIGN INTELLIGENCE ADVISORY BOARD (6)

The President's Foreign Intelligence Advisory Board advises the president on the status of foreign intelligence efforts against the United States.

OFFICE OF POLICY DEVELOPMENT

The Office of Policy Development is a non–security affairs counterpart to the NSC. It consists of two groups, the Domestic Policy Council and the National Economic Council (NEC). (It does not have staff separate from those listed under Domestic Policy Council and NEC.) These two groups advise and assist the president in the formulation, coordination, and implementation of economic and domestic policy. Both serve as a forum in which policy advice to the president can be considered and refined. The policy process is managed in a way that allows the issues particular to each group to be included in policy deliberations being led elsewhere in the EOP or in executive branch departments or agencies.

The Domestic Policy Council (26)

The Domestic Policy Council was established by executive order in 1993. It is the center for all presidential domestic policy initiatives. It coordinates domestic policy advice to the president by pulling from the domestic cabinets their individual policy recommendations and weaving them together into advice for the president. It reconciles differences between the departments and summarizes and analyses them. It also ensures that domestic policy decisions and programs are consistent with the president's stated goals and that those goals are being effectively pursued. Finally, it monitors implementation of the president's domestic policy goals. The National AIDS Policy Group is contained within this council.

National Economic Council (14)

The NEC was also established by executive order in 1993. Its primary functions are to coordinate the economic policy-making process with respect to domestic and international economic issues and to coordinate economic policy advice to the president. It also ensures that the economic policy decisions are consistent with the president's stated goals and that those goals are being effectively pursued.

COUNCIL OF ECONOMIC ADVISORS (33)

The Council of Economic Advisors was established by executive order in 1946. It consists of three members appointed by the president with the advice and consent of the Senate, and one of the members is designated by the president as the chairperson. The council analyzes the national economy and its segments, advises the president on economic developments, appraises the economic programs and policies of the federal government, recommends to the president policies for economic growth and stability, assists in the preparation of economic reports by the president to the Congress, and prepares the Council of Economic Advisors' annual report.

OFFICE OF SCIENCE AND TECHNOLOGY (38)

The Office of Science and Technology provides expert advice to the president in all areas of science and technology. Through the National Science and Technological Council, the office helps the president coordinate science, space, and technology activities and policies across the federal government, including research and development programs related to environmental, national security, and international policy making. The President's Committee of Advisors on Science and Technology ensures public-sector involvement in the work of the Office of Science and Technology and the National Science and Technological Council. The daily work of the Office of Science and Technology consists of advising the president on policy formulation and budget development on all questions for which science and technology are important elements. It also leads an interagency effort to develop and implement science and technology policies and budgets that are coordinated across federal agencies. It articulates the president's science and technology policies and programs to Congress and addresses and defends the need for appropriate resources. It fosters strong partnerships among federal, state, and local governments and the scientific communities in industry and academe. It also furthers international cooperation in science and technology activities.

OFFICE OF THE U.S. TRADE REPRESENTATIVE (144)

The Office of the U.S. Trade Representative develops and coordinates U.S. international trade, commodity, and direct investment policy and leads or directs negotiations with other countries on such matters. The U.S. trade representative is a cabinet member who acts as the principal trade advisor, negotiator, and spokesperson for the president in trade and investment matters. Through an interagency structure, this agency coordinates trade policy, resolves agency disagreements, and frames issues for presidential decision. It provides trade policy leadership and negotiates expertise in its major areas of responsibility, which include all matters within the World Trade Organization;

trade, commodity, and direct investment matters dealt with by international institutions such as the Organization for Economic Cooperation and Development; export and expansion policy; industrial and services trade policy; international commodity agreements and policy; bilateral and multilateral trade and investment issues; trade-related intellectual property; and protection issues and import policy. The agency also has an administrative responsibility for dealing with complaints against unfair trade practices. It has a small office in Geneva, Switzerland, in addition to its main office in Washington. The agency works closely with the private sector through advisory committees whose objective is to consult with the U.S. government on negotiation of trade agreements, to assist in monitoring compliance with the agreements, and to provide input and advice on development of U.S. trade policy.

COUNCIL ON ENVIRONMENTAL QUALITY (19)

In response to growing public concern regarding the quality of the nation's environment in the late 1960s, Congress established the Council on Environmental Quality within the EOP. The council is headed by a chief who is appointed by the president with the advice and consent of the Senate. The Council on Environmental Quality formulates and recommends to the president national policies that further environmental quality. It also consults with federal agencies on legislation and litigation. It brokers interagency disputes. The council analyzes the changes or trends in the national environment, reviews federal programs to determine their contributions to sound environmental policy, and oversees implementation of National Environmental Protection Agency and Council on Environmental Quality regulations for agencies and citizens. It conducts studies, research, and analysis relating to ecological systems and environmental quality. The office is organized along both regional—Africa, Asia and the Pacific, China, Europe and the Mediterranean, Japan, and Western Hemisphere—and subject lines: agriculture, textiles, economic affairs, environmental and natural resources, and industry. Finally, it assists the president in the preparation of the annual environmental quality report to Congress.

OFFICE OF MANAGEMENT AND ADMINISTRATION (140)

The Office of Management and Administration directs the management and administration of the entire White House complex and has oversight responsibilities for all the agencies of the EOP. As part of its responsibility, this office directly supervises many of the White House Office and EOP operating units, including the White House Military Office, Photography Office, Telephone Service, Travel Office, Intern Program, Conference Center, Visitors' Office, White House Administration Office, and the Office of Administration. In addition, the Office of Management and Administration serves as a liaison between the White House and other federal agencies that provide operational support to the White House complex, such as the General Services Administration, the National Park Service, and the Secret Service. John Rogers, profiled in the case studies, was assistant to President Reagan for management and administration.

EXECUTIVE RESIDENCE (6)

The executive residence serves the presidency in three capacities: first and foremost, it is the home of the president and the first family; second, it is the site of official and ceremonial activities of the presidency; and third, it is a museum of our American heritage, open to the public during scheduled hours. The executive residence is headed by the chief usher, who is assisted by a staff of about one hundred people from different government departments. The chief usher also oversees the Office of the Curator, whose job it is to keep the public rooms on the first floor in museum quality. The National Park Service takes care of the grounds in the immediate vicinity of the White House Residence.

VICE PRESIDENT'S RESIDENCE (1)

The vice president's residence is located on the grounds of the Naval Observatory. It serves as the home for the vice president and family and as a facility for hosting official functions. The residence was presented to the United States by Nelson Rockefeller, a former vice president.

OTHER SERVICE ORGANIZATIONS (51)

Other service offices under the EOP include the Usher's Office (6), General Services Administration (14), U.S. Postal Service (21), White House Curator (4), and White House Fellowships (6).

SECRET SERVICE (5,000)

The Secret Service employs approximately 2,100 special agents, 1,200 Uniformed Division Officers, and 1,700 other technical, professional, and administrative support personnel. The Secret Service Uniformed Division protects the following:

> ➤ The White House complex, the Main Treasury Building and Annex, and other presidential offices
> ➤ The president and members of the president's immediate family
> ➤ The official residence of the vice president in the District of Columbia
> ➤ The vice president and the vice president's immediate family
> ➤ Foreign and diplomatic missions in the Washington, D.C., metropolitan area, throughout the United States, and its territories and possessions

The Secret Service also has agents assigned to approximately 125 offices located in cities throughout the United States and in foreign countries. To protect the president, the Secret Service calls on other federal, state, and local agencies to assist on a daily basis. For example, when the president is at the White House, the Secret Service Uniformed Division, the Metropolitan Police Department, and the U.S. Park Service Police patrol the streets and parks nearby. When the president travels, an advance team of Secret Service agents works with the host city and state law enforcement and public safety officials to jointly establish the security measures to protect the president. The Secret Service also has a Protective Research Division, which lists 40,000 Americans who are potential threats, 400 of whom are on the official watch list. The Secret Service is also responsible for issuing passes to all persons who work in or visit the EOP complex.

White House Pay

Working in the White House does not usually pay very much compared with private-sector jobs with similar responsibilities and hours. It can, however, lead to much higher paying jobs later. In August 2001, the *Washington Post* did a story about the pay of White House staffers in the George W. Bush administration. It found that the highest salary was $140,000 and went to such staffers as the chief of staff, the deputy chief of staff, the press secretary, the White House counsel, the national security advisor, the secretary of the cabinet, assistant to the president for presidential personnel, assistant to the president for domestic policy, and senior political advisor to the president.[1] The following list shows rates for other jobs.

- ➤ $120,000: director of speechwriting, deputy counsel
- ➤ $110,000: chief of staff to the first lady, director of intergovernmental affairs, director of scheduling, director of the Domestic Policy Counsel, director of media affairs, director of oval office operations, director of advance, director of the White House Military Office, and director of public liaison
- ➤ $90,000–$100,000: ethics advisor, White House social secretary, principal deputy press secretary, associate counsel, deputy director of presidential personnel, and director of correspondence
- ➤ $80,000–$90,000: assistant speech writer, White House travel specialist, director of the Office of Administration, special assistant to the president for legislative affairs (House) and (Senate), and correspondence analyst
- ➤ $70,000–$80,000: deputy directors of public liaison, advance press, advance event coordination, administrative assistant to the staff secretary, special assistant to the president for intergovernmental affairs, and deputy director for communications for planning
- ➤ $60,000–$70,000: White House telephone service chief operator, director of the Office of Management and Administration, senior financial manager, executive assistant to the press secretary, director of correspondence for the first lady, assistant director of presidential support, director of scheduling and advance for the first lady, and director of White House personnel
- ➤ $50,000–$60,000: supervisor of data entry unit, senior correspondence analyst, associate directors of political affairs, director of mail analysis, and the president's personal secretary
- ➤ $40,000–$50,000: executive assistant to the assistant to the president for presidential personnel, director of presidential personal correspondence, deputy social secretary, associate director of public liaison, assistant press secretary, director of the White House Comments Line and Greetings Office, executive assistant to the chief of staff, and senior trip coordinator
- ➤ $30,000–$40,000: White House telephone operator, director of the Gift Unit, director of special projects, press advance, administrative assistant, senior writer, trip coordinator, director of legisla-

tive correspondence, coordinator of White House intern program, and associate director of the Volunteer Office

➤ $20,000–$30,000: caseworker, associate director of the White House Comments Line and Greetings Office, correspondence analyst, staff assistant, printer, and records management analyst

Note

1. *Washington Post,* "White House Paychecks," www.washingtonpost.com/wp-srv/onpolitics/transcripts/whitehousesalaries.htm (August 31, 2001).

6

EXECUTIVE BRANCH DEPARTMENTS

Want to work on health issues? Want to work on education, foreign affairs, defense, tax, housing, trade, space exploration, small business—and hundreds of other issues? It's the executive departments and agencies—among them, Health and Human Services, the Departments of Defense, Treasury, Housing and Urban Development, Commerce, the National Aeronautics and Space Administration (NASA), the Small Business Administration, and others (see complete list later in this chapter)—not the White House, that deal with these issues on a day-to-day basis. In fact, it's the sum of what an administration's political appointees do in these jobs that determines whether an administration has been successful in accomplishing its goals. The White House oversees what these people do and works with them when appropriate, say, to stage a press conference at the White House to announce a new initiative. But day to day, day after day, it's the appointees who head these departments who are responsible for getting the jobs done. More than half the people profiled in the case studies in Chapter 8 worked as political appointees. They include Richard Armitage, Catherine Bertini, Jon-Christopher Bua, Andrew Card, Jim Dyer, Maria Echaveste, Marlin Fitzwater, Wendy Greuel, Patricia de Stacy Harrison, Mickey Ibarra, Susan King, Roger Majak, Sylvia Mathews, Andrew Natsios, Sean O'Keefe, Leon Panetta, John Rogers, Ed Rollins, and Paul Wolfowitz.

Many people work in a presidential campaign hoping that if their candidate wins, they will be able to get jobs in executive departments in which they have expertise and a career interest. Other people transfer to the departments from Capitol Hill jobs. Still others transfer from the White House, anxious to finally have a small area in which they can actually run something. And finally, some people come from private-sector jobs for a year or two in order to help change the way the government does things.

After their stints in the departments, some return to where they came from. Those who return to the private sector can often leverage their knowledge of how the government works and the contacts they have made into high-paying jobs. A few are able to convert their political appointee status to permanent civil service and remain with the department for the rest of their working careers (see "Burrowing In" later in this chapter). Some come back to their department or go to other departments in future administrations. They all work as the president's representatives, interfacing with civil service "lifers." A large part of the appointees' effectiveness hinges on how well they get along with these folks.

The *Plum Book:* A Guide to Jobs

Every four years, just after the presidential election, a book officially called *United States Government Policy and Supporting Positions*, and unofficially called the *Plum Book*, is published alternatively by the Government Reform and Oversight Committee of the U.S. House of Representatives or the Governmental Affairs Committee of the U.S. Senate. You can get it from the U.S. Government Printing Office. It lists all of the most important political jobs in the federal government, including many of those in the White House, the 15 executive branch departments, and the 86 independent agencies and government corporations.

There are several categories of these jobs, ranging from the most elite category, presidential appointment with Senate confirmation, to the largest category, Schedule C excepted appointment ("Schedule Cs"). Jobs in this latter category are exempted by the president or by the director of the Office of Personnel Management (the Civil Service Commission) from normal civil service application requirements because of their confidential or policy-determining nature. They are effectively controlled by the White House Office of Presidential Personnel (see Chapter 5).

There is no civil service job security in these jobs. When your administration leaves office, you are expected to submit a letter of resignation. If another party wins the election, your resignation will almost certainly be accepted, and you will be out on the street. That may even happen if your own party wins.

The *Prune Book*

A take-off on the *Plum Book* is the series of *Prune Books* produced since 1988 by the Council for Excellence in Government (John Trattner, author). A "prune" is a ripened, wiser plum. The *Prune Book* series, unlike the *Plum Book*, gives extensive position profiles and essays from persons who have held political appointments. It deals with many fewer positions than the *Plum Book*, however, generally only presidential appointments that require Senate confirmation. The *Prune Books* are written as guidebooks for those in an administration responsible for making political appointments and for the political appointees themselves, as well as for Congress and the media so that they all might better understand the positions and the process. These are the highest policy jobs in Washington, and although they may not be the kind of jobs a person right out of school could aspire to, working for someone in one might be. There are six editions of the *Prune Book*:

➤ *The Prune Book: The 100 Toughest Management and Policy-Making Jobs in Washington* (1988)
➤ *The Prune Book: The 60 Toughest Science and Technology Jobs in Washington* (1992)
➤ *The Prune Book: 50 Jobs That Can Change America* (1992)
➤ *The Prune Book: The 45 Toughest Financial Management Jobs in Washington* (1993)
➤ *The Prune Book: Making the Right Appointments to Manage Washington's Toughest Jobs* (1997)
➤ *The Prune Book: How to Succeed in Washington's Top Jobs* (2000)

Based on a survey of both the *Plum Book* and the *Prune Books*, the following political appointments are considered to be the most important in the federal government:

    I.   ECONOMIC POLICY, TECHNOLOGY, AND TRADE
          U.S. Trade Representative
          Department of Commerce
             • Undersecretary of commerce for export administration

- Assistant secretaries for export administration (licensing) and trade development
- Undersecretary for intellectual property and director, U.S. Patent Office and Trademark Office
- Director, National Institutes of Standards and Technology
- Assistant secretary for U.S. Foreign and Commercial Service
- Undersecretary for international trade
- Undersecretary for technology
- Assistant secretary for import administration

Department of Defense
- Director, Defense Advanced Research Projects Agency

Department of Energy
- Chairperson, Federal Energy Regulatory Commission
- Assistant secretary for energy efficiency and renewable energy
- Assistant secretary for political and international affairs
- Undersecretary

Department of Justice
- Assistant attorney general, Antitrust Division

Department of the Treasury
- Commissioner, Internal Revenue Service
- Assistant secretaries for economic policy, tax policy, financial markets, and financial institutions
- Comptroller of the currency
- Commissioner, U.S. Customs Service
- Undersecretary for domestic finance
- Undersecretary for international affairs

Federal Emergency Management Agency
- Director

Securities and Exchange Commission
- Chairperson

Department of Agriculture
- Undersecretary for farm and foreign agricultural services

Department of State
- Undersecretary for economic, business, and agricultural affairs

Independent Agencies
- President, U.S. Import-Export Bank

- Chairperson, Federal Reserve System

Council of Economic Advisors

- Chairperson

United States Small Business Administration

- Administrator

II. FOREIGN POLICY, NATIONAL SECURITY, AND DEFENSE

Agency for International Development

- Administrator

Department of Defense

- Secretaries of the U.S. Army, Air Force, and Navy
- Undersecretary for acquisition, technology, and logistics
- Director, defense research, and engineering
- Assistant secretary for command, control, communications, and intelligence
- Chief information officer
- Undersecretary and comptroller
- Assistant secretary for special operations/low intensity conflict
- Chairperson, Joint Chiefs of Staff
- Director, operational test and evaluation
- Undersecretary for personnel and readiness
- Undersecretary for policy

Department of State

- Permanent U.S. representative to the United Nations
- Undersecretary for arms control and international security affairs
- Undersecretary for political affairs
- Regional assistant secretaries of state (Europe, Africa, Near East, South Asia, East Asia and Pacific, Western Hemisphere)
- Undersecretary for global affairs
- Undersecretary for public diplomacy

Central Intelligence Agency

- Director

III. HEALTH, SAFETY, AND ENVIRONMENT

Consumer Products Safety Commission

- Chairperson

Department of Agriculture
- Undersecretary for food safety

Department of Energy
- Assistant secretary for environmental management

Department of Health and Human Services
- Commissioner, Food and Drug Administration
- Director, National Institutes of Health
- Administrator, Health Care Financing Administration
- Administrator, Substance Abuse and Mental Health Service Administration
- Assistant secretary for planning and evaluation

Department of Labor
- Assistant secretary for occupational safety and health
- Assistant secretary for mine safety and health

Department of Transportation
- Administrator, National Highway Transportation Safety Administration

Nuclear Regulatory Commission
- Chairperson

Environmental Protection Agency
- Assistant administrator, air and radiation
- Assistant administrator, enforcement and compliance assurance
- Assistant administrator, policy and planning
- Assistant administrator, prevention, pesticides, and toxic substances
- Assistant administrator, research and development
- Assistant administrator, solid waste and emergency response
- Assistant administrator, water

Surgeon General of the United States

IV. EMPLOYMENT POLICY, INCOME SECURITY, AND WELFARE

Department of Agriculture
- Undersecretary for food, nutrition, and consumer services

Department of Health and Human Services
- Assistant secretary for children and families

Department of Labor
- Assistant secretary for pension and welfare benefits

- Assistant secretary for employment standards
- Administrator, wage and hour division
- Director, Women's Bureau
- Solicitor

Social Security Administration
- Commissioner

Department of Housing and Urban Development
- Assistant secretary for fair housing and equal opportunity
- Director, Federal Housing Enterprise and Oversight
- Director, Multifamily Housing Assistance Restructuring

Department of the Interior
- Assistant secretary for Indian affairs
- Chairperson, National Indian Gaming Commission

Department of Veterans Affairs
- Undersecretary for Veterans Benefits Administration

V.   EDUCATION, TRAINING, AND LIFELONG LEARNING

Department of Education
- Assistant secretaries for elementary and secondary education, postsecondary education, special education and rehabilitation services, vocational and adult education, and educational research and improvement
- Undersecretary

Department of Labor
- Assistant secretary for employment and training

VI.   LAW ENFORCEMENT

Department of Justice
- Solicitor general
- Administrator, Drug Enforcement Administration
- Assistant attorney general, Civil Division
- Assistant attorney general, civil rights
- Assistant attorney general, Criminal Division
- Assistant attorney general, environment and natural resources
- Assistant attorney general, Office of Justice Programs
- Assistant attorney general, Office of Legal Affairs
- Assistant attorney general, Tax Division
- Director, Bureau of Justice Assistance

Department of State
- Assistant secretary for International Narcotics and Law Enforcement Affairs

Department of the Treasury
- Undersecretary for enforcement

Federal Bureau of Investigation
- Director

Immigration and Naturalization Service
- Commissioner

Independent Agencies
- Director, Office of National Drug Control Policy

VII. NATIONAL INFRASTRUCTURE

Department of Commerce
- Director, Bureau of the Census
- Undersecretary for oceans and atmosphere

Department of Housing and Urban Development
- Assistant secretary for housing
- Federal Housing commissioner
- Assistant secretary for community planning and development

Department of the Interior
- Director, National Park Service
- Assistant secretary for fish and wildlife and parks
- Assistant secretary for land and minerals management
- Assistant secretary for water and science
- Director, Fish and Wildlife Service
- Director, U.S. Geological Survey

Department of Transportation
- Administrator, Federal Aviation Administration
- Administrator, Federal Highway Administration
- Administrator, Federal Transit Administration
- Assistant secretary for Aviation and International Affairs
- Assistant secretary for transportation policy
- Associate deputy secretary

National Aeronautics and Space Administration
- Administrator

Federal Communications Commission
- Chairperson

Independent Agencies
  • Director, Office of Government Ethics

VIII.   CENTRAL MANAGEMENT
        Executive Office of the President
          • Director, Office of Management and Budget
        General Services Administration
          • Administrator
        Office of Personnel Management
          • Director

How Departments and Agencies Are Organized

Whether it be one of the 15 executive departments—Agriculture, Commerce, Defense, Education, Energy, Environmental Protection Agency, Health and Human Services, Housing and Urban Development, Interior, Justice, Labor, State, Transportation, Treasury, and Veterans' Affairs—or one of the other agencies or government corporations, the table of organization usually looks like this (pay rates are in parentheses—see explanation under "Pay Rates"):

➤ Secretary (EX-1), chairperson (EX-III), administrator (EX-II–III), director (EX-IV)
➤ Deputy secretary (EX-II), deputy administrator (EX-III–IV), deputy director (EX-III)
➤ Undersecretary (EX-III; exists only in a department)
➤ Assistant secretary (EX-IV), assistant administrator (ES-1–6)
➤ Deputy assistant secretary (ES-1–6), deputy assistant administrator (GS-15)

Departments and agencies usually also contain the following offices:

➤ Chief financial officer (EX-IV)
➤ General counsel (EX-IV)
➤ Director, Office of Communications (ES-1–6)
➤ Director, Office of Congressional (or Legislative) Affairs, Public Affairs, Intergovernmental Affairs, sometimes all combined into one (ES-1–6)

- ➤ Inspector general (EX-IV)
- ➤ Special function offices
- ➤ Regional offices (only in some departments or agencies)

So one could be the undersecretary for natural resources and environment at the Department of Agriculture (EX-III), or the assistant secretary for the Office of Economic Development at Commerce (EX-IV), or a deputy assistant secretary for congressional and intergovernmental affairs at Labor (ES-1–6), or the deputy administrator at the Small Business Administration (EX-IV). Not only is each one of them a political appointee, but his or her immediate staff is, too.

Job Titles and Hierarchy

Each cabinet secretary or equivalent will have a personal staff that consists of other political appointees, usually a chief of staff (ES-1–6), a deputy chief of staff (GS-15), and one or more speechwriters (GS-13–15), schedulers (GS-13), and executive secretaries (GS-7–12). After that, there are the counselor to the secretary (different from counsel to the secretary, which is a lawyer's position), senior advisors, and special assistants. These jobs can vary greatly depending on the desires of the secretary. Whereas the titles counselor and senior advisor usually connote jobs in the GS-14–15 range or higher, special assistant is usually in the GS-12–15 range. Staff assistant is usually below that range, often GS-9–12.

In sum, most people seeking a political appointment are probably going after a Schedule C position in the GS-9–15 range, probably as a special assistant (usually some kind of administrator), speechwriter, or scheduler, and working on the staff of a cabinet secretary or an assistant secretary or the equivalent.

Pay Rates

The following are the federal salary schedules as of February 2002; they are adjusted upward annually due to inflation.[1] There is also an adjustment for where you live, ranging from 8.64 percent to 19.04 percent (Washington is 11.48 percent):

Executive Schedule (EX)

Level I	$166,700
Level II	$150,000
Level III	$138,200
Level IV	$130,000
Level V	$121,600

Senior Executive Service (ES)

ES-6	$130,000
ES-5	$130,000
ES-4	$129,800
ES-3	$123,700
ES-2	$118,300
ES-1	$113,000

General Schedule (GS)

GS-15	$82,580–$107,357
GS-14	$70,205–$91,265
GS-13	$59,409–$77,229
GS-12	$49,959–$64,944
GS-11	$41,684–$54,185
GS-10	$37,939–$49,324
GS-9	$34,451–$44,783
GS-8	$31,191–$40,551
GS-7	$28,164–$36,615
GS-6	$25,344–$32,949
GS-5	$22,737–$29,539
GS-4	$20,322–$26,415
GS-3	$18,103–$23,530
GS-2	$16,592–$20,876
GS-1	$14,757–$18,456

How to Get a Political Appointment

In a nutshell, to get a political appointment, you have to be both accepted by the department in question and approved by the White House. The process often takes many months—after the many months it may have taken to hire your boss first.

Say you are interested in the position of special assistant to the secretary of state at the State Department, a GS-15 position. It's a pretty loosely defined position: some speechwriting for the secretary, some troubleshooting, some event organization. Normally, when a vacancy occurs in a political job, the agency's White House liaison informs the White House Office of Presidential Personnel. The White House liaison is someone who has close ties to the White House, possibly because he or she once worked there before getting transferred to the department. The Office of Presidential Personnel sends back several names that it recommends for the job. Besides professional qualifications for the job, getting on that list usually boils down to what you did for the president in the last campaign. And because many people who worked on the campaign would love to have a high-ranking job at the State Department, competition will probably be tough.

For a job like this, in addition to superior professional job qualifications, you probably have to do something significant in the president's campaign, such as help run one of the state campaigns, be an outspoken surrogate speaker for the candidate on foreign affairs, or be a fund-raiser or a donor—or closely connected to someone who did these things. This often means spending many months, with or without pay, working on the campaign.

But that's not all. Getting on the White House list may also depend on which constituency you represent, how visible you are in that constituency, and who your rabbi is. For example, it could help if you come from a labor union background, a business background, or are an African American, a woman, or a Hispanic, an Asian, or a Native American. This is so the administration can advertise to its supporters that it is indeed rewarding them by placing one of their own in an important job. To get a GS-15 slot, you're probably going to have to be a fairly prominent member of your constituency. And you're going to need a strong rabbi—maybe a member of Congress whose vote the administration needs for an important piece of legislation. To get you this high a position, the rabbi is probably going to have to carry a lot of weight and be willing to call up the director of presidential personnel and strongly recommend you.

All right, so maybe a GS-15 is a bit out of reach right now. You're young and you just haven't had time to build the kind of resume that it requires. Nor are your rabbis that strong. But you're sharp, you worked hard on the campaign, you got to know a lot of people there and they all think highly of you, and you still want to work at the State Department. Here's a

GS-12 staff assistant slot open in the deputy secretary of state's office. Or a GS-9 slot as a staff assistant in the Bureau of Legislative Affairs. Maybe there's nothing at the State Department right now, but there's something interesting in Commerce that has to do with foreign trade, and you go for that. So it goes; you negotiate.

Once you get on the White House list, then it's up to the State Department (or whichever department you're applying to) to pick you out from the others on the list. The secretary, or more likely the secretary's top aides, have to like you and believe that your professional qualifications will be useful to them.

It doesn't take much to see that any personal contacts you have at both the agency in question and the White House could be immensely helpful to you here. Working on the campaign is a good way to build these contacts.

Sometimes the process is reversed; that is, the department knows you and likes you and submits your name to the White House. If you pass muster at the White House, the White House can simply okay your getting the job. But the White House could hold it up, preferring instead that someone else get the job. Things can drag on while it all gets sorted out.

Once you are accepted by all concerned and report to work, you have to undergo an elaborate security check, which could conceivably (but not likely) result in your being removed from the job, say, for failing to disclose that you once used drugs. Usually, it's not the act itself that is disqualifying but the fact that you failed to disclose it.

It Takes a Long Time

Starting from the date of a president's election, it takes such a long time to get a job through the political appointment process—often many, many months—that you should try to have something else to do while waiting. The problem starts at the top, with the Senate-confirmed jobs. Only when those are filled can the slots lower down be filled.

Every administration since President Kennedy's has experienced increasing delays in winning confirmation for its nominees to the top jobs in government. This has created vacancies that last longer and longer. Whereas Kennedy had his cabinet and subcabinet in place by April 1961, President Clinton had to wait until mid-October of 1993, and President George W. Bush more than a year after being sworn in.

Part of the problem is background investigations. Senate-confirmed nominees must fill out time-consuming questionnaires that ask hundreds of personal questions about their lives and their relatives' lives. These then trigger background checks by the White House Office of Presidential Personnel, FBI, and Office of Government Ethics, all of which take increasingly longer.

And part of the problem is political. In an effort to avoid mistakes, administration headhunters are taking more and more time to scrutinize candidates. Candidates need to expect every aspect of their life to be in good order—from finances to the content of any publications. This extensive scrutiny actually gives a slight advantage to younger, less-experienced people, whose history is shorter and thus easier and faster to check. But all candidates should expect a thorough review of their activities and should be prepared to explain any lapses in their personal or professional good judgment.

Getting appointments through the Senate eats up even more time as senators put holds on nominees, holding them temporarily hostage so they can negotiate favors from the administration.

Understandably, this labyrinth discourages top people from being candidates for such jobs. Having to relocate to the D.C. area for a job that only lasts on average a year and a half, and probably pays less than what they were earning in the private sector, is probably not something a senior executive is going to want to do.

Reforms are being considered, of course, including streamlining the financial disclosure forms, accelerating background checks by giving investigating offices more staff, cutting the number of presidential appointments subject to confirmation, and getting the Senate to limit holds to two weeks and to wrap up the confirmation process in a month and a half. There are also deliberations about reducing the number of political jobs in government, increasing the pay scale of political appointees, and providing relocation assistance. But at the moment, be ready for a long haul.

Get in the System

Once you get that first job as a political appointee, you're in the system, so to speak, and it's much easier to transfer to another job. A surprising number of people do this. In other words, you could view your first job as a stepping stone to your ideal job, even if that job is not in the same department. In order to make transfers of this sort, you normally would have to work in close contact with people in the job you want to move to and then, if they express interest in hiring you, simply request a transfer to the new job. It's even possible to get detailed to the White House like this (see Chapter 5), although in that case, your department continues to pay your salary while you work at the White House. Thus, the department is going to want to gain something from sending you there—probably closer contacts with the White House while you are there and when you come back to your department of origin.

Women Political Appointees

The situation for women as political appointees is similar to their situation on Capitol Hill: currently, their percentage is less than men, but it is steadily rising. The following list shows the percentage of women in each administration beginning with Lyndon B. Johnson. It was compiled from information from the Brookings Institution, the Women's Appointment Project, the National Academy of Public Administration, and Wenews Analysis.

Johnson	4 percent
Nixon	4 percent
Ford	6 percent
Carter	15 percent
Reagan	10 percent
G. H. W. Bush	24 percent
Clinton	37 percent

Presidential Management Intern Program

Other than the White House Fellows Program (see Chapter 5), there is no internship for someone wishing to work specifically for a political appointee in the administration. The closest thing is the Presidential Management Intern Program, which essentially puts you on the fast track as a civil servant. After going through a multiphase winnowing process, you may get to work directly with political appointees; but then again, you may not. If you have received or are scheduled to receive a graduate degree, and the director of your graduate academic program nominates you, you might be able to do a two-year internship in a government department. In order to get into the program, you should display a clear interest in, and commitment to, a career in the analysis and management of public policies and programs. You enter as a GS-9, and after successfully completing the program, the appointment can be converted to a permanent government appointment at the GS-12 level. You can learn more about this program at the Web site www.pmi.opm.gov/pmimain.htm. In addition to this program, many departments have their own internship programs, such as the one at the State Department that you can learn about through www.state.gov/www/careers/rinterncontents.html.

Getting Along with the Mechanics

Civil servants, the permanent personnel who watch countless presidential appointees come and go, are the "mechanics" of government, the ones who actually run it. Political appointees supervise them in the sense of trying to implement policy changes, creating and publicizing new programs, making changes in old programs, or in some cases, eliminating them altogether.

The career government employees know the ins and outs of their departments or agencies far better than the new presidential appointees, who cannot run the place without these civil servants. As a result, slowly but surely, many presidential appointees start thinking more like the career people. Then, the political appointees start defending their bureaucrats. As a result, within a year, the political appointees will often start sounding an awful lot like those of previous administrations.

Even if this doesn't happen, any political appointee who hopes to be effective has got to make peace with the civil servants. If not, the appointee will have a tough time getting things done. A good way to look at it is to regard the civil servants as the mechanics for this big bureaucratic Cadillac that is the federal government. They spend a lifetime learning about how that Cadillac runs, what kind of gas works best, and when it needs oil. They spend a career polishing it and protecting it. All the while, political battles in the form of elections swirl around the mechanics, with politicians vying for power and for the right to drive that big Cadillac. But the mechanics are suspicious of the new drivers. Do they really appreciate the federal vehicle? Sure, they want to take it out for a spin. But do they know how to handle it? Are they going to wreck it? Do they really know what's best for it?

Before the mechanics are going to help that new driver, they want some assurances that the driver is responsible. They won't overtly confront the driver; it's more subtle than that. The driver just notices that sometimes the headlights don't work right, or the windshield wipers need to be fixed, or the engine won't start. But if the driver takes care to consult the mechanics, bring them into the loop, value their input, share credit with them, then miraculously, that car just seems to work great.

Many people who have served as political appointees feel that this relationship between the civil service "experts" and political leaders is the critical juncture in the operation of the executive branch. Thus it is important that political appointees be prepared to receive the support of civil servants as well as to "guide" and "manage" them. If this nexus does not work, the result can be more heat than light, and a rather unsatisfying experience for all concerned. Political appointees would do well to study up on the civil service system and the civil servants that they expect to be working with.

Getting Along with the White House

On top of getting along with the mechanics, political appointees have to pay particular attention to White House needs and cultivating White House contacts. Although each incoming president talks about the need for "cabinet government," the trend has been for most presidents to insist on making the key decisions in the White House because of reelection politics. This means that on big policy-making decisions, lesser-known White House aides—probably key campaign aides—are going to have as much or more clout than cabinet secretaries and their aides, even if the cabinet secretary is a former governor, top business executive, or general. This may be less true at the Departments of State, Defense, Justice, and Treasury than at other departments and also less true in areas that do not carry as much political importance for the president. But the upshot is that political appointees from cabinet secretary on down have to be extremely sensitive to White House desires or they may find that on key matters, they will be simply implementing and administering policy, not helping to decide it.

Another reason to build White House contacts stems from quite a different need, the desire to get more attention for something the department is doing. Once a department has produced a new program or policy, there is then the matter of getting public attention for it. Having presidential involvement at a press launch or similar activities can be a major boost in this regard. Personally knowing the White House aides who can take this request to the president is often the difference between getting the president's help and not.

It is essential to remember how useful good contacts with White House aides can be. These sorts of contacts are not simply a matter of "who you know" but "how well you know them," which means that starting early, such as in the election campaign, can be a big advantage. Officially, the White House Office of Cabinet Affairs is the interface between the departments and the president. But because other political advisors are probably going to be even more important, it behooves political appointees to know these other political advisors, too.

Regional Offices

Many federal departments maintain regional offices as well as a headquarters office in Washington. Some political appointees prefer to serve in these regional offices so that they can continue to live at home. Some serve first in Washington and then switch to a regional office, whereas others start out in a regional office and then move to Washington. Most get their jobs the same way political appointees in Washington do: by helping the president get elected. As with political appointees serving in Washington, appointees working in regional offices lose their jobs when their administration is voted out of office. Appointees working in the regions help develop and carry out the policies of the Washington office.

For example, the Department of Agriculture has 49 state executive directors and 45 state directors. Commerce has 12 regional directors; Health and Human Services, the U.S. Small Business Administration, and the Environmental Protection Agency each have 10. The Department of Education and the Department of Housing and Urban Development both have 10 secretary's regional representatives. And the Department of Justice has almost a hundred U.S. attorneys scattered around the country. The Department of Immigration and Naturalization, the U.S. Marshall's Office, the Department of Labor, and the Federal Emergency Management Agency (FEMA) all have similar field arrangements for political appointees.

Typical cities in which these regional offices are located include Boston, New York, Philadelphia, Atlanta, Chicago, Kansas City (Missouri), Dallas, Denver, San Francisco, and Seattle. The head person in such an office is usually a GS-15 or higher, and most have staffs that include other political appointees.

Burrowing In

There is a method called *burrowing in*, through which an average of about fifty persons a year who start out as political appointees in a department or even as congressional staffers can become career civil servants, thus preserving a job even if the elected official they are serving loses a reelection bid. This procedure is formally covered under the Ramspeck Act and is normally used by a limited number of appointees or congressional staffers who have deep substantive knowledge and who, in the opinion of the department, would be valuable permanent additions to the department. A few people have asked me whether the reverse is possible; that is, whether someone can leave the civil service and get a political appointment—and then revert back to civil service when it's over. The answer is yes, it's possible, but very few people do it. The ones who do this tend to do so at the end of their careers, so that after the political appointment expires, they can retire or go into the private sector. Marlin Fitzwater in the case studies is an example of this. A few people actually revert back to civil service jobs after a political appointment, but they are so few in number that it should not be regarded as a career pattern.

Excellence in Management

What is excellence in government service? What is the difference between merely holding the title and actually making a difference in what you do? The Council for Excellence in Government has spent a lot of time thinking about this and studying what does and doesn't work.[2] It has found that the most important thing is perhaps the most obvious thing: getting something visible, something tangible, done that affects people's lives. Of course, this is harder to measure than, say, the amount of money a company makes.

The first lesson, the council contends, is not the resources you put into pursuing the mission—how much money you spent, how many meetings you held, how many members of Congress you met with—but outcomes: How many lives did you touch? One of the council's seminars for incoming political appointees highlighted four people who, it is commonly felt, have made a real difference in running their agencies:

> ➤ James Lee Witt, director of FEMA, is credited with turning FEMA from an ineffective organization into one of the best in government.
> ➤ Dan Goldin, administrator of NASA, is credited with devising simpler, less-expensive ways for NASA to do business. He has also overseen projects such as the Hubble telescope and the Mars Pathfinder, which have provided a wealth of data in the scientific and medical areas.

➤ Janet Woodcock, director of the Center of Drug Evaluation and Research at the Food and Drug Administration, is credited with dramatically reducing the time it takes to get new drugs on the market and thus saving lives.

➤ Franklin Raines, director of the Office of Management and Budget, is credited with helping to restore the public's trust in government by helping to balance the federal budget and do more with less.

In discussing their best practices, these people made the following points, which can serve as a primer on how to be an excellent political appointee:

➤ Listen to stakeholders' needs, both internal and external. These are the needs of your customers on the one hand and your employees on the other.

➤ Get a clear vision of the goals, the mission. Focus it down to a manageable number of results and steps that can bring about those results. Co-opt the stakeholders by involving them in the process of defining the goals.

➤ Concentrate on speed. Do this not because speed is always the most important value but because it serves to focus people's attention the best.

➤ Get a clear definition of roles and responsibilities.

➤ Find the natural leaders, the people who get things done. There are immensely talented leaders throughout the government. Your job as a political appointee is to find them, enlist them in your cause, and position them where they can get your job done. Conversely, weed out the people in positions of importance who are not leaders.

➤ Communicate the mission constantly; making sure everyone on the team knows the mission and how their job relates to it. People learn in different ways, and you can't assume that just because you said something one way, everyone got the message. You have to keep repeating it in many different ways.

➤ Focus on defining the "what" and the "why" in great detail, but leave the "how" more to your managers.

➤ Set up accountability at each level. Have each manager sign a program commitment agreement, trust them to deliver on it, and do what they said they were going to do. Delegate, don't micromanage.

➤ The leader must assume responsibility for risk and thus free subor-
dinates from it, so they know risk taking is acceptable.

➤ Get to know the congressional staffers on the key committees that
deal with your agency. Keep them abreast of what is happening in
your agency. Don't surprise members of Congress: if representatives
of your agency are visiting places in a member's district; tell the
member beforehand. Don't introduce legislation and then ask
Congress's opinion of it; consult before you introduce it.

➤ Keep in mind the administration's budget cycle and congressional
authorizing and appropriations cycles as you come up with ideas for
new programs. The president's budget is formulated in the summer,
finalized in the fall, and sent to Congress in January. Congress usually authorizes programs during the first part of the year and passes
its appropriations bills in the late summer. You need to get your
idea into the president's budget and then shepherd it through the
rest of the process.

Other characteristics of successful managers chronicled in other works
of the Council for Excellence in Government include the following:

➤ Good people and communications skills
➤ Accessibility
➤ Intellectual independence
➤ Objectivity
➤ Commitment
➤ A sense of excitement
➤ A talent for reaching consensus
➤ Ability to earn loyalties

Notes

1. United States Office of Personnel Management Salaries and Wages, www.opm.
gov/oca/payrates/index.htm.
2. Council for Excellence in Government, www.excelgov.org (November 11,
2002). Unpublished transcript of seminar for the orientation of incoming presidential appointees (Center for Excellence in Government, Washington, D.C.,
May, 1998).

7

RELATED JOBS

This chapter reviews several different Washington industries that are related to the jobs discussed in the previous chapters: think tanks, several categories of lobbyists, political consultants, the media, and state and local governments. Each of these groups not only influences what people in the political parties, on Capitol Hill, in the White House and the administration do in their jobs; they are also revolving doors for people coming into and out of those jobs. Almost all of them have Internet sites where you can learn more about them. Most of them also have intern programs through which young people can get a foot in the door.

One of the signs of effective staffers on the Hill or in the administration is their knowledge of whom to call in these organizations in order to get information or help in selling a point of view. Often, for every issue or industry, there are interest groups and lobbying entities on both sides, and you simply need to know which ones fit your issue and political requirements.

Think Tanks

Washington think tanks—such as the Brookings Institution, the American Enterprise Institute, and the Heritage Foundation—have mushroomed since the 1960s and have become tremendously influential. They originally began as nonpartisan communities of scholars, much like academic institutions, that were interested in studying how to improve government, the United States, and even the world. Many are still nominally nonpartisan, although some are more often cited by Democrats than Republicans and vice versa. Think tanks produce carefully researched materials such as papers and books. They usually consist of a number of senior fellows or scholars at the top, augmented by a larger number of researchers, analysts, event organizers, press officials, and other administrators. Some people first work in a think tank and then switch over to a political job. Some go the other way, going to a think tank after a stint in a political job. Examples from the case studies include David Hoppe and Gene Sperling.

Working in a think tank can be a great way to build issue expertise. Many think tanks have internship programs that you can learn about by consulting the organization's Web site (see the list that follows). Many hire research assistants to help senior researchers in areas such as health, housing, immigration, population studies, human resources, crime, and tax policy. At the entry level, these assistants generally conduct literature reviews, statistical analyses, and programming tasks, as well as edit and write and participate in reporting research findings and presenting data.

The following are some of Washington's best-known think tanks. The designation "(often cited by Democrats)" or "(often cited by Republicans)" is added to show which party cites a particular think tank's research most frequently:

> *The American Enterprise Institute (often cited by Republicans)*. Sponsors original research on government policy, the U.S. economy, and U.S. politics that aims to preserve and strengthen the foundations of a free society, limited government, competitive private enterprise, vital cultural and political institutions, and vigilant defense, through rigorous inquiry, debate, and writing. www.aei.org

> *American Policy Center (often cited by Republicans)*. Grassroots action and education foundation, dedicated to the promotion of free enterprise and limited government regulations over commerce and individuals. www.americanpolicy.org

> *The Brookings Institution (often cited by Democrats)*. Brookings seeks to improve the performance of American institutions, the effectiveness of government programs, and the quality of U.S. public policies. www.brookings.edu

> *The Cato Institute (often cited by Republicans)*. Seeks to broaden the parameters of public policy debate to allow consideration of more options about the proper role of government that are consistent

with the traditional American principles of limited government, individual liberty, and peace. www.cato.org

➤ *Center for Policy Alternatives (often cited by Democrats)*. Devoted to community-based solutions that strengthen families and communities. www.stateaction.org

➤ *Center on Budget and Policy Priorities (often cited by Democrats)*. Conducts research and analysis on a range of government policies and programs, with an emphasis on those affecting low- and moderate-income people. www.cbpp.org

➤ *Economic Policy Institute (often cited by Democrats)*. Seeks to broaden the public debate about strategies to achieve a prosperous and fair economy. www.epinet.org

➤ *The Heritage Foundation (often cited by Republicans)*. Research and educational institute whose mission is to formulate and promote conservative public policies based on the principles of free enterprise, limited government, individual freedom, traditional American values, and a strong national defense. www.heritage.org

➤ *The Urban Institute (often cited by Democrats)*. Founded in 1968 to sharpen thinking about society's problems and efforts to solve them, improve government decisions and their implementation, and increase citizens' awareness about important public choices. www.urban.org

➤ *The Worldwatch Institute (often cited by Democrats)*. Dedicated to fostering a sustainable society—one in which human needs are met in ways that do not threaten the health of the natural environment or future generations. To this end, the institute conducts interdisciplinary research on emerging global issues, the results of which are published and disseminated to decision makers, the media, and the public. www.worldwatch.org

Lobbying Entities

There are several categories of entities that lobby Capitol Hill and the administration: interest groups, trade associations, unions, hired lobbyists, and some political consultants. Only some of these—about 18,800 as of the year 2000—fit the criteria for formally having to register as federal-level lobbyists. The primary criteria for registering is if an organization pays more than a certain amount of money for an agent to spend more than a certain percentage of the agent's time contacting members and employees of Congress, White House employees, and senior officials and employees of the executive departments and agencies of government. If so, both the agent and the organization must register as lobbyists and file semiannual reports listing what governmental organization they have contacted, the issues that were lobbied on, and how much money was spent on the effort. The following Web site contains these reports: sopr.senate.gov. Organizations engaging in lobbying that does not fit these criteria do not have to register. The *Washington Representatives Directory* (2001), published by Columbia Books, states that 8,728 registered lobbyists are actually based in the D.C. metropolitan area, while another 9,404 unregistered lobbyists are located there. That means that another 10,000 registered federal-level lobbyists are based elsewhere in the country.

From a staffer's point of view, lobbyists are a godsend, allies who provide quick, predigested information to sell a point of view. Much of a staffer's job is distilling other people's ideas, and that takes time—time the staffer often doesn't have. A good lobbyist presents the material to the staffer already distilled and with the politics already factored into it.

The public, however, does not always regard lobbyists this way. The public often sees them as enemies of the public good, pushing private good instead. The public fears that if a politician is inclined to take whatever a lobbyist presents without much scrutiny, there is a danger the lobbyist will trick the politician. But there is a built-in defense against this: lobbyists are usually interested in having a long-term relationship with a politician. A lobbyist can get away with lying to a contact only once. After that the politician won't speak to the lobbyist again. So lobbyists will present all the positive reasons to support the client's point of view and if not asked, might not present the other side. But when asked directly about the other side, the lobbyist will probably be candid.

On top of being conduits of information that help staff understand specialized matters, lobbyists are influential with Hill staffers and White House and administration officials because lobbyists are also effective in mobilizing supporters or opponents. They know how to organize public relations campaigns inside and outside a member's district, ranging from "spontaneous" grassroots letter-writing campaigns to paid national television advertising. In addition, some of them make campaign contributions to members' campaigns—or to their opponents.

One of the keys to being an effective lobbyist is personal contacts—who you know and how well you know them. Just being knowledgeable about the process is not enough. As a lobbyist, your success will probably be more of a function of how strong and recent your contacts are with the key decision makers and their aides—who can you call and be sure they will return your call.

Interest Groups

Interest groups are like think tanks in that both study issues and produce research materials relating to their issues. But interest groups are usually more aggressive in lobbying for their more narrow interests. Most of them have Web sites, and many have intern programs. Interest groups are a great source of political activists who eventually find their way into jobs on Capitol Hill, the White House, and the administration. Washington has hundreds of interest groups dedicated to opposing sides of almost any issue you can think of. The following are three pairs of interest groups that illustrate this; the first mentioned in each pair is the Republican-oriented group, and the second is the Democratic-oriented group.

> *American Conservative Union.* The nation's oldest conservative lobbying organization in support of capitalism, belief in the doctrine of original intent of the framers of the Constitution, confidence in traditional moral values, and commitment to a strong national defense. www.conservative.org
> *Americans for Democratic Action.* The nation's oldest independent liberal political organization dedicated to individual liberty and building economic and social justice at home and abroad. Takes early, principled stands on a wide range of issues. adaction.org/

> *National Rifle Association (NRA).* Founded in 1871 and with nearly 3 million members today, the NRA defends the gun industry and Second Amendment rights (the right to bear arms). www.nra.org
> *Brady Center to Prevent Gun Violence.* Formerly called Handgun Control, this organization works to enact and enforce common-sense gun legislation, provide public education about gun violence, and reform the gun industry. www.bradycenter.org

> *National Right to Life Committee.* Largest pro-life organization in the United States, with 50 state affiliates and more than 3,000 local chapters. www.nrlc.org
> *The National Abortion and Reproductive Rights Action League.* Political arm of the pro-choice movement and a strong advocate of reproductive freedom and choice. www.naral.org

The following are some more of the better-known interest groups in Washington:

➤ *AARP.* Formerly known as the American Association of Retired Persons. Represents 35 million members and addresses issues important to the 50+ population, such as long-term solvency of Social Security, protecting pensions, prescription-drug coverage in Medicare, patient protections in managed care, long-term care, and living independently. www.aarp.org

➤ *Alliance for Justice.* National association of environmental, civil rights, mental health, women's, children's and consumer advocacy organizations working to advance the cause of justice for all Americans, strengthen the public interest community's ability to influence public policy, and foster the next generation of advocates. www.afj.org

➤ *American Civil Liberties Union.* Nonpartisan organization that protects civil rights by litigating unpopular causes. www.aclu.org

➤ *American Rivers.* Protects and restores America's rivers. www.american rivers.org

➤ *Amnesty International.* Campaigns to free all prisoners of conscience; ensure fair and prompt trials for political prisoners; abolish the death penalty, torture, and other cruel treatment of prisoners; end political killings and "disappearances"; and oppose human rights abuses generally. www.amnestyusa.org

➤ *Center for Defense Information.* Independent military research organization. www.cdi.org

➤ *Center for Responsive Politics.* Tracks money in politics and its effect on elections and public policy in an effort to create a more-educated voter and a more-responsive government. www. crp.org

➤ *Children's Defense Fund.* Advocates for American children, particularly poor and minority children and those with disabilities. www.childrensdefense.org

➤ *Christian Coalition.* Founded in 1989 by Pat Robertson to give Christians a voice in government. Offers people of faith the vehicle to be actively involved in shaping their government. www.cc.org

➤ *Citizens for Tax Justice.* Dedicated to fair taxation at the federal, state, and local levels. It has often produced studies critical of Republican tax plans. www.ctj.org

➤ *Common Cause.* Works to end special-interest politics and reform government ethics. www.commoncause.org

➤ *Concord Coalition.* Advocates fiscal responsibility while ensuring Social Security, Medicare, and Medicaid are secure for all generations. www.concordcoalition.org

➤ *Democratic Leadership Council (DLC)*. Founding organization of the New Democrat movement, the DLC promotes debate within the Democratic Party and the public at large about national and international policy and political issues in an effort to modernize the progressive tradition in U.S. politics. The DLC describes its agenda as one "based on progressive ideas, mainstream values, and non-bureaucratic approaches to governing." Bill Clinton was one of its founders. The Progressive Policy Institute is the DLC's in-house think tank. www.dlcppi.org

➤ *Empower America*. Encourages public policy solutions that maximize free markets and individual responsibility. www.empower.org

➤ *Families USA*. Dedicated to the achievement of high-quality, affordable health and long-term care for all Americans. www.familiesusa.org

➤ *Friends of the Earth*. Environmental organization dedicated to preserving the health and diversity of the planet. www.foe.org

➤ *Greenpeace*. A leading environmental group that uses peaceful and creative activism to protect the global environment and protest assaults on it. www.greenpeace.org

➤ *Human Rights Campaign*. Works for lesbian and gay equal rights by lobbying the federal government and educating the public about equal rights for all people. www.hrc.org

➤ *League of Women Voters*. Encourages the informed and active participation of citizens in government. www.lwv.org

➤ *Log Cabin Republicans*. Republican gay and lesbian organization. www.lcr.org

➤ *National Association for the Advancement of Colored People*. The nation's oldest civil rights organization, established in 1909. www.naacp.org

➤ *National Center for Tobacco-Free Kids*. Tries to protect children from tobacco addiction by raising awareness about tobacco use. www.tobaccofreekids.org

➤ *National Council of La Raza*. Established in 1968 to reduce poverty and discrimination and improve life opportunities for Hispanic Americans. www.nclr.org

➤ *National Organization for Women*. Established in 1966 to bring women into the full participation in the mainstream of American society in equal partnership with men. www.now.org

- ➤ *National Taxpayers' Union.* Conservative organization that works for lower taxes and spending. www.ntu.org
- ➤ *National Urban League.* Assists African Americans to secure economic self-reliance, parity and power, and civil rights. www.nul.org
- ➤ *National Resources Defense Council.* Group of lawyers, scientists, and policy experts that often litigates on behalf of the environment. www.nrdc.org
- ➤ *Nature Conservancy.* Protects endangered species and ecosystems through land acquisition and research. www.tnc.org
- ➤ *People for the American Way.* Conducts research and advocacy for a wide variety of liberal causes in pursuit of fairness, justice, civil rights, and the freedoms guaranteed by the Constitution. www.pfaw.org
- ➤ *Planned Parenthood Federation of America.* Promotes the right of women and men to decide freely the number and spacing of their children and the right to the highest possible level of sexual and reproductive health. www.plannedparenthood.org
- ➤ *Public Citizen.* Consumer advocacy organization founded by Ralph Nader in 1971 to represent consumer interests in Congress, the executive branch, and the courts. www.citizen.org
- ➤ *Rainbow PUSH Coalition.* Multiracial, multi-issue, international membership organization, founded by the Reverend Jesse L. Jackson, that works for social, racial, and economic justice. www.rainbowpush.org
- ➤ *Sierra Club.* One of the most influential environmental groups, with 700,000 members. www.sierraclub.org
- ➤ *Zero Population Growth.* Works to slow population growth and achieve a sustainable balance between the Earth's people and its resources. www.zpg.org

Trade Associations and Labor Unions

For many industries there is a trade association that represents the management side of an issue and a union that represents the workers' side of that issue. Although both represent the same industry, their concerns, and therefore their politics, are quite different. Management often is most concerned about industry profits and tends to vote Republican. Unions, on the other hand, are more concerned with the lives of the workers and tend to vote Democratic. Many trade associations and unions are extremely influential politically, maintaining PACs that contribute money to their candidates and providing campaign workers as well. Both trade associations and labor unions employ researchers, analysts, and lobbyists to push their agenda before Congress and the executive branch and to publicize it in the media. Other employees organize conventions and other educational meetings and generally help to run the organization. Most have intern programs. Many people move from jobs with trade associations or unions into jobs at the political parties, Capitol Hill, the White House, and the administration and vice versa. For examples of people who followed this pattern, see the profiles of Catherine Bertini, Andrew Card, and Mickey Ibarra in Chapter 8.

Here is a sampling of trade associations and labor unions. The first of each pair names a trade association (usually Republican); the second names a corresponding labor union (usually Democratic) for that industry:

> ➤ *U.S. Chamber of Commerce.* www.uschamber.org
> ➤ *American Federation of Labor–Congress of Industrial Organizations (AFL-CIO).* www.aflcio.org

> ➤ *Air Transport Association of America.* www.air-transport.org
> ➤ *Airline Pilots Association.* www.alpa.org

> ➤ *American Trucking Associations.* www.trucking.org
> ➤ *International Brotherhood of Teamsters.* www.teamster.org

> ➤ *Steel Manufacturers' Association.* www.steelnet.org
> ➤ *United Steelworkers of America.* www.uswa.org

> ➤ *Aerospace Industries Association of America.* www.aia-aerospace.org
> ➤ *International Association of Machinists and Aerospace Workers.* www.iamaw.org

Other prominent trade associations include the following:

> ➤ *American Electronics Association.* www.aeanet.org
> ➤ *American Farm Bureau.* www.fb.org
> ➤ *American Hospital Association.* www.aha.org
> ➤ *American Medical Association.* www.ama-assn.org
> ➤ *American Petroleum Institute.* www.api.org
> ➤ *Associations of Trial Lawyers of America.* www.atla.org
> ➤ *Business Roundtable.* www.brtable.org
> ➤ *Health Insurance Association of America.* www.hiaa.org
> ➤ *International Dairy Foods Association.* www.idfa.org
> ➤ *Motion Picture Association.* www.mpaa.org

➤ *National Association of Manufacturers*. www.nam.org
➤ *National Automobile Dealers Association*. www.nada.org
➤ *National Federation of Independent Business*. www.nfibonline.com
➤ *National Restaurant Association*. www.restaurant.org
➤ *Nuclear Energy Institute*. www.nei.org
➤ *Recording Industry Association of America*. www.riaa.com

Other prominent labor unions include the following:

➤ *American Federation of Teachers*. www.aft.org
➤ *American Federation of Government Employees*. www.afge.org
➤ *American Postal Workers Union*. www.apwu.org
➤ *Communications Workers of America*. www.cwa-union.org
➤ *International Association of Fire Fighters*. www.iaff.org
➤ *International Brotherhood of Electrical Workers*. www.ibew.org
➤ *Laborers' International Union of North America*. www.liuna.org
➤ *National Association of Letter Carriers*. www.nalc.org
➤ *National Education Association*. www.nea.org
➤ *Union of Needletrades Industrial and Textile Employees*. www. uniteunion.org
➤ *United Association of Journeymen and Apprentices of Plumbing and Pipe Fitting Industry of the United States and Canada*. www.ua.org
➤ *United Brotherhood of Carpenters and Joiners of America*. www. carpenters.org
➤ *United Food and Commercial Workers International Union*. www. ufcw.org
➤ *United Mine Workers of America*. www.umwa.org

Lobbyists-for-Hire

In addition to the aforementioned organizations dedicated to advancing specific causes, there are also Washington "hired guns," often law firms, that can be employed to promote any cause you like—if you can afford their fees. Examples from the case studies of people who have moved from political jobs into this form of lobbying or the other way around include John Podesta, Ralph Reed, and Anne Wexler.

Everybody hires Washington lobbyists, even education officials. In 2001 the Illinois Board of Education—in partnership with the two boards overseeing the state's higher education system—paid $182,000 for a five-month contract with a top Washington lobbying firm owned in part by a former chairman of one of the national political parties. The firm has represented such corporate giants as Phillip Morris and Microsoft. The Illinois Board of Education officials hired the firm to press for more federal funding even though Illinois already had a federal liaison on staff, as well as a congressional delegation to lobby for them for free. The Illinois superintendent of schools explained that he hired the firm because of concerns that the state was being shortchanged compared with other states in obtaining federal aid for education. In its contract with the firm, the board specified that they expected the firm to help increase its federal education funding by 6 percent over FY 1999 funding levels.

But let's look at the big bucks: the drug industry. In June 2001 Public Citizen reported that in the 1999–2000 election cycle, the drug industry hired 625 different lobbyists and paid them a total of $92.3 million. Of the 625 lobbyists, more than half were either former members of Congress (21) or had worked in Congress or other federal agencies (295). Thirty-three of these lobbyists had served as chief of staff to members of Congress, 32 had worked in the White House, and 11 others had worked for the powerful House Ways and Means Committee.

The following are the biggest lobbying firms in Washington:

- ➤ *Cassidy & Associates.* Former congressmen Fred Rooney of Pennsylvania and Marty Russo of Illinois both work for this firm, whose clients have included Boeing, Exxon, and a number of colleges and universities.
- ➤ *Verner, Liipfert.* Verner, Liipfert, Bernhard, McPherson and Hand is home to former Senate majority leaders George Mitchell and Bob Dole and former Texas governor Ann Richards.
- ➤ *Patton, Boggs.* Patton, Boggs, which counts former congressman Greg Laughlin of Texas in its ranks, has represented the Association of Trial Lawyers, MCI Worldcom, and US Airways. Thomas Boggs, the firm's top rainmaker, is the son of Hale Boggs, House Democratic majority leader until he was killed in a plane crash, and former U.S. representative Lindy Boggs, who was elected to fill her husband's seat. He is also the brother of Cokie Roberts, a noted television reporter and commentator.
- ➤ *Akin, Gump, Strauss, Hauer & Feld.* This firm's staff of political insiders includes Robert Strauss (former chairman of the DNC) and Vernon Jordan (friend and advisor to President Clinton). The firm has about a thousand attorneys in 10 U.S. and 4 international offices. Along with its lobbying staff and expanding intellectual property practice, Akin, Gump's expertise ranges from corporate

law to white-collar criminal defense. The firm also is expanding its technology practice.

In 1999 Influence, Inc., ranked the top 117 firms that reported at least $1 million in income for 1998.[1] It also showed the amount of campaign contributions of each and even what the breakdown was between Democrats and Republicans. Some firms are overwhelmingly for one side; some are split evenly between the two. Table 7.1 shows the top 25 from that list.

WHAT LOBBYISTS-FOR-HIRE DO

Lobbyists help clients formulate strategies for dealing with Congress, the White House, and the administration. They prepare legislative strategies based on a knowledge of politicians' needs. They organize "grassroots" campaigns in the districts of key members to show them their constituents care. Lobbyists develop media strategies to complement the above. They introduce clients to key members of Congress and other officials and their aides. If they are bipartisan, lobbyists can do this on both sides of the aisle. They help clients identify and then organize potential supporters from allied groups and trade associations. They advise clients on the legislative and regulatory process. Lobbyists help defeat legislation and proposed regulations their clients don't like and pass legislation and regulations they do.

WHERE THEY COME FROM

Members of the House or Senate are considered the biggest catch by a lobbying firm. In 1999 the Center for Responsive Politics identified 129 former members of Congress who were active as lobbyists. In 1998 the figure was 138. Despite the Republican takeover of Congress, the center found, 66 former members who lobby are Democrats, compared with 62 Republicans and one independent.

After former members of Congress in importance are senior White House and agency officials, such as those from Commerce, Treasury, and the Office of Management and Budget. They also include senior congressional staff—such as chiefs of staff, legislative assistants, and committee and subcommittee staff directors—former trade association officials, and persons who have served in state and local government. Others come from backgrounds of coalition building and grassroots organization. Many have also had extensive experience in political campaigns and are even active in current campaigns.

Table 7.1.   Top 25 Lobbying Firms in 1998

Rank/ Organization	1998 Lobbying Receipts (in millions)	1999 Lobbying Receipts (in millions)	Campaign Contributions (in millions)	% to Democrats	% to Republicans
1. Cassidy & Associates	$19.9	$17.6	$0.4	63%	37%
2. Verner, Liipfert	$18.8	$18.8	$0.7	58%	42%
3. Patton, Boggs	$14.4	$10.0	$0.2	74%	26%
4. Akin, Gump	$11.8	$10.2	$0.8	52%	48%
5. Preston, Gates	$10.2	$9.5	$0.3	44%	55%
6. Barbour, Griffith	$7.4	$5.2	$0.1	0%	100%
7. Washington Counsel	$7.3	$6.4	$0.06	46%	54%
8. Wms & Jensen	$7.1	$6.3	$0.4	40%	60%
9. Baker, Donalson	$6.8	$3.9	$0.03	23%	77%
10. Hogan & Hartson	$6.6	$6.4	$0.3	51%	49%
11. Pricewaterhouse- Coopers	$6.6	$2.4	$1.6	34%	66%
12. Van Scoyoc Associates	$6.5	$5.2	$0.1	39%	61%
13. Timmons & Company	$5.9	$5.3	$0.1	50%	50%
14. Podesta.com	$5.4	$3.6	$0.08	82%	18%
15. Alcalde & Fay	$4.7	$3.7	$0.03	79%	21%
16. Arnold & Porter	$4.7	$2.9	$0.1	63%	37%
17. Dutko Group	$4.6	$4.2	$0.07	72%	28%
18. Black, Kelly	$4.7	$5.2	$0.1	33%	67%
19. Capitol Associates	$4.4	$3.7	$0.06	61%	39%
20. Mayer, Brown & Platt	$4.3	$3.4	$0.1	66%	34%
21. Boland & Madigan	$4.2	$3.8	$0.04	1%	99%
22. Griffin, Johnson	$4.2	$5.3	$0.04	99%	1%
23. McDermott, Will & Emery	$4.1	$3.6	$0.2	44%	56%
24. Arter & Hadden	$4.1	$4.1	$0.1	24%	76%
25. Wexler Group	$4.0	$2.9	$0.1	48%	52%

There are, it should be noted, laws and ethics regulations that restrict the lobbying of government officials by former members of Congress, senior staff, and White House and administration appointees. The rules generally bar lobbying by these persons for a certain number of years after they leave office. This, however, does not mean that such persons cannot immediately be hired as strategists and advisors to lobbying firms; it just means that they cannot personally lobby government officials until the expiration of their restriction time.

Many lobbying firms have interns. These positions can be excellent training ground for individuals who want to serve later as congressional staff or political appointees, especially for people who may not immediately find a political position. But people who do this need to pick the issue and lobbying firm carefully to avoid becoming tainted by an unpopular or "wacky" issue or firm—of which there are many. It's best to stay with mainstream issues and firms. There is even a school for would-be lobbyists in Washington, called The Bryce Harlow Institute on Business and Government Affairs. This is a probusiness internship and education program that examines the history and philosophy of government regulation and focuses on the changes that have occurred in lobbying and the public policy process during the past quarter century. The course also outlines the growth of political activism in corporate America and the development of a Washington, D.C., business-government affairs community. The Institute's Web address is www.dcinternships.org/bhibga.

Political Consultants

Elections and campaigns have gotten so specialized that political consultants are often hired to assist with them. As a result, people who work in political jobs are more and more likely to run into consultants. In the Wild West atmosphere of campaigns, these are the swashbuckling hired guns who tell politicians how to run campaigns, giving them everything from strategic advice to polling to research. They also decide which issues to use, how to write the best television and radio ads, and when and where to place them. Consultants advise on how to conduct everything from telemarketing to direct mail, fund-raising, media relations, communications, computer use, and more. Politicians are not the only ones to hire political consultants; increasingly, corporations, public interest groups, and labor unions do, as well.

Sometimes the consultants are more famous than their candidates, for example, Democrats Paul Begala, James Carville, and the late Bob Squier and Republicans, Ed Rollins, Mary Matalin, and the late Lee Atwater. And then there's Dick Morris, who worked for both Republicans and Democrats. Many of them have enormous influence. At Bob Squier's height in the 1980s, for example, one-third of U.S. senators were paying for his advice. Today, however, the industry has become increasingly competitive. Although no one knows for sure, it is thought that there are about three thousand political consultants in the United States. Out of public view, campaign consultants team up with each other, gang up on each other, and sometimes blow up relationships with candidates over money or strategy. In the rough and tumble of politics, they are often the most colorful actors. In a world in which the perception of power is power itself, hiring a big-name consultant can coax more donations out of campaign contributors. Conversely, firing one can lower confidence in the campaign and dry up donations.

There have always been people who have acted as political consultants off and on, but the first person to call himself a full-time political consultant was Joseph Napolitan, who started in 1956 and now has offices in Springfield, Massachusetts, and New York City. As the old political machines died out in the 1960s, professionals such as Napolitan moved in to run campaigns. Napolitan worked on the campaigns of John F. Kennedy and Lyndon Johnson and was director of media for Hubert Humphrey's 1968 presidential bid. He is also a veteran of more than a hundred U.S. Senate, House, gubernatorial, and big-city mayoral campaigns. His activities are not limited to this country; he has served as a personal consultant to nine foreign heads of state. Napolitan gave advice to Costa Rican president Oscar Arias that helped the leader win the Nobel Peace Prize in 1988.

Napolitan is also the founder of the nonpartisan American Association of Political Consultants in Washington, D.C. This organization, which can be contacted through its Web site, www.theaapc.org, not only maintains a list of its eight hundred member consultants; it conducts annual seminars to assist students in learning about the industry and even finding internships and jobs in it. Its members include political consultants, media consultants, pollsters, campaign managers, corporate public affairs officers, professors, fund-raisers, lobbyists, congressional staffers, and vendors and is open to everyone associated with politics, from the local level to the White House.

The American Association of Political Consultants claims that there are more than 50,000 public elections held in the United States each year. Add to that elections for leaders of private, professional, academic, business, labor, public interest, and other organizations, as well as public votes on local and state referenda, initiatives, and constitutional amendments, and the number jumps to more than 500,000 elections each year.

Some of these consultants make big money. A recent survey of consultants found that 20 percent made more than $200,000 a year; a smaller group made $500,000 a year, and a handful of media strategists in each party made

$1 million or more a year. But in order to earn this kind of money in an increasingly competitive industry, some firms have had to handle as many as 40 campaigns in a single election cycle. Whereas at one time a Bob Squier could say, "The fee is 15 percent; take it or leave it," in today's more competitive world, the fee for a media consultant is more likely to be 6 to 7 percent in a high-spending race. As a result, most firms have cultivated new markets by using their renown in the political world to secure even more lucrative corporate work that is akin to lobbying. More than three-quarters of consultants do corporate work, and sometimes half their income comes from it.

In recent years, the specialized political adman has squeezed out the general consultant as the maker of the really big bucks. Bob Squier, whom Joe Napolitan once called the "best of all time," was the first to maximize a tradition in which media consultants receive a commission for every television advertisement a campaign buys. Napolitan never charged a commission on anything. The commission system gives consultants an incentive to drive up the amount of television advertising a campaign does. And consultants are the ones who decide how much advertising is appropriate. Television advertising can sometimes eat up as much as 70 percent of a campaign's budget, with the consultant making 7 to 15 cents on every television dollar, although usually consultants' fees and profit margins are carefully guarded trade secrets. Consultants also make money by charging add-ons to base costs—for example, fundraising consultants charging extra for the number of political action committee donations they collect and polling consultants charging extra for special analytical services they can provide beyond the basic poll. Politicians may not like the expense, but because they feel there is no other way to get elected, they pay.

But the ground rules may be shifting for the future. The influence of conventional television advertising is waning, which will open new opportunities for political consultants. Television advertising is still superior to other types of advertising, but it takes ever-increasing amounts of it to make the desired impact. There is a school of thought that the Internet is the wave of the future. Not enough people use it now to produce a really broad audience, but observers feel that will change in the future and that a new breed of political consultant, the "net consultant," will be needed.

Such consultants can help a candidate mobilize online through such methods as simplifying write-in campaigns by conducting them via e-mail. Voting records can be displayed online, volunteers can be recruited online, and money can even be raised online. Rapid response to critics' attacks can be posted online. Net consultants can prevent the misuse of the Internet from hurting a candidate, too. For instance, they could prevent a campaign from sending out unsolicited political ads via e-mail, which can make voters angry. All in all, the Internet promises to change the rules in a way to make room for new consultants.

═════▶ The Media ◀═════

Besides being well-known members of the media, what else do these Republicans have in common—G. Gordon Liddy (nationally syndicated radio talk show host), John McLaughlin (host of *The McLaughlin Group*), Peggy Noonan (author and editorialist), William Safire (*New York Times* columnist), Dianne Sawyer (cohost of *Good Morning America*), and Tony Snow (syndicated columnist and host of *Fox News Sunday*)?

The answer is that they all served in the White House earlier in their careers, as did Democrats Bill Moyers (television personality and journalist) and George Stephanopoulos (ABC News analyst).

Many other members of the media also worked first on Capitol Hill, including Democrats Chris Mathews (host of MSNBC's *Hard Ball*) and Tim Russert (host of *Meet the Press*) and Republican Pete Williams (NBC News correspondent).

Much more than the public may realize, there's a busy two-way street between the media and the government. Williams, for example, also was an assistant secretary of defense for Public Affairs, and Moyers, Noonan, Sawyer, Snow, and Williams worked in the media prior to getting their government jobs. David Gergen of *U.S. News and World Report* worked in the Nixon, Ford, Reagan, and Clinton White Houses.

This relationship between politics and the media exists not only at the national level but also at state and local levels. Whereas a top White House aide, for instance, may later land a job with the national media, aides in Congress frequently go on to lucrative careers with local television stations or newspapers back home. They may also develop journalistic careers with some of the many specialized publications and news services in the Washington area. Conversely, many reporters who work for these publications later land jobs with Congress and the hundreds of government departments and agencies.

It's clear that a job in the media can often help further a career in politics. The reason is that journalists offer several talents that politicians value highly:

➢ *Communications skills and the knowledge of how to craft and deliver messages.* Because a large part of politics is communicating and ex-

plaining policy decisions, it's not surprising that presidents, cabinet secretaries, senators, and representatives hire people from the
media for this important purpose.

> *The ability to write quickly and well.* The ability to write quickly and
well, in journalistic style as opposed to academic style, can be a
valuable asset to agencies that routinely put out press releases on
their activities. Good journalists are familiar with techniques for
explaining complex issues, a talent that many politicians lack.

> *Knowledge of what interests the public and what doesn't.* Television
specialists know how to craft stories for maximum effect on viewers. They know about short, punchy, sound-bite style, good com-
plementary use of visuals, and high-energy delivery. Those with
television experience can use these skills either to speak for a
politician or to advise a politician on how to make better use of
television.

> *Skill in dealing with the working press, some of whom may be former
colleagues.* For a representative who sits on the House Banking
Committee, for example, it can be an advantage to hire a journalist who has former colleagues at influential banking industry publications.

How can a job in politics further a career in the media? In general, political experience helps when the skills you learn in politics can also be used
in television, radio, and print media. But just as a Republican administration
is unlikely to hire someone who worked for a liberal magazine, a conservative television network isn't likely to hire an aide to a liberal representative.
Even some middle-of-the-road media companies may shy away from hiring
an applicant whose background includes work at a highly partisan organization, whether Democratic or Republican.

Political talents that the media value include the following:

> *Access.* Once you've worked in politics, you'll develop hundreds of
contacts and a bulging Rolodex, assets that many reporters will tell
you are their most useful. While another journalist struggles to find
a source who can explain the intricate workings of steel quotas, for
instance, you might simply phone an old friend at the Department
of Commerce who gives you not only a thorough explanation but
also an important insight. Your editor is impressed.

> *The ability to assess information.* A journalist without experience in
politics can easily miss the importance of what a government

source says. And few things irk a politician more than giving a journalist a scoop, only to realize later that the journalist didn't appreciate the value of the information given. Take, for example, what is called the poison pill amendment. On the surface this appears to be a small proposed change to a piece of legislation going through Congress. But in reality, the change would effectively gut the bill.

➤ *Knowledge of the political process.* Although television, radio, and the print media all report on legislative developments, many journalists would be at a loss to explain just how that process works. Knowing the process saves precious time in a deadline-dependent profession and makes the final story far more understandable to the viewer or reader. Working in politics can also teach you the ground rules by which reporters and politicians interact. For example, if something is explicitly agreed upon as being off the record, a reporter cannot use it directly in the story. But if the source forgets to stipulate that the comments are off the record, the reporter has the right to use them. On the other hand, if it's important to maintain a long-term relationship with a source, a reporter experienced in politics can often decide more wisely whether to "burn" the source by quoting the source directly or to attribute the information to "a knowledgeable source" and thereby preserve the relationship.

Failure to observe these basic principles has gotten a lot of sources in trouble and has led to the saying, "Don't ever say anything to a reporter that you wouldn't mind seeing on the front page of the newspaper." But in politics, it's often more complicated than that. Sometimes you want the message on the front page of the paper; you just don't want the world to know how it got there. This inevitably leads to complicated arrangements between some sources and reporters; reporters who don't report everything they know about a story for fear of permanently cutting off a source, and sources who don't tell reporters everything they ought to know about a story for fear of undermining the message. This becomes a game between the politicians and the reporters; the politicians are trying to manage the news so they look good, while the reporters are trying to find something sensational to write about. Both sides use the other, and both are completely aware of it. Although they pretend to the public they aren't.

This is the reason that in most politicians' offices, only the press secretary or other officially authorized personnel are allowed to talk to the press. Other staffers are supposed to refer all press inquiries to those officials.

~Target Groups~

The relationship between politics and the media is a critical element in the way our country operates, and the relationship is constantly evolving. Both politicians and the media, for example, have target groups. Politicians target the groups that they think will give them votes. Democrats are constantly trying to assemble and hold together their coalition, and Republicans do the same with theirs. But Democratic and Republican officials in the south may have somewhat different coalitions than those in the north. Similarly, different media sources target the demographic groups—readers or viewers—that they believe will bring in the most advertising dollars.

The Pew Research Center for the People and the Press has provided important insights into the relationship between politics and the media. In November 1999 the organization published a study of 10 sectors of the voting public and where they got their news.[2] The findings of this study, summarized in the following sections, show which groups politicians and the media target, what messages those groups most likely want to hear, and what type of media would be most likely to reach them.

DEMOCRATS

Voters identified as Democrats range from liberal to the "partisan poor."

Liberal Democrats

Liberal Democrats make up 10 percent of registered voters. Of these, 78 percent always or nearly always vote. They are, for the most part, secular progressives, consistently liberal on economic, social, and international issues. Overall, 82 percent follow public affairs most of the time or some of the time, 55 percent regularly read a newspaper, 37 percent regularly watch the network nightly news, 35 percent regularly watch news magazine shows, 36 percent regularly watch cable news networks (tied with staunch Republican conservatives as the largest percentage to do so), 15 percent regularly listen to call-in radio shows, and 70 percent go online, the second-largest percentage to do so.

Socially Conservative Democrats

Socially conservative Democrats make up 14 percent of registered voters. Within this sector, 78 percent always or nearly always vote. Think of them as latter-day New Dealers. They hold conservative opinions about freedom of expression, homosexuality, and immigrants but have strong ties to unions. They are more financially satisfied than many other Democrats and may go Republican—these were the "Reagan Democrats." Eighty percent follow public affairs most of the time or some of the time, 58 percent regularly read a newspaper, 53 percent regularly watch the network nightly news, 41 percent regularly watch news magazine shows, 34 percent regularly watch cable news networks, 13 percent regularly listen to call-in radio shows (among the lowest percentages to do so), and 56 percent goes online.

New Democrats

The New Democrats make up 9 percent of registered voters, of which 78 percent always or nearly always vote. This was Bill Clinton's base. New Democrats have less compassion than others in their party for the disadvantaged and are less critical of business. Yet like most Democrats, they express support for government and are more socially tolerant than the conservative wing of the Democratic Party. They would consider voting for a Republican. Within this sector, 83 percent follow public affairs most of the time or some of the time, 54 percent regularly read a newspaper, 46 percent regularly watch network nightly news (the largest percentage to do so), 47 percent regularly watch news magazine shows (by far the largest percentage to do so), and 40 percent regularly watch cable news networks (again, by far the largest percentage to do so). Only 13 percent listen to call-in radio shows, among the lowest percentage to do so, and 53 percent go online.

Partisan Poor

Ten percent of registered voters fall under the label "partisan poor." Within this group, 77 percent always or nearly always vote. You can consider them social welfare loyalists. This most racially mixed bloc looks to government for solutions to its problems and remains strongly loyal to the Democratic Party. Of this group, 74 percent follow public affairs some or most of the time, 51 percent regularly read a newspaper, 39 percent regularly watch the network nightly news, 41 percent regularly watch news magazine shows, 30 percent regularly watch cable news networks, 17 percent regularly listen to call-in radio shows, and 32 percent go online, the smallest percentage to do so.

REPUBLICANS

As with the Democrats, Republicans come in a variety of flavors.

Staunch Conservatives

Staunch conservatives make up 12 percent of registered voters. Of these, 90 percent always or nearly always vote, by far the largest percentage to do so. Classified as white male hard-liners, they are consistently conservative on economic, social, and international issues. In this group, 93 percent follow public affairs most of the time or some of the time (the largest percentage to do so), 64 percent regularly read a newspaper (again, the largest percentage to do so), and 45 percent regularly watch the network nightly news. Only 30 percent regularly watch news magazine shows, the lowest percentage, except for the bystanders (see under "Independents"), 36 percent regularly watch cable news networks, 35 percent regularly listen to call-in radio shows (the largest percentage to do so), 59 percent go online.

Moderate Republicans

Moderate Republicans represent 12 percent of registered voters. In this group 81 percent always or nearly always vote, a percentage second only to staunch conservatives. They are often characterized as affluent centrists. They are less critical of government, more interventionist, more environmentalist, more tolerant, and less probusiness than staunch conservatives. They are also less loyal to the Republican Party. Of moderate Republicans, 86 percent follow public affairs most of the time or some of the time (a percentage second only to staunch conservatives), 52 percent regularly read a newspaper, 42 percent regularly watch network nightly news, 36 percent regularly watch news magazine shows, 29 percent watch cable news networks, 17 percent regularly listen to radio call-in shows, and 58 percent go online.

Populist Republicans

Often characterized as the Republican Party's poor cousins, populist Republicans account for 10 percent of registered voters. Within this sector, 74 percent always or nearly always vote. Populist Republicans are highly religious and socially conservative. But they have more-moderate opinions about government and less-favorable opinions of business corporations than staunch conservatives. They would consider voting for a Democrat. Seventy percent follow public affairs most of the time or some of the time, 35 percent regularly watch network nightly news, the lowest percent to do so, except for bystanders (see under "Independents"), 49 percent regularly read a newspaper, and 34 percent regularly watch news magazine shows. Only 27 percent regularly watch cable news networks, the lowest percentage to do so, except for bystanders, 16 percent regularly listen to call-in radio shows, and 42 percent go online.

INDEPENDENTS

The different varieties of independents include so-called new prosperity independents, the disaffected voters, and bystanders.

New Prosperity Independents

Eleven percent of registered voters are considered "new prosperity independents." Of these, 72 percent always or nearly always vote. They are characterized as young to middle-aged voters whose affluence, Internet savvy, and stock market investments lead them to strongly endorse the status quo. This group strongly favors both handgun control and a capital gains tax reduction. Overall, 77 percent follow public affairs most of the time or some of the time, 59 percent regularly read a newspaper (second only to staunch conservatives), 38 percent regularly watch the network evening news, 33 percent regularly watch news magazine shows, 33 percent regularly watch cable news networks, 22 percent regularly listen to call-in radio shows, and 75 percent go online, by far the largest percentage to do so.

Disaffecteds

The so-called disaffected voters make up 10 percent of registered voters. Of these, 63 percent always or nearly always vote, far lower than any other group, except for the bystanders, who don't vote at all. Working class and alienated, the disaffecteds are at the opposite end of the socioeconomic spectrum than new prosperity independents and are alienated and cynical rather than confident and upbeat. Nevertheless, they actually hold many political views that are similar to the new prosperity independents. But they are less important as voters because of their limited participation. Seventy percent follow public affairs most of the time or some of the time, a percentage tied with populist Republicans as the lowest (except for bystanders), 46 percent regularly read a newspaper (the lowest of any group except bystanders), 38 percent regularly watch the network nightly news, 33 percent regularly watch news magazine shows, 33 percent watch cable news networks, 17 percent listen to call-in radio shows, and 40 percent go online.

Bystanders

Bystanders make up zero percent of registered voters. Democracy's dropouts, bystanders do not vote. They are the lowest in most categories: 34 percent follow public affairs most of the time or some of the time; 26 percent regularly watch network nightly news; 25 percent regularly watch news magazine shows; 13 percent watch cable news networks; and 12 percent listen to call-in radio shows. But interestingly, 46 percent go online, which is more than four of the other groups do.

CONCLUSIONS

You can see from the foregoing analysis that television in some form (network news, news magazine shows, cable television) is the main source of political news for a large majority of Americans. But over the years, the percentage of people relying on either network or local television has been steadily falling while the percentage watching cable television news has been steadily rising. Newspapers, once the main source of news about politics for many Americans, have also been dropping, while use of the Internet has been rising. During presidential elections, significant numbers of people also say they learn about the election from television news magazines, political shows on network and cable television and public television, and talk radio. A smaller group, mostly young people, say they learn something about the campaign through late night talk shows, such as those hosted by Jay Leno and David Letterman, or comedy shows, such as *Saturday Night Live*.

As media strategists contemplate how to reach the desired groups, they will consider a number of factors, including the circulation of a newspaper or the viewership of a television station and what its political bent may be. At the national level, a network news broadcast is going to reach far and away the largest number of people. *NBC Nightly News,* for example, which is thought to have a liberal bent, reaches about 11 million people each night. ABC and CBS are in the same range. The figure for cable networks, such as the more conservative Fox News Channel, is much lower, at 656,000; CNN (596,000) and MSNBC (296,000) are lower still. Sunday shows, such as NBC's *Meet the Press* (4–5 million) and ABC's *This Week* (3 million) are in between.

Any individual newspaper will not reach nearly as many people as a network news program will, but the newspaper story is usually more in-depth and therefore may often be more influential among opinion makers and certain stakeholders. *USA Today* (which you can read for free online at www.usatoday.com) is the nation's top-selling newspaper, with an average daily circulation of 2.3 million. Liberal-leaning papers include the *New York Times* (www.nytimes.com), with a circulation of 1.1 million, and the *Washington Post* (www.washingtonpost.com), with a circulation of 800,000. The more-conservative *Wall Street Journal* (public.wsj.com; but you have to pay) has a circulation of 1.9 million, whereas the *Washington Times* (www.washtimes.com) has a circulation of only about 100,000.

Together with the *New York Times, Wall Street Journal, Washington Post,* and *USA Today,* the following papers make up the top 10 papers in the United States:

New York Post (www.nypostonline.com)
Los Angeles Times (latimes.com)
Chicago Tribune (www.chicagotribune.com)
Boston Globe (www.boston.com/globe)
Baltimore Sun (www.sunspot.net)
Dallas Morning News (www.dallasnews.com)

In addition to general newspapers, wire services such as the Associated Press (AP) supply stories to thousands of subscriber newspapers.

These top 10 newspapers and the wire services are not the only print news sources, of course; there are also thousands of smaller, local newspapers. Today, thanks to the Internet, you can read most of them free online by clicking onto www.newspapers.com. These newspapers can be a great source for more-local stories, the kind that could have an impact within a congressional district or a state but not necessarily reach a national news source. There are also many specialty publications relating solely to issues such as taxes, business, health, and many others.

Reporters get jobs at these news sources either through a journalism degree in college or graduate school, accompanied by practical work experience. The work experience can come from an internship at a big paper, such as the *Washington Post,* or at one of the major networks, or from first working at smaller papers or local television stations.

Examples from the case studies of people who moved between the media and government include Roger Majak and Susan King.

State and Local Government

State officials move into Washington political jobs at all levels. A former state governor who wins the presidency will put former state employees on the White House staff and in the administration. State representatives or state senators who get elected to the U.S. House or U.S. Senate bring staff with them from those jobs. At the local level, an employee of the D.C. mayor who has had a business relationship with the House Appropriations Committee might get asked to serve as staff for that committee. Catherine Bertini, Andrew Card, Andrew Natsios, and Bob Nash, profiled in the case studies, all made this type of move.

Furthermore, state officials are one of the major constituencies that persons holding political jobs in Washington have to deal with on a day-to-day basis. It could be in the form of casework that a congressional office has to do, such as a local government applying for a federal grant, or a governor working through the White House Office of Intergovernmental Affairs to win disaster relief funds. Or it could come in the form of state officials coordinating with officials in many federal departments to win federal matching funds for a variety of programs.

The skills that these people bring to Washington political jobs are many. If they come from state legislatures, they know how a legislative body works, what the lives of politicians are like, and what makes a good staffer. If they come from a governor's office, they know about the executive role and what that entails. In both cases, they know about state constituency groups, and they have plenty of political contacts in the state. In both cases, they may know their boss rather well and thus have his or her special confidence.

Getting jobs in state and local governments is generally easier than at the federal level because there is less competition. Although there is wide variation, the pace at the state level tends not to be as frantic as at the federal level. But the pay is usually less at the state level. Many of the strategies for getting state and local political jobs are similar to the ones discussed in this book for getting political jobs in Washington.

Notes

1. Center for Responsible Politics, "Top Overall Lobbying Firms," www.open secrets.org.pubs/lobby/98/topoverall.htm (September 17, 2002).
2. Pew Research Center, www.people_press.org/report/display.php3?reportid=50.

8

~~⚔~~

CASE STUDIES

In this chapter are 36 case studies, or short biographies, of people who have held the jobs described in this book. These people are here primarily because I knew them to be excellent at what they did or I knew someone who suggested them to me for that reason. I admit that this was not a particularly scientific process. And this is certainly not meant to be the definitive list of "who's who in Washington." Rather, it is simply a good representation of the kinds of careers that exist in Washington. Another list, with perhaps entirely different names, could have been created with equally good results. Some on this list are famous; most are not. Some are at the end of their careers; some are partway through them. They are fairly evenly divided between Republicans and Democrats and represent many of the themes in U.S. national politics today.

A few trends jump out. First is the vast difference in the social background of those who get political jobs in the United States. It ranges from migrant worker to Mayflower descendant. Second is education. Most have college degrees, and 63 percent have advanced degrees: 33 percent have master's degrees, 19 percent have law degrees, and 11 percent have doctorates. College majors are all over the lot—international relations, dramatic arts, engineering, psychology, sociology, anthropology, political science, biology, U.S. history, and mathematics. The general background seems to range from specific subject knowledge at one end to knowledge about po-

litical organizing at the other. You can get subject knowledge through an
advanced degree, but you can't get knowledge of political organizing that
way. You have to get it through practical experience. At least 70 percent of
the group had significant campaign experience that helped them get a political job.

Of this group, four of the men (11 percent of the whole group) served
in the military. None of the women did.

Most of these people have held more than one job within the federal
political system. They didn't just take one job at the beginning of a career
and stay with it for life—although they may well associate with a mentor for
a long period of time.

One trend about people working in the political parties is that not
even the top leadership tends to stay there very long. A few may go from one
party job to another. But by and large, people tend to stay a few years and
then move on either to the Hill, the White House, the administration, or to
other political campaigns, sometimes setting themselves up in business as
campaign consultants.

Several trends emerge about people working on the Hill. A few people
are widely respected career-Hill types. They come in two kinds. The first is
the person who stayed close to home, hitched a star to that of a local politician who rose through the ranks, eventually becoming an important committee chair or a member of the leadership, and who was the staffer's mentor,
taking the staffer along for the ride. Jim Dyer is an example of this type. The
second career-Hill type transfers from one representative or senator to another, known around the network as being particularly competent and thus
having no trouble getting job offers from other representatives and senators.
Both types have one thing in common: they've worked in Congress for a
long time. It's rare for someone to be one of the most-respected Hill staffers
without having been there for quite a while.

But the normal Hill type is a transient, someone who works there only
a few years before moving on to something else—the White House, the administration, or the private sector, often as a lobbyist. Thus, while representatives and senators are often in office for decades, the staff is turning over
much faster, except for a few senior aides.

On the surface, everyone who works in the White House or the administration appears to be a transient, too, including the president. A presidential term only lasts four years, eight if you're really good. So these people
need something else to do when they're out of office—a business to return
to, a law degree so they can join a law firm, lobbying, going back to the Hill,
and so on. But when you look deeper, you see that the higher the position,

the more likely it is that the person has had experience in a previous White House or administration. So there is a certain continuity there.

To work in a think tank, you usually have to have a great technical expertise as opposed to great knowledge of the "three Ps"—process, politics, and the people. With the highly paid lobbyists, it's the other way round; before they got their lobbying jobs, they all seem to have extensive experience with the process, politics, and the people involved in the federal system.

The one thing all the people discussed here have in common is that for much of the time they are serving a specific clientele, not necessarily just "the national interest." Lobbyists, obviously, are the most like that, in that they serve a specific client first and foremost but try to argue that their client's interests are actually in the national interest. Each political party has its own political agenda, which argues, in essence, that the national interest is best served by paying more attention to its coalition's needs than to those of the other party. Some of the time, the elected officials—the representatives, senators, presidents and their staffers—are occupied with matters that are truly in the national interest. But much of the time, they are making sure their constituents get their share of the federal pie; representatives look out for the interests of 435 districts, and senators the interests of 50 states. Perhaps a president spends the most amount of time on matters that are in the national interest, but even the president has to pay strict attention to the interests of the numerous groups that helped him get elected.

Career Patterns

The following are the career patterns that emerge from the case studies and from the rest of the book:

GETTING THE FIRST JOB

Campaigning is the method by which the majority of people get their first job in politics and consequently it is discussed in great detail in this book. But it is certainly not the only way. The others include the following:

> ➤ *Connections*. One way to get a political job is through being closely connected to someone else who helped the candidate get elected. This could be a relative, a campaign worker, or a donor.

➤ *Working at no expense to the politician.* This includes volunteering, being an intern, or winning a fellowship. You can volunteer to work in a representative's office or even in the White House. You can achieve the same result by going through one of the many formal internship programs for the Hill or the White House Internship program. Some lobbying firms even have intern programs. There are paying fellowships for the Hill, the White House Fellows Program for the White House, and the Presidential Management Intern Program for administration jobs.

➤ *Transferring in.* Some people are able to transfer into political jobs from a related job. For example, some develop issue expertise, either through association with an academic institution or (more likely) through positions in the General Accounting Office, civil service jobs, lobbying groups, or think tanks, interest groups, trade associations, or labor unions.

TYPE OF WORK IN POLITICAL JOBS

From the case studies, one can see that there is a large range of jobs you can hold in politics, but the following are the four main areas:

➤ *Political organization.* The most obvious form of this is running campaigns, but it also means assembling coalitions to pass legislation, either as a Hill aide, a White House aide, a member of the administration, or even as a lobbyist.

➤ *Establishing policy.* One of the benefits of winning an election is winning a mandate to pursue certain policy objectives. So if you work in a political job, there is a good chance that you will participate in determining your team's policy. This participation comes in two general roles: reportorial (gathering facts and reporting them to superiors) and advisory (using those facts to actually advise a politician on what a policy ought to be and on how to sell it). Reportorial jobs are usually easier to get than advisory jobs, but many people work their way from one to the other.

➤ *Communications.* A large part of political jobs involves internal and external communications—communicating to other actors in the political process what the policy is to be and communicating it to the public so that your team can win a stronger mandate to continue.

➤ *Administrative.* Holding an administrative job in a political setting means building and using a network to get things done. If you work in a political job, you will be in a perfect position to learn how the system works, learn the substance and politics of issues, and make contacts with the main actors in the political process. You will probably keep building and using this network for the rest of your career.

WHERE POLITICAL JOBS LEAD

Once you've gotten your first political job, as the case studies will show, you are likely to head down one of the following roads:

➤ *Another political job.* If you are a Hill aide starting out as a legislative assistant, one well-beaten path is to work your way up to chief of staff. From there, you can become a subcommittee staff director. Or you might get to this position just from having been a legislative assistant. Another path is to transfer to an administration job or the White House. Some people come back to government jobs after having been in the private sector for a while.

➤ *Lobbyist.* Many people leave government jobs to join firms that represent clients' interests at various junctures of the political process, such as getting a client's project included in the president's budget proposals or getting Congress to enact it.

➤ *Another area of the private sector.* Some people who have held political jobs go to work for private sector firms that do not engage in lobbying but which make use of their issue or process knowledge. Examples of these include international trading companies, law firms, schools and universities, the media, and general communications work. But it is likely that they will go to jobs that make more specific use of their government experience, such as director of government relations or law work representing clients with business before the federal government. If they have served long enough in both government and the private sector, they may get pensions from both.

Individual Case Studies

The following case studies give a glimpse of the variety in the careers of those who have held political jobs in Washington.

RICHARD L. ARMITAGE (REPUBLICAN)

In March 2001 the Senate confirmed Richard Armitage as deputy secretary of state. Prior to that time, starting in May 1993, he was president of Armitage Associates and had been engaged in a range of worldwide business and public policy endeavors, as well as frequent public speaking and writing engagements. Previously, he held senior troubleshooting and negotiating positions in the Departments of State and Defense and Congress.

Born in 1945, Armitage graduated in 1967 from the U.S. Naval Academy, where he was commissioned an ensign in the U.S. Navy. He completed three combat tours with the riverine/advisory forces in Vietnam. Fluent in Vietnamese, he left active duty in 1973 and joined the U.S. Defense Attaché Office in Saigon. Immediately prior to the fall of Saigon, he organized and led the removal of Vietnamese naval assets and personnel from the country.

In May 1975 Armitage came to Washington as a Pentagon consultant and was posted in Tehran, Iran, until November 1976. Following two years in the private sector, he was administrative assistant to Senator Robert Dole (R-KS) from 1978 to 1980. For the 1980 Reagan campaign, he was senior advisor to the Interim Foreign Policy Advisory Board, which briefed Reagan on major international policy issues, and from 1981 to 1983, he was deputy assistant secretary of defense for East Asia and Pacific Affairs.

From 1983 to 1989, Armitage served as assistant secretary of defense for International Security Affairs, representing the department in developing politico-military relationships and initiatives throughout the world. He spearheaded the U.S. Pacific security policy, including the U.S.-Japan and U.S.-China security relationships, managing all Defense Department security assistance programs and providing oversight of policies related to the law of the sea, U.S. special operations, and counterterrorism. He played a leading role in Middle East security policies.

From 1989 to 1992, he was presidential special negotiator for the Philippines Military Bases Agreement and special mediator for water in the Middle East. During the 1991 Gulf War, President Bush sent him as a special emissary to Jordan's King Hussein.

From 1992 to 1993 until his departure from public service, Armitage directed U.S. assistance to the newly independent states of the former Soviet Union, holding the personal rank of ambassador. In January 1992 the Bush administration's desire to jump-start international assistance to these states led to Armitage's appointment as coordinator for emergency humanitarian assistance. During his tenure in these positions, he completed extensive international coordination projects with the European Community, Japan, and other donor countries.

CATHERINE BERTINI (REPUBLICAN)

In April 2002 Catherine Bertini finished her term as the executive director of the United Nations' (UN) World Food Programme (WFP), the largest global food aid agency. When she was appointed to the post in 1992, she was the first American woman to head a UN organization and the first woman to lead WFP. She was reappointed for a second five-year term as executive director in 1997. In March 2000 she was named the secretary-general's special envoy to the Horn of Africa, and she immediately embarked on a mission there to avert a drought-induced famine. Under her leadership, WFP's share of global food aid rose from 22 percent in 1993 to 36 percent in 1998. Some 83 million people received WFP food aid in 2000. At the same time, voluntary contributions from governments, nongovernmental organizations, and the private sector, which are the sole source of WFP's funds, reached a record $1.9 billion in 2001. Under Bertini, WFP has underscored the role women play in food aid and pioneered the use of food aid to empower them. Also under her, overhead costs are low; with more than 80 percent of its staff working in the field, WFP has the smallest number of people based at headquarters of any major UN agency.

Before she took up her WFP post, Bertini was the assistant secretary for food and consumer services in the Department of Agriculture from 1989 to 1992. While there, she directed 13 food assistance programs, which benefited one in six Americans, including 25 million children in more than 90,000 schools. In 1992 Bertini founded the Breastfeeding Promotion Consortium, which saw an increase in the number of nursing mothers in the United States from 38.3 percent to 50.4 percent over the next five years.

From 1987 to 1989, Bertini was acting assistant secretary of the family support administration in the Department of Health and Human Services. Charged with implementing welfare reform, she oversaw changes to federal regulations that created educational opportunities for long-term welfare mothers, many of whom consequently entered the job market for the first time. The revised regulations also put greater pressure on absent fathers to pay child support to their indigent spouses.

Before that, from 1977 to 1987, she supervised government relations, philanthropic activities and public affairs for the Container Corporation of America.

From 1975 to 1976 she worked for the RNC and from 1971 to 1975 was youth director for the New York Republican State Commission. Earlier, as a college senior, she worked full time in the last gubernatorial campaign of Nelson Rockefeller (R-NY). When he was reelected, she went to work as a confidential assistant in the governor's office. Before that, she had been a legislative aide to her hometown state senator. Bertini was born in 1950 in Syracuse, New York, and graduated from the State University of New York at Albany in 1971. She is married to Thomas Haskell, an international photographer who has donated many of his pictures to WFP.

JON-CHRISTOPHER BUA (DEMOCRAT)

Jon-Christopher Bua now runs his own Washington-based consulting firm after having served as the communications director in three federal agencies during the Clinton administration. Born in 1948, Bua grew up in New York City and loved watching political events unfold on television. As a teenager, he volunteered in the campaigns of John F. Kennedy (for president), Robert Kennedy (for U.S. senator), and John V. Lindsay (for New York City mayor). A career as an actor and acting coach intervened before he got involved in politics again—this time in 1991 for Bill Clinton.

Impressed with Clinton's performance in a television debate, Bua called the Little Rock headquarters to see how he could get involved with the campaign and was referred to the campaign headquarters in Manhattan. There he was asked to put together a group of male attorneys and train them to speak around New York State as surrogates for Governor Clinton.

Using the skills he had developed over 20 years as an actor (including appearances in John Cassavetes' film *Gloria* and daytime television's *All My Children*) and as an acting teacher, theater director, and speech coach, he revised the surrogate materials, talking points, and message delivery system prescribed by the campaign in Little Rock. He also spoke to 20,000 Haitians, in Creole, at a rally in front of the UN and on Creole radio. In addition, he resurrected street-corner speaking, training scores of speakers and perching them on soapboxes all over Manhattan, where they exhorted passers-by to vote for Bill Clinton and Al Gore.

As a result of this campaign work, in 1993 Bua was recommended for a job in Washington as the surrogate scheduler for the National Health Campaign, a project of the DNC. There he scheduled thousands of individuals to speak in support of the president's health care initiative. He subsequently became a permanent member of the DNC staff and set up a Talk Radio Strategy to counter the right-wingers who dominated talk radio at the time. In that capacity, he booked over two thousand pro-Democratic speakers, making an estimated 150 million voter contacts. He appeared on hundreds of shows himself. Altogether, he served at the DNC from 1993 to 1997.

Following Clinton's reelection in 1996, Bua was the communications director of the U.S. Small Business Administration (1997–1999), the Office of Personnel Management (1999–2000), and the managing director for intergovernmental and public affairs at the Overseas Private Investment Corporation (2000–2001). In March 2001 he established Jon-Christopher Bua Strategic Communications and now works with a wide range of clients from the public and private sectors on message creation, preparation, delivery, and reporting.

Bua earned a bachelor's degree in dramatic arts from the City College of New York in 1971, and was enrolled at NYU in a Master of Fine Arts Program in Acting in 1971–1972. He is married to Michele D. Ross, a partner in a Washington law firm.

ANDREW H. CARD (REPUBLICAN)

On November 26, 2000, Andrew Card was appointed chief of staff for President George W. Bush. In this job, his days begin at 6:15 A.M. and end between 8:30 and 10:30 P.M. One of his earliest tasks was trimming White House staff and salaries. "From a management perspective," he explained, "I want to leave some room to grow during the administration."

Card has a long record of service in both the public and private sector, including in the administrations of two former presidents. He has witnessed the changing of the guard under seven former Republican chiefs of staff, including James Baker, Don Regan, and John Sununu. As Bush's deputy chief of staff, Card even had to fire Sununu, his boss at the time, after the outspoken and controversial Sununu overstepped his bounds one time too many.

In 2000 Card served as chairman of the Bush-for-President operation at the convention. From 1993 to 1998, he was president and chief executive officer (CEO) of the American Automobile Manufacturers Association and then General Motors' vice president of governmental relations. He is thus the only chief of staff in the last 20 years to move directly from lobbying to the White House, and he is the highest-ranking auto executive to serve in government since Ford Motor Company's Robert McNamara became John F. Kennedy's defense secretary in 1961.

In 1992 Card briefly considered running for the U.S. Senate against Ted Kennedy, but his parents' failing health quickly changed his mind: "Serving in a political office is selfless," as he put it, "but running is selfish." Instead, that year Card was named secretary of transportation under President George H. W. Bush. In August 1992 Bush sent Card to Florida to take charge of relief efforts and repair the political damage caused by what some perceived as a leisurely government response to the $25 billion Hurricane Andrew disaster. Later, Card directed President Bush's transition office during the transition from the Bush administration to the Clinton administration.

Prior to serving as secretary of transportation, Card served as assistant to the president and deputy chief of staff, in which capacity he managed the day-to-day operations of the White House staff and helped develop economic, foreign, and domestic policy. In 1988 Card directed Bush's New Hampshire victory over Senator Bob Dole.

From 1983 to 1987 Card held two official positions under President Ronald Reagan: special assistant to the president for intergovernmental affairs and later, director of intergovernmental affairs, where he was the president's primary liaison to governors, state legislators, and mayors. In 1982 Card ran unsuccessfully for Massachusetts governor. Before that, starting at age 26, he served four terms in the Massachusetts House of Representatives (1975–1983). His first attempt to get elected to that office had failed. As a state representative, Card worked with the Democratic majority on issues such as political corruption in state construction work and earned a reputation as a conciliator and peacemaker. In 1982 he was named Legislator of the Year by the NRLA.

In 1979 Card first began his association with the Bush family when he was the Massachusetts campaign chairman for George H. W. Bush's attempt to win the Republican nomination for president. Card drove the elder Bush through Massachusetts in a kind of mobile office during the early days of his bid. Although Bush lost the nomination to Ronald Reagan, he did win the Massachusetts primary.

Card was born in 1947, in Brockton, Massachusetts, before his parents finished high school. Consequently, he spent a lot of time with his grandmother; his introduction to politics began with her involvement in local politics and the school committee. Card began attending town meetings when he was eight years old. The family then moved to Holbrook, which Card described as "a blue-collar, working-class community, kind of on the wrong side of the tracks." Although he is a Mayflower descendant, he calls himself a "swamp Yankee" because of his family's lower-middle-class standing.

Card held a Reserve Officers' Training Corps (ROTC) scholarship at the University of South Carolina, from which he graduated with a bachelor's degree in engineering in 1971. He then worked as a structural engineer for five years. He entered the Merchant Marine Academy but dropped out in 1979 to enroll at Harvard's Kennedy School of Government. He left there after a year to participate in George H. W. Bush's first presidential campaign.

Card and his wife of 34 years, Kathleen, have three children and four grandchildren. She is a minister at Trinity United Methodist Church in McLean, Virginia, and Card is one of her parishioners.

JIM W. DYER (REPUBLICAN)

Jim Dyer is majority clerk and staff director for the U.S. House Committee on Appropriations. He was born in 1943 in Scranton, Pennsylvania, and received his bachelor's degree from the University of Scranton in 1966. He started his political career as an advance man for the Pennsylvania Republican Committee in 1966–1967.

Between 1967 and 1970 Dyer was assistant to Pennsylvania lieutenant governor Raymond J. Broderick. From 1971 to 1975, Dyer was legislative and press aide to Representative Joseph M. McDade (R-PA) and then served as McDade's administrative assistant (1975–1981) and as associate staff member of the House Appropriations Committee under McDade (1981–1984).

From 1984 to 1985 he was the director of government affairs for the Power Systems Division of United Technologies Corporation.

Starting in 1985 Dyer held a number of positions in the Reagan administration, beginning at the State Department as deputy assistant secretary of state for legislative affairs, House of Representatives. In 1986 he was acting assistant secretary of state for legislative and intergovernmental affairs. Starting in 1987 he switched to the White House, where he served as deputy assistant to the president for legislative affairs (1987–1988) and then as deputy assistant to the president for legislative affairs in the House of Representatives (1988–1989). In 1989 he became a budget consultant to the secretary of the navy.

He then left government and from 1989 to 1991 was director of Washington relations for Phillip Morris. But in 1991 he returned to government, this time as a part of the Bush administration, and from 1991 to 1993 worked as deputy assistant to the president for legislative affairs in the Senate.

After the Bush administration, Dyer became a governmental affairs consultant at Hand, Arendall, Bedsoe, Greaves and Johnston, ETA Associates, Washington, D.C. (1993–1994). He returned to Capitol Hill in 1994, this time as Republican professional staff assistant with the House Appropriations Committee, becoming staff director in 1995. He is married to Margia L. Carter.

MARIA ECHAVESTE (DEMOCRAT)

Forty-eight-year-old Mexican-American Maria Echaveste served in a variety of administration jobs before President Clinton made her deputy chief of staff, the highest position ever attained by a Hispanic woman. Echaveste was the eldest of the seven children who grew up following ripening crops across California, picking cotton, strawberries, grapes, tomatoes, and carrots. Although she had few material possessions, she spent as much time as possible in libraries in the communities where she worked. She eventually won a scholarship to Stanford, where she majored in anthropology. She then spent a year in Washington interning with the U.S. Commission on Civil Rights. Envisioning a government job, she earned a law degree from the University of California at Berkeley. But instead of returning to Washington, she became a corporate attorney in New York City, a job she found both lucrative and enjoyable.

In New York she married a Bronx attorney and converted to his religion, Orthodox Judaism. She subsequently divorced but remained Jewish because she felt Judaism, more than Catholicism, allowed its followers to concentrate on the here and now rather than the hereafter. In New York she became active in Democratic politics and served as president of the city's board of elections. During the 1992 presidential campaign, she left her law firm to become the national Latino coordinator for the Clinton team.

When Clinton got elected, Echaveste joined his administration, becoming wage and hour administrator at the Labor Department, overseeing minimum wage laws, child labor laws and the newly passed family medical leave act. She led a project that obtained $8 million in back wages for poor workers who had been illegally underpaid by their employers. And she pushed an anti-sweatshop crusade to press retailers and clothes makers to improve the working conditions at the facilities of their apparel contractors.

At the start of Clinton's second term in 1997, Echaveste moved over to the White House as director of public liaison, responsible for boosting support for presidential policies and initiatives. In 1998 she was promoted to deputy chief of staff, which entailed everything from deciding who gets raises to coordinating the State of the Union speech to planning the Wye River summit to negotiating Mideast peace and the 50th anniversary NATO conference.

MARLIN FITZWATER (REPUBLICAN)

Marlin Fitzwater is the only press secretary in U.S. history to be appointed by two presidents. He served for almost a decade in this position to Presidents Reagan and George H. W. Bush, one of the longest records in history. He is also an example of someone who converted from civil service status to political appointee to do so, a rare occurrence for such a sensitive job. During the Gulf War, Fitzwater became known to millions of Americans as the voice of the 26-nation coalition prosecuting the war. He gave over 850 press briefings in six years, winning praise from the news media and the public. His White House press operation became a model for many of the emerging democracies of Eastern Europe and Latin America. He has participated in three presidential campaigns and worked with all the major Republican political figures involved in the 1996 campaign. He is the author of three books: *Call the Briefing,* a best-selling memoir and behind-the-scenes look at Presidents Reagan and Bush; *Esther's Pillow,* a fictional view of a small town in America based on a true story; and *In His Speech,* in which he uses his experiences within the White House fishbowl to put today's media events into perspective.

Fitzwater grew up on a small farm in Kansas, graduated from Kansas State University in 1965 with a degree in journalism, and worked on newspapers in Abilene, Manhattan, Topeka, and Lindsborg, Kansas, before moving to Washington, D.C., in 1966 to serve as a GS-5 newsletter writer at the Appalachian Regional Commission. But in 1968, because of Vietnam, he was activated from the Air National Guard to serve in the regular U.S. Air Force.

Returning home from the air force in 1974, Fitzwater exercised his right under the law governing those activated into the armed services to return to a government job. While he had been away, the Department of Transportation had been formed. Several of his friends from the Appalachian Regional Commission had transferred there and "rehired" him at the Department of Transportation, where he worked as a speechwriter from 1970 to 1972.

Between 1972 and 1980, he was one of the chief spokesmen for the newly created Environmental Protection Agency (EPA), still as a civil servant, as the United States started a massive cleanup of the environment. His name started appearing in the papers. His speeches and statements laid out the rationale for stopping acid rain, ozone depletion, and toxic waste dumping. He was named Outstanding Civil Servant in government in 1980.

That same year, Ronald Reagan got elected president, an event that was to have far reaching consequences on Fitzwater's career. When Donald Regan came in as secretary of the treasury in the new administration, Fitzwater was detailed for a few weeks to help bring the secretary up to speed on press relations and Washington. Regan took a liking to Fitzwater and hired him as the chief spokesman for the Treasury, again as a civil servant. But after 17 years, this was to be his last civil service job.

In 1983 Fitzwater got a call from David Gergen, then in Reagan's communications office. Gergen said he had seen Fitzwater's name in the papers defending supply-side economics and was impressed. He asked whether Fitzwater would like to be deputy press secretary to the president. Fitzwater jumped at the chance. He was so excited, he didn't even ask what the salary was—it turned out that he had to take a $7,000 pay cut to take the job. Chief of staff Jim Baker took him to meet Reagan, who welcomed him on board. On his way out of the meeting, Fitzwater said "Yes!" under his breath as he was passing one of the secretaries. When asked what this meant, Fitzwater exclaimed that no matter what happened next, he would always be able to say he was a press secretary to the president of the United States, at least for a little while. It turned out to be quite a long while, a decade.

Fitzwater thus gave up his civil service protected job status in order to become a political appointee and started his White House career as deputy press secretary, where he was a spokesman for Reagan's tax cuts and investment incentives. How did he overcome the normal tendency to prefer someone with long loyalty to the president, based on prior service with him or service in a campaign? Fitzwater believes it was a combination of his name being in the papers vigorously supporting the Reagan policies, the fact that he had Donald Regan's endorsement, and that he was known as being one of the best professionals in the business.

Fitzwater became press secretary to Vice President Bush in 1985, was press secretary to President Reagan from 1987 to 1989, and then worked as press secretary to President Bush from 1989 to 1992. While a presidential press secretary, Fitzwater insisted on, and was never denied, complete access to the president. He also learned what every press secretary learns: people in the White House seldom tell you everything they know about a matter—which can lead to your getting blindsided by enterprising reporters.

After leaving the White House, Fitzwater formed the public relations firm Fitzwater and Tutwiler, Inc., and has since also been an author and lecturer. In addition, he has been a consultant to the television show *West Wing*, a job he loves because it portrays a president and his aides making mistakes but always trying to do good. About six weeks before each new show appears, the producers call him, tell him about the scenario they are contemplating for the next show, and ask him to check details and provide any vignettes that support the plot lines. Six weeks later, Fitzwater sees his stories on television. Fitzwater often speaks around the country and has many young people ask him about politics and the White House, but he says it's sad that they never ask him about civil service jobs in the executive branch. Fitzwater is married and has two children.

WENDY GREUEL (DEMOCRAT)

In 2002 40-year-old Wendy Greuel won the Second District seat on the Los Angeles City Council and started work on this full-time job. The Van Nuys resident won the race by only 242 votes in one of the most bitter contests in local elections in some time. Close observers predict she will one day be a candidate for mayor of Los Angeles.

Prior to winning the city council seat, Greuel had been in the Corporate Affairs Department of DreamWorks SKG in Los Angeles, starting in August 1997. While there, she worked on the company's government/political relations and charitable giving. She also served as the liaison with the Glendale community and coordinated DreamWorks' legislative and governmental activities at the local, state, and national levels. Greuel's extensive experience with elected officials and community organizations enhanced the company's commitment to be a good corporate citizen.

Prior to DreamWorks, Greuel served in Washington and Los Angeles as a member of the Clinton administration as the field operations officer for southern California for Andrew Cuomo, the secretary of Housing and Urban Development (HUD). In that job, she championed projects offering opportunities for homeownership, job creation, economic development, and social services for the less fortunate. She also coordinated HUD's earthquake emergency response and recovery programs, the Los Angeles Homeless Initiative, and was instrumental in the establishment of the Los Angeles Community Development Bank.

Greuel's first experiences with public service began as student body president at Kennedy High School in Los Angeles. She won a youth leadership award and an internship in the office of City Councilman Joel Wachs (whose seat she now holds). She also won an internship in Mayor Tom Bradley's office. During the summer of 1981, she represented Los Angeles in its Washington, D.C., office and then interned for Bradley in Los Angeles during her last years in college. These internships, says Greuel, changed her life. Before them, she had been contemplating going into the family business, but the internships opened a new, exciting world to her.

Following her college graduation, Bradley offered her a full-time job. She worked for him for 10 years, from 1983 to 1993, as a grants coordinator and as his liaison to the city council, city departments, and the community in general on social policy and political issues including child care, AIDS, the homeless, the elderly, and health issues. Bradley's deputy mayor at the time was Mark Fabiani, who was to serve later in the Clinton White House.

In 1993 Bradley was leaving office, and Greuel was trying to decide what to do next. Working in Washington was a possibility, she thought, but how to pursue it? In Los Angeles she happened to meet Andrew Cuomo, who would soon become confirmed as secretary of HUD. Mark Fabiani helped her get a resume to Cuomo. A few weeks later, Cuomo called her on a business matter but also asked what her plans for the future were. He suggested that she come to D.C. and work for him, which she did.

Later, Greuel transferred to the HUD office in Los Angeles. She had always had in the back of her mind that she might want to run for city council, and working back home, she reasoned, might be a good launching pad. She happened to be in Los Angeles when one of the big earthquakes struck and was asked to stay for a few days to help sort out the recovery efforts. Six weeks later, she was still there, living out of a hotel, and was finally asked to transfer there permanently, which she did. She stayed in that job until 1997, when the opportunity arose for her at DreamWorks. When she took that, she had pretty much given up the idea of ever being able to run for office, but when the chance came later, she grabbed it.

Greuel received her bachelor's degree from the University of California, Los Angeles in 1983, after changing her major three times, from psychology to economics to political science.

PATRICIA DE STACY HARRISON (REPUBLICAN)

Patricia de Stacy Harrison was sworn in as the assistant secretary of state for educational and cultural affairs on October 2, 2001. As an entrepreneur, author, and political leader, she has more than 20 years experience in communication strategy, coalition, and constituency building. Prior to her job at the State Department, she served as the first Italian-American cochair of the RNC and the first cochair not previously a member of the RNC.

As founder and president of the National Women's Economic Alliance, she worked to identify women and minorities for leadership roles in business and politics. Through the "Decade for Democracy," a mentoring exchange program sponsored by the U.S. Department of Commerce and the U.S. Small Business Administration, she worked with women entrepreneurs in emerging democracies to help them achieve success within their new free enterprise systems.

Harrison was also a founding partner of E. Bruce Harrison Company, among the country's top 10 owner-managed public affairs firms prior to its sale in 1996. While there, she created and directed programs working for better environmental solutions.

In 1990 President Bush appointed her to the President's Export Council at the U.S. Department of Commerce, where she worked to strengthen export promotion programs on behalf of U.S. business. In 1992 she was appointed to serve on the U.S. Trade Representative's Service Policy Advisory Council. Harrison is the author of *A Seat at the Table* and *America's New Women Entrepreneurs* and is a graduate of American University. She is married and the mother of three children.

DAVID HOPPE (REPUBLICAN)

David Hoppe is chief of staff to Senate majority leader Trent Lott (R-MS). He has spent about a quarter-century on the Hill, dating back to the late 1970s when he was first associated with Lott in the House of Representatives. Hoppe is one of the most knowledgeable and influential Hill staffers.

Hoppe's efforts are widely credited with breaking the logjam that threatened passage of the Individuals with Disabilities Education Act Amendments of 1997, which overhauled the law on special education policy for 5.6 million disabled children in America's public schools. Hoppe had a special stake in the outcome; he is the parent of a child with Down's syndrome.

For two years, the bill had been caught between leaders of the Republican revolution, who wanted to help schools cut costs and curtail classroom disruptions caused by disabled students, and those who advocated expanded education opportunities for the disabled. It took the deeply religious, conservative Hoppe to bring the two sides together. Based in large measure on his credibility as a parent with a disabled child, Hoppe brought about a compromise that made it easier for schools to discipline disabled students but did not let states cut off their education. The law also upgraded teacher training, gave parents a greater role, and improved planning and mediation. President Clinton specifically thanked Hoppe in his signing ceremony speech about the bill.

Born in 1951, Hoppe received his bachelor's degree from the University of Notre Dame (1973) and a master's degree from the Johns Hopkins University School of Advanced International Studies (1975). His first paying job in politics was as a research associate with the House Republican Study Committee (1976–1978). In 1978 he was a political consultant. Then, from 1979 to 1980, he worked as the executive director of the House Republican Research Committee.

From 1980 to 1984, Hoppe first worked for Trent Lott, who was then a U.S. representative and House Republican whip, as Lott's administrative assistant. Hoppe became the executive director of the House Republican Conference (1984–1987) and then worked as staff director (1987–1988) to U.S. representative Jack Kemp (R-NY), then a potential presidential candidate.

In 1988 Hoppe left government and was vice president for governmental relations at the Heritage Foundation. But one year later, he moved to the Senate, serving as administrative assistant to Senator Dan Coats (R-IN) from 1989 to 1992. In 1993, however, he moved back to his former boss, Trent Lott, now a U.S. Senator and secretary of the Senate Republican Conference. Hoppe worked as Lott's staff director from 1993 to 1995. From 1995 to 1996 he was Lott's chief of staff after Lott became Senate Republican whip. Hoppe assumed his current position in 1996. He has written two publications on China.

Hoppe has been married to Karen Suzanne Davis since 1976. The two conservative idealists met in a carpool when she was working at the Heritage Foundation. They have three children.

MICKEY IBARRA (DEMOCRAT)

Mickey Ibarra, a long-time political activist, currently runs his own political consulting firm called Ibarra and Associates in Bethesda, Maryland, specializing in government relations, public affairs, marketing, and economic development. He is Latino, and Latinos, now at 35 million, are the fastest-growing segment in the U.S. population. Prior to setting up his own business, he served in the Clinton White House as the director of intergovernmental affairs (1997–2001), an office first established by President Nixon in 1969. Ibarra was one of only 20 people to hold the formal title "Assistant to the President" in the Clinton administration. In his White House position, Ibarra and his staff sought to maintain a partnership with state and local governments and build support among them for the president's initiatives while at the same time responding to their concerns.

Originally from Utah, and the son of a Mexican migrant worker, Ibarra was born when his mother was 16 years old. He spent his youth in foster homes, at one point living with a couple in Provo for several years. Ibarra received his bachelor's degree from Brigham Young University, paid through the GI bill for his service in the U.S. Army. He spent five years as a teacher, beginning teaching in Utah County in 1977 at a public alternative high school for at-risk students and then moving to Salt Lake County. He attended the University of Utah while he continued teaching, getting his master's degree in education in 1980. As a teacher, Ibarra became involved in the Utah Education Association and later with the National Education Association (NEA). From the NEA's state office in New Mexico, he moved to the main office in Washington, D.C., in 1984. By 1990 he was the campaigns and elections manager at the NEA, good training for his eventual position in the White House. In 1996 he took a leave of absence from the NEA and joined the Clinton-Gore campaign as the senior campaign advisor and director of special projects. He also served on the political affairs staff of the Presidential Transition Office following President Clinton's election in 1992.

SUSAN KING (DEMOCRAT)

Susan King is currently vice president of public affairs at the Carnegie Corporation of New York, where she is responsible for the corporation's communications, including its publications, Web site, and dissemination programs. Before joining Carnegie, King served in two capacities during the Clinton administration. In 1995 she was the Labor Department's first executive director of the Commission on the Family Medical Leave Act, which reviewed how changes in the law were being implemented and made recommendations for changes. From 1996 to 2001 she was assistant secretary for public affairs at the Department of Labor. There she oversaw media relations and public education efforts for the department's 16 agencies and was its frontline strategist on methods to inform the public about policies affecting the workplace. In 1995, for example, she spearheaded the "No Sweat" media initiative—an innovative public service, education, and consumer awareness campaign that called attention to labor abuses in the garment industry, a campaign that she felt effected change more than journalism alone could have done. Once, in describing how to respond to the media during a crisis, King said: "Bring all the key players into a room and get the facts straight. Never tell more than you know, don't freelance what you think, and constantly update reporters. Reporters have to get information, and if you don't give them anything, they will report rumors."

Prior to working in government, King spent 20 years as a journalist covering national and international issues. From 1987 to 1993 she anchored WJLA-TV newscasts in Washington, covering the 1988 presidential campaign, the Nicaragua conflict, and the 1990 elections, as well as Supreme Court nominations and the local political scene. From 1983 to 1987 she worked at WRC-TV in Washington to anchor the 6:00 P.M. news and produce "Cover Story" for the 11:00 P.M. news, a three-minute daily analysis of major news stories. She took "Cover Story" to WJLA in 1987, where she anchored the 5:00 P.M. and 11:00 P.M. newscasts (1987–1993).

In 1993, after almost 20 years building her broadcast career in Washington, King was made an "offer" by WJLA that was, in her words, "tantamount to being fired." The station, as a cost-saving measure, planned to demote its top talent in order to force their departure instead of firing them and being responsible for compensation packages. King brought arbitration against the station to make it live up to its collective bargaining agreement. She won her case and in so doing re-established the rules for all journalists and set a national precedent. WJLA and arbitration behind her, she became an independent journalist for CNN, ABC Radio, the *Diane Rehm Show*, NPR's *Talk of the Nation*, and CNBC's *Mary Matalin Show*.

King began her career in 1970 as an editorial assistant to Walter Cronkite at CBS News in New York. She moved to WGR-TV in Buffalo, New York, where, from 1973 to 1975, she was the first women to anchor regular newscasts. From 1975 to 1979 she reported and anchored the news for WTOP-TV (now WUSA-TV9) in Washington alongside some of today's local anchor institutions, including Maureen Bunyan, Gordon Peterson, Max Robinson, and Andrea Mitchell. King is the founder and former cochair of the International Women's Media Foundation, which is dedicated to a free press and to promoting women's role in it. She is a 1969 graduate of Marymount College and earned a master's degree in communications from Fairfield University in 1973.

ROGER MAJAK (DEMOCRAT)

Roger Majak currently works for Open Harbor, Inc., a venture capital computer software company based in Silicon Valley. The firm assists companies in managing their international trade business via computer programs that contain all necessary international trade regulations and that analyze each transaction.

Prior to that, from 1997 to 2001, he served as assistant secretary of commerce for export during the Clinton administration. In that capacity he helped manage control of exports having national security implications and also worked on converting defense industries to commercial businesses.

Majak grew up in Chicago and earned a bachelor's degree in journalism from Northwestern University in 1963. After a short period as a journalist in Chicago, he got a master's degree in international affairs from Ohio State in 1965. While still working as a journalist, he completed all coursework toward a doctorate by 1968, with the exception of writing a thesis.

In 1968 Majak was awarded a one-year congressional fellowship from the American Political Science Association, which was what got him onto Capitol Hill. He worked six months as a general legislative assistant for Senator Joe Tydings (D-MD) and six months in the same capacity for Representative Jonathan Bingham (D-NY). In 1969, as the fellowship ended, Bingham hired him as a regular legislative assistant in the office. Shortly thereafter, the administrative assistant left the office and Bingham appointed Majak as interim and then permanent administrative assistant when Majak was only age 23. He held this position until 1974. That year, in an effort to further burnish his international relations credentials, he served on the staff of the one-year Murphy Commission, which studied how the United States got into the Vietnam War.

In 1975 Representative Bingham became chairman of the International Relations Committee's Subcommittee on International Economic Policy. Majak expressed interest to Bingham about being the staff director of the subcommittee, Bingham agreed, and Majak served in this capacity for 10 years, until 1985. This put him in the international trade field, where he has stayed for the rest of his career. In 1985, thinking that it was time to work in the private sector, Majak took a job as director of government relations for Tektronix Corporation, in its Washington office. He stayed there for five years.

In 1992 and 1996, Majak wrote issue papers for the Clinton campaigns. When Clinton won, Majak was working with Stuart Eizenstat, former chief domestic advisor to President Carter, at the law firm of Powell, Goldstein, Fraser and Murphy. After serving as U.S. ambassador to the European Union in the first Clinton term, Eizenstat became undersecretary of commerce in 1996 and was among those who recommended Majak for the open position of assistant secretary for export administration. It helped also that the undersecretary to whom Majak would be reporting (William Reinsch) was his Senate counterpart when Majak was Bingham's subcommittee staff director, and the two had worked together amicably on trade and other issues. For added White House support for his appointment, Majak requested and obtained the endorsement of the Democratic Leadership Council, which had close ties to President Clinton and which shared Majak's views on business regulation and international trade. Majak resides in Alexandria, Virginia, with his wife, Sally, and a son and daughter.

SYLVIA MATHEWS (DEMOCRAT)

Sylvia Mathews is currently executive vice president of the Bill and Melinda Gates Foundation, where she oversees finance, administration, legal, government relations, public affairs, and other foundation activities. She helps to shape overall foundation strategy and evaluate the effectiveness of current programs, as well as coordinates the foundation's strategy of building partnerships with governments, industry, UN agencies, foundations, and nongovernment organizations.

Prior to that, starting in 1998, Mathews was deputy director of the Office of Management and Budget, where she helped develop administration policy and was responsible for coordinating administration efforts on budget and appropriations matters, as well as other legislative and management issues. Prior to this position, in 1997, Mathews was appointed assistant to the president and deputy chief of staff to the president, where she supervised the work of several White House offices, including the NEC, the Domestic Policy Council, the Council on Environmental Quality, and the Offices of Public Liaison, Intergovernmental Affairs, and Communications. She also helped review staff recommendations and managed the flow of information from staff to the president.

Before working for the president, she served as chief of staff to the secretary of the treasury, Robert E. Rubin, from 1995 to 1997, advising Rubin on foreign and domestic policy, management, and communications issues, helping implement the secretary's priorities throughout the department, and serving as the secretary's liaison to the White House and other government agencies.

Mathews first joined the Clinton administration in December 1992 as the manager of the president-elect's Economic Transition Team. In January 1993 she became staff director for the NEC and special assistant to Rubin, then assistant to the president for economic policy. Her responsibilities included advising Rubin on economic and long-term planning issues, working closely with senior White House and administration officials, and overseeing the day-to-day work of the NEC staff.

Before joining the federal government, she worked in the private sector for the McKinsey and Company management consulting firm. From 1990 to 1992 she was an associate with McKinsey in New York, where she performed analytical research, primarily in the areas of finance and telecommunications.

She was the deputy director of economic policy for the 1992 Clinton-Gore campaign. Four years earlier, she was a researcher in the 1988 Dukakis-Bentsen presidential campaign, in which capacity she fact checked debate preparation materials. Prior to that, she was an aide to Massachusetts governor Michael Dukakis (D-MA) and served as a Lyndon B. Johnson Intern for Congressman Nick Rahall (D-WV). She graduated from Harvard College with a bachelor's degree in government in 1987, after which she was a Rhodes Scholar, receiving an honors degree in philosophy, politics, and economics in 1990 from Oxford University.

JANICE MAYS (DEMOCRAT)

Janice Mays is the minority (Democratic) chief counsel and staff director for the House Ways and Means Committee. She is therefore one of the most senior women staffers on the Hill, having come to Ways and Means in 1975.

Mays grew up in Georgia and was the only person in her class in Macon's Wesleyan College to major in political science. As a result, she was eligible for a number of independent study programs, one of which was a three-month legislative internship on the agriculture committee in the Georgia house of representatives.

Following graduation from Wesleyan in 1973, Mays entered the University of Georgia School of Law in Athens, from which she graduated in 1975 and was admitted to the Georgia bar. While in law school, she decided she did not want to be a litigator and remembered that she had particularly enjoyed her experience as a legislative intern. She then applied to be a legislative assistant to several of the Georgia U.S. representatives, but there were no vacancies.

Luck then intervened. Mays had gone to school with the daughter of U.S. Representative Phil Landrum (D-GA), and he recommended her for a position on the Ways and Means Committee staff. Luck intervened again as the committee was just beginning to expand its staff as a part of post-Watergate reforms. Representative Wilbur Mills (D-AK), the prior committee chairman, had relied on the staff of the Joint Committee on Taxation to handle tax matters for him. His Ways and Means tax staff consisted of only one or two people, who dealt mostly with constituent requests. However, the new chairman, Al Ullman (D-OR) wanted his own tax staff, and Mays had had all of the requisite tax courses in law school, although she had been only an average student.

Mays got the job and served on the Ways and Means tax staff from 1975 to 1987, until she became chief tax counsel, the first woman ever to reach that level. In addition, she became staff director for the Subcommittee on Select Revenue Measures.

In 1981 she received a master's of law in taxation from the Georgetown University Law School after three years of night classes. She enrolled in the program not because she felt she needed it for her Ways and Means work but because she thought it would help her concentrate in a specialty area that might be valuable to her should she leave the Hill and return to Georgia to practice law, which she was then contemplating.

In 1993 Ways and Means Committee chairman Dan Rostenkowski (D-IL) promoted her to chief council and staff director for the full Ways and Means Committee, again the first woman to reach that position. When the Republicans took control of Congress in the 1994 election, she reverted to Democratic staff director.

Especially in her early years on the committee, Mays viewed her job as a nonpartisan tax job, not as a political one. She now manages a staff that has perhaps the widest, most important jurisdiction of any in Congress, overseeing the nation's tax laws, trade import issues, Social Security, Medicare, and welfare (now called Temporary Assistance for Needy Families). Hers is a "full-service" staff, responsible for helping the Democratic members of the Committee to write bills and amendments on these issues.

Mays is proud of her long service to the House, an institution she reveres. She is especially proud of her role in helping to craft such legislation as the 1986 Tax Reform Act, which simplified the tax rules, took 6 million people off the tax rolls, and still remained revenue neutral.

In hiring Ways and Means Committee staff, Mays looks for common sense as much as academic accomplishments. She does not ask what an applicant's political affiliation is, but she usually wants the applicant to have done an apprenticeship somewhere before coming to the committee. This would most likely be in an executive branch department dealing with the issues that Ways and Means handles because that would provide good contacts as well as knowledge of the issues. She also hires some people from law firms who have attained special expertise. She feels that the role of women is increasing on the Hill and finds that the women she hires generally stay longer than the men.

MINYON MOORE (DEMOCRAT)

Minyon Moore has been the chief operating officer of the DNC. Prior to that, she served as the transition director for incoming DNC chairman Terry McAuliffe. Before that, from 1997 to 2001, she served in the Clinton White House successively as director of public liaison, deputy director of political affairs, and then assistant to the president and director of political affairs. She was an active member of the task force that helped develop the President's Initiative on Race. Prior to joining the White House, Moore distinguished herself in the areas of voter education, coalition building, and community outreach at the DNC. There, she served as political director and constituency and outreach director (1993–1996). In those capacities, she worked closely with local and state leaders as well as leaders of community groups, including the National Rainbow Coalition. She coordinated voter registration efforts with the DCCC, as well as with the DGA and the DSCC. In these efforts, she, along with other black women, such as Donna Brazile, Al Gore's campaign manager, and Regena Thomas, now New Jersey secretary of state under Governor Jim McGreevey (D-NJ), has been responsible for turning out black voters at the polls in unprecedented numbers. Before joining the DNC, Moore worked for the Reverend Jesse Jackson, first at his organization People United to Save Humanity (PUSH) and then when he ran for president. She is a native of Chicago and attended the University of Illinois at Chicago.

MICHAEL J. MYERS (DEMOCRAT)

Michael Myers is staff director and chief counsel to the U.S. Senate Committee on Health, Education, Labor, and Pension that is chaired by Senator Edward M. Kennedy (D-MA). Myers is rated as one of the most influential staffers on Capitol Hill. The committee has a sweeping and diverse jurisdiction that includes such matters as biomedical research, occupational safety, private pension plans, domestic activities of the American National Red Cross, equal employment opportunity, mediation and arbitration of labor disputes, and many others.

Myers was born in 1955 in Cleveland, Mississippi. He graduated from Columbia University with a bachelor's degree in 1979. From 1979 to 1981 he was an International Fellow at Columbia and received a master's degree in 1981.

From 1979 to 1980 Myers was the program director for the UN high commissioner for refugees in Hanoi, Vietnam, the first of several jobs he was to have concerning refugees. This position's main role is to protect millions of the world's refugees, through such measures as providing them with food, clean water, shelter and medical care. It also seeks to find permanent solutions for refugees, preferably through repatriating them to their original homes.

From 1981 to 1986 Myers was the representative for Church World Service, in Washington, D.C. The Church World Service is the relief, development, and refugee assistance ministry of 36 Protestant, Orthodox, and Anglican denominations. It meets emergency needs, aids refugees, and helps address the root causes of poverty and powerlessness. Within the United States, it helps communities respond to disasters, resettles refugees, and promotes fair national and international policies, among other things.

In 1987 Myers took a job as counsel to the Senate Judiciary's Sub-committee on Immigration and as foreign policy advisor to Senator Kennedy. He served in this position until 1993, leaving the Senate that year to become the director of policy for humanitarian and refugee affairs for the Department of Defense. He served in this post until 1996. The Office of Humanitarian and Refugee Affairs directs the Defense Department's demining programs and oversees the civic assistance activities of the U.S. military. It is also responsible for Defense policy regarding humanitarian law treaties and for policy oversight of migration-related activities. In addition, it coordinates transportation support for humanitarian and disaster relief efforts and acquires and donates excess property to recipients around the world.

In 1997 Myers returned to the Senate and spent a year as minority staff director for the Senate Judiciary's Subcommittee on Immigration, again under Senator Kennedy. In 1998 he switched to another Kennedy committee, becoming minority counsel for the Senate Committee on Health, Education, Labor and Pension. In 2001, when the Democrats took back control of the Senate, he was upgraded to majority counsel.

BOB J. NASH (DEMOCRAT)

Bob Nash is currently a vice president with the Shorebank Corporation in Chicago. From 1995 to 2001, he served as assistant to the president and director of presidential personnel. His responsibilities included directing the presidential appointment process for the Clinton administration, including boards, commissions, cabinet and subcabinet members, senior executive service employees, ambassadors, U.S. attorneys, and U.S. marshals.

Prior to this, Nash was the undersecretary of agriculture for small community and rural development. In this position, he was responsible for an $8 billion budget and 12,000 federal employees. He authorized loans, grants, and equity investments in rural America for business development, housing, water, sewer, telephone, and electric facilities, as well as health care and other community facilities. During this time, he was also chairman of the Rural Telephone Bank Board and a board member of the U.S. Department of Agriculture's Commodity Credit Corporation.

Nash was born in Texarkana, Arkansas, and received a bachelor's degree in sociology from the University of Arkansas at Pine Bluff in 1969. He earned a Certificate in Management from the U.S. Department of Agriculture graduate program in 1971 and his master's degree in urban studies from Howard University in 1972.

Nash began his public service career while attending Howard University at night. He served as management analyst in the executive office of the deputy mayor of Washington, D.C., then as assistant to the city manager of Fairfax City under a management internship program. He later served as administrative officer for the National Training and Development Service, located in Washington, D.C., where he was responsible for the administrative operations of this national training organization for state and local government management.

In 1974 Nash returned to Arkansas, and served as director of community and regional affairs under Governors Dale Bumpers and David Pryor. He was responsible for local land use planning assistance and grants management for city and county government infrastructure projects. In 1975 he accepted a position as vice president of the Winthrop Rockefeller Foundation in Little Rock, Arkansas, where he was responsible for rural economic development, civic education, grants management and administrative operations.

Nash continued his public service career with Governor Bill Clinton in 1983, when he took a job as Governor Clinton's senior executive assistant for economic development, responsible for developing the state's economic policy, industrial and business recruitment, and expansion. He left the governor's office in 1989 and was appointed by the governor as president of the Arkansas State Development Finance Authority. There, he was responsible for managing a $3 billion public-sector finance institution and generating capital in the private markets to support the state's housing, small business, and public facilities needs.

Nash's wife, Janis F. Kearney, was President Clinton's personal diarist. The couple has three children.

ANDREW S. NATSIOS (REPUBLICAN)

Andrew Natsios was sworn in on May 1, 2001, as administrator of the U.S. Agency for International Development (USAID), the government agency that administers economic and humanitarian assistance worldwide. He had served earlier at USAID, first as director of the Office of Foreign Disaster Assistance (1989–1991) and then as assistant administrator for the Bureau for Food and Humanitarian Assistance (now the Bureau for Humanitarian Response) (1991–1992).

Prior to becoming administrator of USAID, Natsios was chairman and CEO of the Massachusetts Turnpike Authority (2000–2001). Before that, he was secretary for administration and finance for the Commonwealth of Massachusetts (1999–2000). From 1993 to 1998 he was vice president of

World Vision U.S., and from 1987 to 1989 he was executive director of the Northeast Public Power Association in Milford, Massachusetts.

Natsios served in the Massachusetts house of representatives from 1975 to 1987 and was named Legislator of the Year by the Massachusetts Municipal Association (1978), the Massachusetts Association of School Committees (1986), and Citizens for Limited Taxation (1986). He also was chairman of the Massachusetts Republican State Committee for seven years.

Natsios is a graduate of Georgetown University and Harvard University's Kennedy School of Government, where he received a master's degree in public administration. He has taught graduate and undergraduate courses at Boston College, the University of Massachusetts, and Northeastern University. He is the author of numerous articles on foreign policy and humanitarian emergencies, as well as the author of two books: *U.S. Foreign Policy and the Four Horsemen of the Apocalypse* (Center for Strategic and International Studies, 1997), and *The Great North Korean Famine* (U.S. Institute of Peace, forthcoming).

After serving 22 years in the U.S. Army Reserves, Natsios retired in 1995 with the rank of lieutenant colonel. He is a veteran of the Gulf War.

A native of Holliston, Massachusetts, Natsios and his wife, Elizabeth, have three children.

J. BONNIE NEWMAN (REPUBLICAN)

In the summer of 2001, J. Bonnie Newman, a former assistant to Presidents George H. W. Bush and Ronald Reagan, a senior public affairs and government relations consultant, and former University administrator, was named executive dean at Harvard's John F. Kennedy School of Government. In that position, she is the senior administrative officer of the Kennedy School and joins the senior management group in developing the school's strategic direction.

Before coming to the Kennedy School, Newman was the founder and managing director of The CommerceGroup, LLC, a strategic communications consultancy. She was also active as a private investor in the financing and development of early stage entrepreneurial opportunities. Prior to the establishment of The CommerceGroup, she served as interim dean of the Whittemore School of Business and Economics at the University of New Hampshire (1998–1999), where she established a distance learning program and worked with faculty to initiate technology upgrades for the school. From 1991 to 1995 she was the owner of Coastal Broadcasting Corporation, licensee of WZEA-FM radio of Hampton, New Hampshire.

From 1989 to 1991 she was assistant to President George H. W. Bush for the Office of Management and Administration, where she oversaw all administrative operations for the White House and EOP during the transition to the administration of President Bush.

In 1983, President Reagan nominated Newman to be assistant secretary of commerce for economic development, where she served with Secretary Malcolm Baldrige. Previously, she served as associate director of the Office of Presidential Personnel at the White House (1982–1983).

From 1981 to 1982 Newman was chief of staff for new U.S. representative Judd Gregg (R-NH), whom she first met in 1976 through the Reagan presidential primary campaign in New Hampshire. She was working on the campaign as a volunteer, her first job in politics. Four years later, when Gregg ran for Congress, he approached Newman to manage his campaign, which she did. When he won, Gregg made her his chief of staff. (Gregg is now a U.S. senator.)

Before working for Gregg, Newman was executive director of the Forum on New Hampshire's Future, a citizen participation program for industrial development and community planning. And prior to that, from 1972 to 1978, she was dean of students at the University of New Hampshire. She had been assistant dean since 1969.

Looking back over her career, Newman notes, "So much of life is serendipity. You volunteer for a campaign, you meet a nice guy, four years later he runs for Congress, you go to Washington for a few weeks to help set up his office." Yes, but how, one might ask, do you position yourself so that these opportunities come your way? "You've got to be willing to extend yourself, take risks, be flexible," Newman says, "work hard and do a good job."

Newman received her bachelor's degree in social science from St. Joseph's College in 1967 and a master's degree in education from Pennsylvania State University in 1969.

DANNY O'BRIEN (DEMOCRAT)

In December 2001 Danny O'Brien began as chief of staff to Senator Robert G. Torricelli (D-NJ), a member of two of the Senate's most prestigious committees, Finance and Foreign Relations, but who was also facing reelection in 2002. O'Brien became the "mayor of Torricelliville," overseeing the senator's legislative priorities that were carried out by a legislative staff in Washington, as well as constituency services that were performed primarily in two New Jersey offices, but also in the Washington office. O'Brien oversaw the senator's political interests through a Washington and New Jersey press operation and handled matters concerning Torricelli's reelection campaign. He also oversaw the senator's political relationships with the DSCC, the DNC, House and Senate colleagues, the Senate leadership, and other national and state allies, such as labor, environmentalists, and financial supporters. Torricelli offered him the job after interacting with him during the Jim McGreevey (D-NJ) for Governor campaign in 2001.

In that campaign, O'Brien served as both McGreevey's director of field operations and as an agent of the Democratic State Party's Coordinated Campaign, which was trying to win state senate and assembly races in addition to the governor's race. In these capacities, O'Brien created and ran an innovative, statewide, grassroots field campaign that not only resulted in a 14-point win for McGreevey but also helped the Democrats take back control of the state assembly and tie for control of the state senate.

Prior to the McGreevey campaign, O'Brien ran the coordinated campaign in Nevada for Al Gore's presidential run in 2000. He was drafted for this post from his position in the White House Office of Public Liaison, where he was the director of ethnic affairs from 1999 to 2000. In this job, he managed the domestic politics concerning such Clinton administration initiatives as the Northern Ireland peace process, bringing peace to Serbia-Croatia, and the Middle-East peace process by consulting with leading ethnic organizations, such as the Irish American Unity Conference, the National Albania-American Council, and the Arab-American Institute, respectively.

O'Brien comes from an air force family and grew up on military bases around the country. He graduated from high school in Redlands, California, in 1981, where he first was attracted to public service and social issues, serving as either student body or class president all four years. He also developed into a highly competitive tennis player, which he feels taught him how to manage a team of people through strong communications skills, the ability to lay out objectives, and the ability to build bonds. Before he entered college, however, O'Brien spent 1981–1982 as an American Field Service exchange student in Merida, Venezuela, solidifying his interest in international affairs.

Returning to the United States, O'Brien entered the local University of Redlands in 1982 and earned a bachelor's degree four years later, majoring in political science and Spanish, with an additional emphasis on western European history. He was also a member of two National Championship Division III tennis teams and was deeply inspired by his coach, Jim Verdieck, the winningest coach in college tennis to date. After college, O'Brien's parents gave him a one-way ticket to Washington, D.C., where he taught tennis until he landed a job with the EPA's Superfund program in 1986. He stayed there until 1988, preparing information on the progress of Superfund sites for EPA management and congressional offices.

After this experience, however, O'Brien wanted to focus more on international affairs. Consequently, he did a short internship with the Organization of American States in Washington. There he learned of the AFL-CIO's political organizing programs in Latin America that were funded through USAID. O'Brien had no labor background but sold the AFL-CIO's International Affairs Department on his multicultural, language, and organizing skills. The AFL-CIO then sent him to Argentina in 1989 to promote organized labor's role in Argentina's transfer from dictatorship to democracy and a free-market system. He subsequently served in Panama, Brazil, and Paraguay. Then, in July 1994 he was sent to Sofia, Bulgaria, where he developed one of the largest AFL-CIO programs in the region, which he then replicated portions of in Romania, Poland, and Croatia. On at least one occasion, however, he had to leave a country because of threats on his life. Thus it was that not in the United States but during six years abroad, O'Brien learned the essentials of campaigns and field organization, which he describes as the following:

> ➤ Enjoying people and particularly enjoying motivating them to get involved politically.
> ➤ Having strong communication skills.
> ➤ Mastering strategic planning.
> ➤ Being committed to detail and follow-through.
> ➤ Always looking for opportunities for innovative outreach methods to target disaffected voters.
> ➤ Being willing to do the physical as well as the mental aspects of the job, handling everything from cleaning the campaign headquarters to writing plans and speeches.

But by 1995 O'Brien was deeply troubled by what he perceived as the radical direction that the newly elected House Speaker, Newt Gingrich, and his Republican-controlled Congress were trying to take the country. He decided to put on hold his international development work and return to domestic politics. In 1996 he took a job in a Nevada congressional race that the DCCC considered top priority. Although this was a losing effort, he made such a reputation as a strong organizer and campaigner that in the spring of 1997, the DNC's political director appointed O'Brien director of grassroots organizing and state party building. This job required him to travel around the country, "living out of a bag," for a year and half doing campaign training and state party building in two dozen states. These efforts were part of the political department's success in the unexpected pick-up of five congressional seats in 1998.

After the 1998 elections, O'Brien got a call from the White House Office of Public Liaison asking whether he would be interested in working there. A former DNC colleague working in that office at the time had recommended him. O'Brien accepted the position, serving until he left to work on the Gore campaign in the spring of 2000.

O'Brien summarizes his career by saying that even though early on he developed a passion for grassroots organizing and community affairs, he never identified a plan leading to the high government positions he has held. But he is proud that this passion has contributed greatly to his efforts in helping government meet people's needs. In hiring people for his Senate office, he looks first to see whether they have had campaign experience. This is because he feels that people who come out of campaigns have a much higher appreciation for the complexity of the relationship between elected officials and their constituents—and the fact that it requires constant nurturing. O'Brien tries to help those who have not had campaign experience find other ways to interrelate more with constituents, so they can always bear in mind that what they are doing relates to real people and not just to abstract notions of good public policy.

SEAN O'KEEFE (REPUBLICAN)

Sean O'Keefe was appointed by President George W. Bush to be the 10th administrator of NASA on December 21, 2001, following Senate confirmation the previous day. He had previously served as the president's deputy director of the Office of Management and Budget since February 2001. Before that, beginning in 1996 O'Keefe had been the Louis A. Bantle Professor of Business and Government Policy at the Maxwell School of Syracuse University, where he also directed the National Security Studies program.

O'Keefe served as secretary of the navy under President George H. W. Bush in 1992 and as comptroller and chief financial officer of the Department of Defense from 1989 to 1992. Before joining Defense Secretary Dick Cheney's Pentagon management team, he served for eight years on the U.S. Senate Appropriations Committee and was staff director of the Defense Appropriations Subcommittee. His public service began in 1978 as a presidential management intern in the Navy Department; he was then recruited for the Defense Appropriations Subcommittee after having worked for the Senate on a detail assignment.

O'Keefe is a Fellow of the National Academy of Public Administration and served as chair of an academy panel on investigative practices in 1999. He was a Visiting Scholar at the Wolfson College of Cambridge University in England in 1994, and he is a member of the Naval Postgraduate School's civil-military relations seminar team for emerging democracies. He has conducted seminars for the Strategic Studies Group at Oxford University. O'Keefe earned his bachelor's degree in 1977 from Loyola University and his master of public administration degree in 1978 from The Maxwell School.

SCOTT PALMER (REPUBLICAN)

Scott Palmer is chief of staff to Speaker of the House Dennis Hastert (R-IL). He started to work for Hastert in 1995, four years before the conciliatory Hastert was chosen Speaker to replace the combative and partisan Newt Gingrich. As chief of staff, Palmer is the "gatekeeper" to the Speaker and advises him on a range of issues about running the House of Representatives, including who should be the chairmen of House committees, who the important representatives are, what their favorite projects are back home, how to assemble temporary alliances in order to pass the Republican agenda, and generally how to lead the House even though there is only a razor-thin Republican majority. Hastert has even shared a Washington apartment with Palmer and another top aide while Hastert's wife has remained in Illinois to continue teaching elementary school.

From 1995 to 1999, Palmer assisted Hastert in the latter's role as chief deputy majority whip, a leadership position in which Hastert was responsible for advancing legislation to the House floor by working with members, developing an achievable policy strategy, lining up support, and counting Republican and Democrat votes to ensure passage. Palmer helped Hastert cultivate a reputation of reaching across the aisle to develop bipartisan legislation and himself cultivated the reputation of being able to manage crisis and conflict well and, unlike many leadership staffers, get along well with aides from every leadership office.

Before working for Hastert, Palmer was the chief of staff for the House Committee on Science, Space and Technology (1993–1994). In that capacity he led a committee responsible for overseeing nondefense scientific research and development programs at such agencies as NASA, the Department of Energy, the EPA, the National Science Foundation, the Federal Aviation Administration, and the Federal Emergency Management Agency. Prior to that, Palmer was a staff member on the House Subcommittee on Investigations, starting in 1980, becoming staff director in 1992.

Palmer was born in 1947 in Cleveland, Ohio. He graduated from Harvard College with a bachelor's degree in 1970, after having left school in 1967–1968 to serve as a VISTA volunteer. He earned a master's degree from Northeastern University in 1975. From 1976 to 1979 he worked as a researcher in marine biology at the University of Delaware, receiving his doctorate in that subject in 1979. That year, he started his first job with the House of Representatives by winning a one-year congressional fellowship from the American Association for the Advancement of Science.

LEON E. PANETTA (DEMOCRAT)

Leon Panetta is the founder of the Panetta Institute at California State University, at Monterey Bay, a nonpartisan center aimed at getting young people involved in public service through such things as internship programs, and lecture tours.

From 1994 to 1997 he served as White House chief of staff under President Clinton. Before that, from 1993 to 1994, he was the director of the Office of Management and Budget, where, among other things, he was instrumental in negotiating the 1993 budget package that led to a balanced federal budget.

Prior to that, from 1977 to 1983, Panetta was a U.S. representative from California's 16th (now 17th) congressional district and was chairman of the House Budget Committee from 1989 to 1993. His major accomplishments while in the House include authoring the Fair Employment Practices Resolution, which extended civil rights protections to House employees for the first time; protecting the California coast from offshore oil and gas drilling; establishing Medicare and Medicaid reimbursement of hospice care for the terminally ill; and working on a variety of education, health, and defense issues. He was a key participant in the 1990 Budget Summit, as well as other budget summits of the 1980s.

Panetta was born in Monterrey, California, in 1938, the son of Italian immigrants. He graduated from Monterey High School, where he served as vice president of the student body as a junior, and president as a senior. He credits these experiences as whetting his appetite for politics.

In 1960 he received his bachelor's degree from Santa Clara University and in 1963 received a law degree from Santa Clara University Law School, where he was an editor of the Law Review. Panetta feels that the skills he learned in law school—the ability to look at both sides of a case, learn what the facts are, and then be able to advocate a position either for or against something—are invaluable assets in politics. From 1964 to 1966 he served as a first lieutenant in the U.S. Army, which was valuable in teaching him leadership skills, particularly the need to take risks. Panetta feels that today's leaders are not willing to take enough risks.

In 1966 he first went to Washington as a Republican as a legislative assistant to Senator Thomas Kuchel (R-CA), the Senate minority whip. The way he got the job with Kuchel, a progressive Republican appointed to the Senate by Governor Earl Warren when Richard Nixon became vice president, is interesting. Just getting out of the army, Panetta wanted a job in Washington. So he wrote Joe Califano, whom he did not know but who was then an assistant to President Lyndon Johnson—a Democrat. Panetta told Califano he had read about him and that he was proud both of them were of Italian extraction. He asked Califano whether he could suggest a way for Panetta to get into politics. Califano set up some appointments for him at the Department of Justice, the Pentagon, and other agencies, and Panetta flew to Washington.

While in Washington for this, however, Panetta walked into Senator Kuchel's office without any introduction. Kuchel happened to be looking for a legislative assistant, liked the fact that Panetta was a lawyer and had been in the army, and hired him.

However, Kuchel voted for so much progressive legislation—civil rights, labor protections—that he offended a lot of Republicans and was subsequently defeated in a Republican primary. Panetta needed to find another job. Luck intervened, and in 1969 the Nixon administration asked him to work at the Department of Health, Education, and Welfare as an assistant to Secretary Finch. Soon after, Panetta was appointed director of the Office for Civil Rights, which enforced school desegregation orders because of his experience working on civil rights legislation for Senator Kuchel. At that time, however, the Nixon administration had developed its "southern strategy," part of which was to go slow on civil rights enforcement because civil rights were controversial in the South. Panetta decided to enforce the laws anyway, which ultimately cost him his job.

After leaving the Office for Civil Rights in 1970, Panetta went to work as executive assistant for John V. Lindsay, who was mayor of New York City and another liberal Republican. It was there, in 1971, that Panetta decided he would become a Democrat. Later that year, he returned to California, where he practiced law with a Monterrey law firm, switched parties, and was elected to Congress in 1976 as a Democrat. He is the author of *Bring Us Together* (1971), an account of his service as director of the Office of Civil Rights.

Looking back over his career as both a job seeker and someone who hired people for a congressional office, a congressional committee staff, the

Office of Management and Budget, and the White House staff, Panetta has these thoughts for young people interested in getting their first political job:

> The most important thing is for you to get to Washington to see it. Get involved in some capacity, get your foot in the door. This is even more important than being in a campaign. You need to get a sense of what Washington is about. A congressional internship is a great way to do this. Another way is just walking in to see your local congressman or senator or state representative and tell them that you'd like to get involved in politics and can they help. Coming to Washington is better than being in a campaign at this stage for two reasons. First, you see that Washington is a human process. This gives you the confidence that you can play in this game. Second, you establish relations with people who create other opportunities for you later. This bond is really important. Once people see Washington like this, I find that they want to stay.

Panetta is married to Sylvia Marie Varni, who administered his district offices during his service in Congress. They have three grown sons and one grandchild.

JOHN PODESTA (DEMOCRAT)

John Podesta, is currently a visiting professor of Law at Georgetown University, a public speaker, and close advisor to Senate majority leader Tom Daschle (D-SD). Prior to that, he held several high posts in the Clinton White House, the most important of which were deputy chief of staff (1997–1998) and then chief of staff (1998–2001). In the latter job, he met with President Clinton several times a day. His primary responsibility was to organize all of the information that flowed to and from the president. He had to ensure that important issues were brought to the president's attention promptly and that White House staff members had the time, information, and resources they needed to handle their work. Podesta oversaw the president's schedule, helping to decide whom the president should see or call and with whom he should correspond. He also briefed the president on policy issues, assisted in the process of appointing individuals to government jobs, and reviewed the president's speeches before they were delivered. He met regularly with other members of the president's staff, including his schedulers, speechwriters, policy experts, budget team, and national security staff.

He also helped the president work with Congress to pass new legislation and traveled all over the world with the president on Air Force One.

From January 1995 to 1997 Podesta was a visiting professor at Georgetown University Law Center, where he taught courses on technology policy, congressional investigations, legislation, copyright, and public interest law.

From 1993 to 1995 he served in the first Clinton administration as staff secretary at the White House, where he managed the paper flow to and from the president, coordinating White House senior staff advice on presidential decision memoranda and approval on all presidential documents. He also served as the principal White House spokesperson on the Whitewater investigation and as the senior policy advisor to the president on government information, privacy, telecommunications, and regulatory policy.

Before joining the Clinton administration, Podesta was president and general counsel of Podesta Associates, Inc. (now PodestaMatoon), a Washington, D.C., government relations and public affairs firm that he founded with his older brother, Tony, in 1988. In fact, while John Podesta was working with President Clinton to get Congress to add a prescription drug benefit to Medicare and enact a patients' bill of rights, Tony Podesta was representing the Pharmaceutical Research and Manufacturers of America, lobbying against the president's Medicare plan. Their relationship as brothers, former business partners, and spokesmen for people who have power and money in America is a tricky one and an extreme example of how Washington power players interrelate. While clients of the lobbying firm wanted the lobbyists to simply pick up the phone to the president's closest aide, the Podesta brothers know that it would be ethically wrong and politically suicidal, so they do not do it. They say that not only did they not lobby each other; they did not even talk policy together.

John Podesta has also had extensive Capitol Hill experience. He served as counselor to Senate Democratic leader Thomas Daschle (1995–1996). He also served as an aide to Senator Patrick Leahy (D-VT) in several capacities: as chief counsel for the Senate Committee on Agriculture, Nutrition, and Forestry (1987–1988); as chief minority counsel to the Senate Judiciary Committee Subcommittees on Patents, Copyrights, and Trademarks; Security and Terrorism; and Regulatory Reform; and as counsel on the majority staff of the Senate Committee on the Judiciary (1979–1981).

Prior to that, he was special assistant to the director of Action, a federal volunteer agency. And in 1976 Podesta worked as a trial attorney in the Land and Natural Resources Division of the Justice Department.

Podesta began his political activity as a college freshman, joining the student senate, and was heavily involved in the anti–Vietnam War student movement. He was the campus coordinator for students for presidential hopeful Eugene McCarthy, and during the summer of his freshman year, he volunteered to work the Iowa caucuses for McCarthy.

Podesta is a native of Chicago and holds a law degree from Georgetown University Law Center (1976) and a bachelor's degree in psychology from Knox College (1971). He is married to Mary S. Podesta, a Washington, D.C., attorney. They have three children.

ROGER B. PORTER (REPUBLICAN)

Roger Porter is IBM Professor of Business and Government at Harvard's John F. Kennedy School of Government as well as a senior scholar at the Woodrow Wilson International Center for Scholars. He has been on the faculty at Harvard since 1977, with interruptions for government service. His teaching and research focus on the relationship between business and government, strategic management, and domestic and international economic policy. From 1996 to 2000 he was director of Harvard's Center for Business and Government.

Porter served for more than a decade in senior economic policy positions for three presidents. His last White House position was as assistant to President George H. W. Bush for economic and domestic policy (1989–1993). In that assignment, he supervised a staff of 35 people working on such issues as taxes, trade, competition, regulation, crime, environmental protection, and product liability reform. From 1985 to 1989 Porter was professor of business and government at Harvard and faculty chairman of the Program for Senior Managers in Government.

During the Reagan administration, Porter served as deputy assistant to the president and director of the White House Office of Policy Development. He also served as executive secretary of the Economic Policy Council and as counselor to the secretary of the treasury. He was executive secretary of the Cabinet Council on Economic Affairs from 1981 to 1985.

Porter first joined the White House staff in 1974, at the outset of the Ford administration, as part of the highly selective White House Fellows program. As a Fellow, he was selected to serve on the staff of Vice President Ford. The day he arrived for work, Ford was sworn in as president. At the end of his fellowship year, Ford asked him to stay on. Porter was appointed special assistant to the president and served as executive secretary of the President's Economic Policy Board.

Porter is the author of several books, including *Presidential Decision Making: The Economic Policy Board; Efficiency, Equity, and Legitimacy: The*

Multilateral Trading System at the Millennium; and *The U.S.-U.S.S.R. Grain Agreement.* He has also served on the board of directors or as a consultant to more than a dozen major U.S. corporations.

Porter's experience in government prior to his White House service involved two summers working on local government modernization. He was interested in economics, history, and government, and he envisioned an academic career. He decided it would be a good idea to see government firsthand, and the White House Fellowship seemed an ideal way to do it. He expected to only stay one year. Once in government, however, he discovered that there were many talented people and abundant opportunities for those willing to work hard.

Porter has stated publicly that he believes the growth in the number of political appointments in the executive branch hinders career civil servants from advancing to top government positions. Methods for attracting and retaining talented civil servants is a major issue at the moment because many are expected to retire soon and it is unclear how they will be replaced. Recruiting new ones will require that they have adequate prospects for advancement.

An alumnus of Brigham Young University, Porter was selected as a Rhodes Scholar and Woodrow Wilson Fellow, receiving his bachelor's degree from Oxford University. He received his doctorate from Harvard University in 1978.

RALPH REED (REPUBLICAN)

It is hard to talk about the impact of the religious right on U.S. politics without talking about Ralph Reed. Currently, he is president of Century Strategies, LLC, a political and corporate consulting company based in Atlanta, Georgia, which assists conservative political and corporate clients in achieving their public policy and public relations objectives. Areas in which the firm has been involved include electricity deregulation, health care reform, banking and financial services, and the high-technology industry. His 1996 book *Politically Incorrect: The Emerging Faith Factor in American Politics* argues that religious faith is essential to democracy.

Reed began in politics in 1976 when he worked for gubernatorial candidates in Georgia, North Carolina, and California, as well as the reelection campaigns of Senator Jesse Helms (R-NC) in 1984 and 1990. During this time, Reed consulted on 25 congressional campaigns across the country. From 1982 to 1984, he served as executive director of the College Republican National Committee, where he supervised a grassroots network of a hundred thousand members on a thousand campuses with a $600,000 budget. In 1984 he founded Students for America, of which he became executive director and built a grassroots conservative student network of ten thousand members on two hundred campuses in 41 states.

From 1989 to 1994 Reed served under Pat Robertson, as the executive director of the Christian Coalition, a nonprofit national organization dedicated to mobilizing and training Christians for effective political action. Under Reed's leadership, the Christian Coalition grew to over 1.7 million members and supporters organized in 1,700 local chapters in all 50 states. Reed has advised House majority leader Dick Armey (R-TX), House Conference chairman J. C. Watts (R-OK), the late Senator Paul Coverdell (R-GA), Senator Richard Shelby (R-AL), and Governor George W. Bush (R-TX). He contributed strategy in the formulation of both the "Contract with America" and the "Contract with the American Family," the two main legislative blueprints for the first Republican Congress in 40 years.

Reed was born in 1961 in Portsmouth, Virginia, and was raised in Florida and Georgia. He received his bachelor's degree in history from the University of Georgia and earned his doctorate in American history from Emory University in Atlanta, Georgia. He is a best-selling author and editor of three books, as well as a frequent television commentator.

JOHN F. W. ROGERS (REPUBLICAN)

In 1997 John Rogers was made a managing director of the investment firm Goldman Sachs. Prior to that, he served as vice president and assistant to the chairman of Goldman Sachs.

Before his work at Goldman Sachs, Rogers served a number of years in Washington, which he declares taught him several important lessons. "First was self-confidence from dealing with very senior people." Another was learning about the "external forces that affect your ability to accomplish things," such as the press. "This gives you a different perspective when you're in business." He also learned about doing good staff work. But the basic lesson he learned was this: "If you succeed in government, you're probably going to succeed in business; if you're a turkey in government, you're going to be a turkey in business, too. Yes, there are differences, but I don't draw a lot of distinction between the two."

In 1991 Rogers was nominated by President George H. W. Bush to be undersecretary of state for management. From 1988 to 1991, he was executive vice president of the Oliver Carr Company. Prior to this, he served in the Reagan administration as assistant secretary of the treasury for management (1985–1987). And prior to that, he served Reagan first as deputy assistant and then as assistant to the president for the Office of Management and Administration (1982–1985), an office that was first created during the Reagan years. In addition to that responsibility, Rogers was the director and general manager of the Committee for the 50th American Presidential Inaugural.

Rogers joined the White House staff in January 1981 as special assistant to the president for administration, responsible for the day-to-day administrative operations at the White House. Before joining the White House staff, he was executive assistant to the director of the White House transition team, James A. Baker III. Prior to the transition, he had been a volunteer in Reagan's presidential campaign. From 1977 to 1980 Rogers served successively as editorial assistant and assistant to the president for administration at the American Enterprise Institute for Public Policy Research.

During the Ford administration, as a college undergraduate at George Washington University, Rogers worked as a volunteer/intern at the White House. This was before the creation of the present-day White House intern program. "I always wanted to go to Washington," he explains, "and that is why he chose George Washington." His congressman, William Walsh (R-NY), for whom he had once campaigned, helped him get the internship, where he started out in the mail room, sorting through telegrams in the wake of the Nixon impeachment controversy. He later got a job as a researcher in the speechwriter's office, working 20 hours a week. After leaving the White House in January 1977, Rogers got a job with the Senate Republican Policy Committee, under Senator John Tower (R-TX) and graduated from George Washington University in 1978.

Rogers was born in Seneca Falls, New York, in 1956. He became involved in politics as a youngster, canvassing for Richard Nixon and for Congressman Walsh (whose son is in Congress now).

EDWARD J. ROLLINS (REPUBLICAN)

Ed Rollins has been an extremely colorful, combative, and controversial political organizer who currently is a news commentator and analyst. He is noted primarily for his role in leading the 1984 Reagan reelection campaign to victory. But he also ran campaigns for Jack Kemp, Christie Todd Whitman, and Ross Perot.

Rollins was born in 1943 and raised in the shipyard town of Vallejo, California. There, he won more than 150 bouts as an amateur boxer before a TKO in 1967 ended his career. He graduated from California State University at Chico State in 1968. He began his political career as a Democrat and a Robert F. Kennedy supporter. It was only when Kennedy was slain in 1968 and a Republican state representative offered him a job that Rollins started to become a Republican. Disagreement with antiwar protestors completed the transition.

In 1972 he became a field operative for Richard Nixon. When Nixon won, Rollins took a job in the Department of Transportation, which he continued through the Ford administration, leaving in 1977. He then accepted a job offer from a colleague at Transportation and became the dean of the faculty at the National Fire Academy. In the spring of 1979, he became the chief of staff for the Republicans in the California assembly.

Shortly thereafter, former President Nixon offered him a job as his chief of staff but at the same time suggested he campaign for Ronald Reagan instead, advice that Rollins took. He campaigned for both Reagan and Republican assembly candidates. Following Reagan's election, Rollins accepted a job in the White House as deputy director of the Office of Political Affairs. Four years later, Reagan chose him to be the national campaign director for his 1984 reelection campaign. Rollins led that effort to the largest electoral landslide in American history, carrying 49 states for the Reagan-Bush ticket. After the campaign, Rollins rejoined the administration as assistant to the president and deputy chief of staff for political and governmental affairs.

In 1985 he left the White House to become a lobbyist. But a year later, he became campaign chairman for the Kemp for President campaign. When Kemp lost out in the primaries, Rollins was forced to sit out his first presidential race since 1972. From 1989 to 1991, he was the first non-congressperson to head the NRCC.

In 1991 Rollins went to work for Sawyer Miller, a public relations and consulting firm in Washington. In 1992, however, he quit and briefly helped run the Ross Perot for President campaign. In 1993 Rollins was a consultant to the Christie Todd Whitman for Governor of New Jersey campaign. In 1994 he campaigned for George Nethercutt (R-WA), who defeated Speaker of the House Thomas Foley in the year the Republicans took back the House of Representatives for the first time in 40 years. Also in 1994 Rollins worked on the unsuccessful Huffington for Senate campaign in California. In 1995 he left politics, started an international consulting firm, and became a political commentator. He and his wife also adopted a child.

In 1996 Rollins wrote a best-selling biography, *Bare Knuckles and Back Rooms: My Life in American Politics,* which chronicles his rise in Republican politics. In the book, he sums up his philosophy about campaigning: "Campaigns aren't the place for the timid or those worried about their reputations."

PETER ROUSE (DEMOCRAT)

In 2001, after more than two decades of service to the U.S. House and Senate, Pete Rouse became the chief of staff to Senate Democratic leader Tom Daschle (D-SD). Daschle and Rouse first worked together as legislative assistants in the office of Senator James Abourezk (D-SD). (Daschle spent five years as an aide to Abourezk.)

Rouse is one of the quietest of Hill staffers, preferring to work in anonymity, but he is also considered by all observers to be one of the two or three most knowledgeable and influential staffers on the Hill. He not only runs Daschle's leadership office; he also runs Daschle's personal senatorial office and oversees the South Dakota office.

A Connecticut native, Rouse has a bachelor's degree from Colby College (1968) and master's degrees from both the London School of Economics (1969) and Harvard University (1977). From 1971 to 1975, he was legislative assistant to U.S. Representative James Abourezk, who in 1970 became the first Democrat since the landslides of President Roosevelt in the 1930s and 1940s to win South Dakota's Second District congressional seat. In taking this job, Rouse began the first of several positions working for politicians from rural areas where agricultural issues—the Farm Bill, family farms, trade agreements—are important.

When Abourezk was elected to the Senate in 1972, Rouse moved with him, again as legislative assistant, staying until 1975. In January of that year, however, he moved back to the House, this time as legislative director to U.S. Representative Berkley Bedell (D-IA), a job he held for two years. Following that, Rouse left the Hill for a year at Harvard's John F. Kennedy School of Government to get a Master of public administration degree. Upon his return, he rejoined Bedell's staff as administrative assistant, a position he held from 1975 to 1979.

Rouse then left Bedell and from 1979 to 1982 worked as chief of staff for Terry Miller, the lieutenant governor of Alaska who died of bone cancer in 1989 at age 46. Miller was a Republican, the only boss Rouse ever had who was not a Democrat. At the age of 30, Miller became the youngest president of the Alaska state senate and was known as a man of conviction who often championed causes that he believed in even when they were not on his party's agenda.

Returning to the Hill again, Rouse was from 1985 to 1986 administrative assistant to then-Representative Richard J. Durbin (D-IL). (Durbin was later elected to the U.S. Senate, in 1996.) In 1987 Rouse moved back to the Senate, this time as administrative assistant to his former colleague, Senator Tom Daschle (D-SD), who was newly elected to the Senate in 1986, after being a U.S. representative since 1979. Rouse served in this position from 1987 to 1994. In 1995, when Daschle was elected Senate minority leader, Rouse was appointed chief of staff for the Office of the Senate Minority Leader. Then, in 2001, when the Democrats gained control of the Senate and Daschle became majority leader, Rouse became chief of staff to the majority leader.

KAPIL SHARMA (DEMOCRAT)

In the summer of 2001, at age 29, Kapil Sharma started his own lobbying firm, KS Group, leaving the position he had held for several years as senior counsel for Senator Robert G. Torricelli (D-NJ). While working for Torricelli, Sharma was responsible for overseeing the senator's legislative agenda as well as for bankruptcy, intellectual property, internet/technology, telecommunications, and transportation issues.

Being of Indian descent, Sharma also felt that the senator should have good relations with the Indian community, which makes up 3 percent of the New Jersey population. Some observers even go so far as to say that Sharma was instrumental in changing the senator's perception of India. Torricelli is a member of the Senate Foreign Relations Committee and the Finance Committee, two of the most powerful in the Senate. In the past, Torricelli voted for anti-India amendments that called for the suspension of American aid to India because of its alleged violations of human rights. More recently, however, Torricelli introduced a resolution expressing sympathy for victims of the 2001 earthquake in Gujarat that claimed thousands of lives and made a statement on the floor of the Senate strongly supporting improved U.S.-India relations. By hiring Sharma, Torricelli made him one of the most senior Indian-American staffers in Congress. And by the summer of 2001, Torricelli had three other Indian Americans interning in his office—two in Washington and one in Newark.

Sharma obtained both a bachelor's and a law degree from Rutgers. Since his junior year in college, he has served as a consultant on numerous congressional, state, and local campaigns. In 1996, after obtaining the law degree, he went to work full time for Congressman Frank Pallone (D-NJ), founder and former cochair of the Congressional Caucus on India and Indian Americans, after having interned for Pallone for several summers. In the summer of 1998, Sharma started work for a leading Washington lobbying firm, Verner Liipfert et al, which had an India contract worth over $600,000 a year. Sharma thus became the first Indian American to work for a major lobbying firm. But in June 2000, he took a considerable pay cut to work for Torricelli.

GENE B. SPERLING (DEMOCRAT)

In January 2001 Gene Sperling, formerly President Clinton's national economic advisor and director of the NEC, joined the Brookings Institution as a guest scholar in the economic, foreign policy, and governmental studies programs. At Brookings, in addition to overall economic and fiscal issues, Sperling focuses on universal education in the world's poorest countries, especially Africa.

As director of the NEC, Sperling coordinated the administration's economic policy and played a key role in the 1993 and 1997 Deficit Reduction Acts and in the policy of saving the surplus for Social Security and debt reduction. During President Clinton's first term, Sperling helped design and pass several of the president's early initiatives, including the increase in the Earned Income Tax Credit, the Direct Student Loan Program, Empowerment Zones and the Community Development Financial Institutions program, and the Technology Literacy Initiative. He also helped create the America Reads child literacy initiative. He was a principal negotiator for the 1997 Balanced Budget Agreement, a principal negotiator with Treasury Secretary Lawrence Summers in finalizing the Financial Modernization Bill, and together with U.S. Trade Representative Charlene Barshefsky, successfully concluded the historic China–World Trade Organization agreement in Beijing. Sperling also coordinated the president's Medicare reform efforts.

Prior to joining the NEC, Sperling served as deputy director of economic policy for the 1992 presidential transition and economic policy director of the Clinton-Gore presidential campaign. From 1990 to 1992, he was an economic advisor to Governor Mario Cuomo of New York. Prior to that, Sperling was a policy consultant and lawyer dealing with appellate constitutional issues, as well as an economic advisor for Democratic officials.

Sperling received a bachelor's degree from the University of Minnesota in 1982 and a law degree from Yale Law School in 1985. He was senior editor of the *Yale Law Journal*. He attended Wharton Business School in 1986–1987. He is a native of Ann Arbor, Michigan, where his parents still reside.

TED VAN DER MEID (REPUBLICAN)

In 1999 Ted Van Der Meid became counsel to House Speaker Dennis Hastert (R-IL) and director of floor operations. In this capacity, he is the chief legal advisor to the Speaker, planner of legislative schedules, and strategist for floor operations to get legislation passed.

Prior to this, between 1995 and 1999, he had the sensitive assignment of staff director and chief counsel to the House Committee on Standards of Official Conduct (the House "Ethics Committee"). In that job he supervised the committee staff during several well-publicized ethics hearings into the activities of members of the House, including the then-House Speaker Newt Gingrich (R-GA). The committee imposed no penalties on Gingrich, concluding that the charges were too stale to prove.

Van Der Meid began his Hill service as a research associate in the House Wednesday Group, a consortium of conservative groups in and out of government. From 1985 to 1987, he worked as an associate staff member for the House Committee on Budget and Legislative Assistant to U.S. Representative Lynn Martin (R-IL). He then was legislative director to U.S. Representative Jan Myers (R-KS) (1987–1988).

After taking a year off to get his master of public administration degree, Van Der Meid became general counsel to House Republican leader, U.S. Representative Robert H. Michel (R-IL) (1989–1995).

Van Der Meid was born in 1957 in Rochester, New York, and received a bachelor's degree from North Park College in 1979, a law degree from Syracuse University in 1983, and a master's degree from Harvard University in 1989. He was admitted to the New York State Bar in 1984.

ANNE WEXLER (DEMOCRAT)

Anne Wexler is president and chairperson of the executive committee of the Wexler Group, a full-service lobbying company she cofounded in 1981. In January 1998 *Washingtonian Magazine* declared: "She is easily the most influential female lobbyist in a field still dominated by men." The Wexler Group provides strategic counseling, direct lobbying, coalition building, and grassroots communications strategies to corporations, associations, and government clients. It generates support for clients in such areas as taxes, trade, insurance, transportation, and legal reform. It has been involved in campaigns supporting the North American Free Trade Agreement and normal trade relations with China, among other issues. Former representative Robert Walker (R-PA) joined the 25-member firm as CEO in 1996. Its client list includes General Motors, Lockheed Martin, American Airlines, and Visa.

Before entering the private sector, Wexler had a long career as a public servant. In 1992 she served as a senior advisor on the Clinton-Gore transition team. During the Carter administration, she was assistant to the president for the Office of Public Liaison, where she was responsible for maintaining liaisons with the business community and other interest groups to build public support for the president's programs and policies.

Prior to that, she served as deputy undersecretary of commerce. In that capacity she coordinated the department's programs and field operations and directed its Office of State and Local Governments. While at the Department of Commerce, she was also chair of the President's Task Force on Women Business Owners.

Earlier, she was the campaign manager for her anti-Vietnam war husband Joe Duffey's unsuccessful U.S. Senate campaign. A worker in that campaign was a young Yale Law School student named Bill Clinton.

Wexler earned a bachelor's degree in history from Skidmore College in 1951. She resides in Washington with her husband, Dr. Joseph Duffey, former head of the United States Information Agency and earlier assistant secretary of state for educational and cultural affairs and chairman of the National Endowment for the Humanities under Presidents Carter and Reagan. They have four sons.

PAUL D. WOLFOWITZ (REPUBLICAN)

Paul Wolfowitz is currently deputy secretary of defense in the Bush administration, his third tour of duty at the Pentagon. He started the government part of his career as a management intern at the Bureau of the Budget in 1966–1967. For seven years prior to his present appointment, Wolfowitz was dean and professor of international relations at the Paul H. Nitze School of Advanced International Studies of the Johns Hopkins University. From 1989 to 1993 he served as undersecretary of defense for policy in charge of the 700-person defense policy team that was responsible to Secretary of Defense Dick Cheney for matters concerning strategy, plans, and policy. During the Reagan administration, Wolfowitz served for three years as U.S. Ambassador to Indonesia, the largest country in the Islamic world. During his tenure, his embassy was cited as one of the four best-managed embassies inspected in 1988.

Prior to that posting, he served three-and-a-half years as assistant secretary of state for East Asian and Pacific affairs, where he was in charge of U.S. relations with more than 20 countries. From 1981 to 1982 he was head of the State Department's policy planning staff. Before that he was deputy assistant secretary of defense for regional programs (1977–1980) and worked in the Arms Control and Disarmament Agency (1973–1977), working on the Strategic Arms Limitation Talks and a number of nuclear nonproliferation issues. From 1966 to 1967 he was a management intern at the Bureau of the Budget in between receiving his bachelor's degree in mathematics from Cornell University in 1965 and his doctorate in political science from the University of Chicago in 1972. He has written widely on the subject of national strategy and foreign policy.

HOWARD WOLFSON (DEMOCRAT)

In 2001, at age 34, Howard Wolfson became the executive director of the DCCC after being the press secretary for Hillary Rodham Clinton's successful U.S. Senate campaign in 2000. At the DCCC, he is paid $150,000 a year to oversee a staff of 60 operatives working to help Democrats win the House of Representatives. Wolfson's former boss from Capitol Hill days, U.S. Representative Nita M. Lowey (D-NY), is chairperson of the DCCC.

Until about a year before the Clinton campaign, Wolfson, the former political reporter–turned–campaign consultant, was planning to help his then-boss, Nita Lowey, run for the Senate seat being vacated by retiring senator Daniel Patrick Moynihan (D-NY). But Lowey decided against the race, and well-known New York political operative and former Clinton White House deputy chief of staff Harold Ickes asked Wolfson to be press secretary for the first lady's campaign instead. Wolfson knew New York election politics well, having served as director of communications for U.S. Representative Charles Schumer's (D-NY) successful Senate campaign against Alphonse D'Amato (R-NY) in 1998, when he was "on loan" from his real boss at the time, Nita Lowey. In his press secretary role, Wolfson had to handle the unprecedented media attention paid to Hillary Clinton from all over the world and himself became an instant celebrity and a regular on such shows as CNN's *Larry King Live*.

Prior to working on the Hillary Clinton campaign, Wolfson worked for Lowey for six years, first as press secretary (1993–1994), and then chief of staff/press secretary (1995–1999). He got his first job in politics in 1992, on the legislative staff of U.S. Representative Jim Jontz (D-IN). Jontz lost his reelection bid later in the year, and Lowey hired Wolfson in 1993.

Wolfson earned a bachelor's degree from the University of Chicago in 1989 and became a newspaper reporter in Fairfax County, Virginia. He tired of reporting and got a master's degree in history from Duke University in 1991. After being both a reporter and an academic, he decided politics was more to his liking. Wolfson is the son of teachers and is a native of Yonkers, New York. He still maintains his home in Manhattan; he lives in a Capitol Hill hotel during the week and takes the Metroliner to New York on Fridays.

REFERENCES
RICHARD L. ARMITAGE

"Richard Armitage." Taiwan Studies Institute home page. <http://www.taiwanstudies.org/election/advisors/armitage.html> (March 15, 2002).

Ruppert, Mike. "Richard Armitage Quietly Confirmed as Deputy Secretary of State." *The Wilderness Publications*. <http://www.fromthewilderness.com/free/politics/armitage_SS.html > (April 10, 2002).

CATHERINE BERTINI

"Catherine Bertini." World Food Program home page. April 4, 2002. <http://www.strength.org/conference/bertini.htm> (September 17, 2002).

JON-CHRISTOPHER BUA

Bua, Jon-Christopher. Personal telephone interview with the author. (March 14, 2002).

ANDREW H. CARD

"Chief of Staff Andrew H. Card, Jr." White House press release. November 26, 2000. <http://www.whitehouse.gov/government/card-bio.html> (April 15, 2002).

Gavel, Doug. "White House Chief of Staff to Address Kennedy School Graduates" KSG Communications press release. June 3, 2001. <http://www.ksg.harvard.edu/press/card_060401.htm> (April 1, 2002).

Hanna, Julia. "Card Talk." *Kennedy School Bulletin*. Autumn 2001. <http://www.ksg.harvard.edu/ksgpress/ksg_news/publications/card.html> (April 15, 2002).

JIM W. DYER

Congressional Yellow Book: Who's Who in Congress. New York: Leadership Directories, 2002.

"Fabulous Fifty Congressional Staff." *Roll Call*. January 21, 2002. <http://www.rollcall.com/pages/features/01/fab50/> (March 17, 2002).

MARIA ECHAVESTE

Dart, Bob. "From Migrant Worker, She Rose to Key White House Role." *Cox News Service.* 1999. <http://www.coxnews.com/washington/ECHAVESTE.HTM> (March 15, 2002).

"Maria Echaveste." *El Centro Chicano's Hall of Fame.* <http://www.stanford.edu/dept/elcentro/hall_of_fame.html> (March 15, 2002).

Ross, Alec. "A View from the Top." *Horizon.* <http://www.horizonmag.com/6/maria-echaveste.asp> (March 15, 2002).

MARLIN FITZWATER

"Marlin Fitzwater." *Talk Show Marketing.* <http://www.talkshowmarketing.com/Fitzwater.htm> (April 4, 2002).

"Marlin Fitzwater, Businessman, Journalist, Civil Servant, Presidential Adviser." *Plano Forum.* October 4, 2001. <http://www.planoforum.org> (March 15, 2002).

"The West Wing: Marlin Fitzwater." *PBS On-Line News Hour.* September 8, 2000. <http://www.pbs.org/newshour/media/west_wing/fitzwater.html> (April 9, 2002).

Personal interview, (May 3, 2002).

WENDY GREUEL

League of Women Voters of California. "Full Biography of Wendy Greuel." February 19, 2002. <http://www.smartvoter.org/2002/03/05/ca/la/vote/greuel_w/bio.html> (March 10, 2002).

PATRICIA DE STACY HARRISON

Northwood University Distinguished Women. "Patricia de Stacy Harrison." 1991. <http://www.northwood.edu/dw/1991/harrison.html> (March 15, 2002).

"Patricia de Stacy Harrison." U.S. Department of State, Bureau of Educational and Cultural Affairs. October 2, 2001. <http://exchanges.state.gov/education/harrisonbio.htm> (March 15, 2002).

DAVID HOPPE

Congressional Yellow Book: Who's Who in Congress. New York: Leadership Directories, 2002.

"Fabulous Fifty Congressional Staff." *Roll Call*. January 21, 2002. <http://www.rollcall.com/pages/features/01/fab50/> (March 17, 2002).

"Heritage Alumni Make Good." *Heritage Today*. <http://www.heritage.org/heritage25/heritagetoday/p20.html> (April 13, 2002).

Wolf, Richard. "How One Boy Moved Congress." *USA Today*. June 27, 1997. <www.ed.gov/offices/OSERS/Policy/IDEA/article1.html> (April 22, 2002).

MICKEY IBARRA

"Announcement." *Politico (Latino Guide of Political Consultants)*. <http://www.politicomagazine.com/ibarra.html> (March 15, 2002).

Desmond, Theresa. "Work Address: 1600 Pennsylvania Avenue." *Continuum, the Magazine of the University of Utah*. Winter 1998–1999. <http://www.alumni.utah.edu/continuum/winter98/ibarra.html> (March 15, 2002).

"President Names Mickey Ibarra as Assistant to the President and Director of Intergovernmental Affairs at the White House." White House press release. May 16, 1997. <http://clinton6.nara.gov/1997/05/1997-05-16-ibarra-to-direct-intergov-affairs-for-white-house.html> (March 15, 2002).

SUSAN KING

Russell, Avery. "Carnegie Corporation Announces New Staff Appointment." June 30, 1999. <http://www.carnegie.org/sub/news/king.html> (March 15, 2002).

"Susan King Sworn In as Assistant Secretary for Pubic Affairs." Department of Labor press release. January 11, 1996. <http://www.dol.gov/opa/media/press/opa/opa9601.htm> (March 15, 2002).

ROGER MAJAK

Majak, Roger. Personal telephone interview with the author. (March 16, 2002).

SYLVIA MATHEWS

"Sylvia Mathews." *Women and Public Policy Program*. 1999. <http://www.ksg.harvard.edu/wappp/students/bios/sylviamathews.html> (March 15, 2002).

"Sylvia M. Mathews." *The President's Interagency Council on Women*. October 21, 1998. <http://secretary.state.gov/www/picw/acwbio_mathews. html> (March 15, 2002).

Neilson, Trevor. "Sylvia Mathews Named Executive Vice President of the Bill and Melinda Gates Foundation." January 2, 2001. <http://www. gatesfoundation.org/aboutus/announcements/announce-337.htm> (March 15, 2002).

JANICE MAYS

Congressional Yellow Book: Who's Who in Congress. New York: Leadership Directories, 2002.

"Fabulous Fifty Congressional Staff." *Roll Call*. January 21, 2002. <http://www.rollcall.com/pages/features/01/fab50/>. (March 17, 2002).

Mays, Janice. Personal telephone interview with the author (March 15, 2002).

MINYON MOORE

Foster, Douglas. "Jesse Jackson: The Mother Jones Interview." *MOJO Wire*. March–April 2000.<http://www.motherjones.com/mother_jones/MA00/ jackson.html> (March 15, 2000).

"President Clinton Announces Minyon Moore as Assistant to the President and Director of Public Liaison at the White House." White House press release. May 29, 1998. <http://clinton6.nara.gov/1998/05/1998-05-29-moore-annouced-as-assistant-white-house-public-liaison.html> (March 15, 2002).

MICHAEL J. MYERS

Church World Service home page. February 6, 2002. <http://www.church worldservice.org/aboutcws.htm> (April 16, 2002).

Congressional Yellow Book: Who's Who in Congress. New York: Leadership Directories, 2002.

"Fabulous Fifty Congressional Staff." *Roll Call*. January 21, 2002. <http:// www.rollcall.com/pages/features/01/fab50/> (March 17, 2002).

Lubbers, Ruud. "In Search of Solutions." BBC News. <http://news. bbc.co.uk/hi/english/static/in_depth/world/2001/road_to_refuge/ return/analysis. stm> (April 16, 2002).

BOB J. NASH

"Bob J. Nash, Under Secretary of Agriculture for Rural Economic and Community Development." U.S. Department of Agriculture press release. May 12, 1993. <http://www.usda.gov/agencies/gallery/nash.htm> (March 15, 2002).

"President Names Officials at Agriculture, Education, and HUD." White House press release. March 9, 1993. <http://clinton6.nara.gov/1993/03/1993-03-09-todays-appointments.html> (March 15, 2002).

ANDREW S. NATSIOS

"Andrew Natsios." *United States Institute of Peace.* <http://www.usip.org/oc/gts/natsios.html> (March 15, 2002).

"Biography of Andrew S. Natsios." *US Agency for International Development.* May 1, 2001. <http://www.usaid.gov/about/bio_asn.html> (March 15, 2002).

J. BONNIE NEWMAN

"J. Bonnie Newman." New Hampshire College home page. May 14, 2001. <http://www.nhc.edu/general/awards/newman.htm> (April 13, 2002).

Mena, Jesus. "J. Bonnie Newman Appointed Executive Dean at the Kennedy School of Government." Kennedy School press release. July 24, 2000. <http://www.ksg.harvard.edu/ksgpress/ksg_news/press_releases/press_newman_release.htm> (March 15, 2002).

"Newman Appointed Executive Dean at Kennedy School." *Harvard University Gazette.* April 21, 2000. <http://www.news.harvard.edu/gazette/2000/08.21/newman_dean.html> (March 15, 2002).

"Nominations." White House press release. January 10, 1984. <http://www.reagan.utexas.edu/resource/speeches/1984/11084b.htm> (April 15, 2002).

DANNY O'BRIEN

O'Brien, Danny. Personal telephone interview with the author. (May 25, 2002).

SEAN O'KEEFE

"President Bush Nominates Sean O'Keefe as Deputy Director of the Office of Management and Budget." White House press release, February

6, 2001. <http://www.whitehouse.gov/news/releases/20010206-5.html> (March 15, 2002).

Thompson, Elvia. "NASA Administrator Sean O'Keefe." February, 2002. <http://www.nasa.gov/bios/okeefe.html> (April 13, 2002).

SCOTT PALMER

Congressional Yellow Book: Who's Who in Congress. New York: Leadership Directories, 2002.

"Fabulous Fifty Congressional Staff." *Roll Call.* January 21, 2002. <http://www.rollcall.com/pages/features/01/fab50/> (March 17, 2002).

Gizzi, John. "Hastert Aide Promotes GOP Moderates, Opposes Hyde, Crane Chairmanships." *Human Events Online.* 2000. <http://www.humanevents.org/articles/12-22-00/gizzi.html> (April 10, 2002).

VandeHei, Jim. "Speaker Hastert's Inner Circle." *Roll Call.* 1998. <http://www.rollcall.com/election/hastertcirc.html> (March 20, 2002).

LEON E. PANETTA

"Conversations with History." *Institute of International Studies* (University of California, Berkeley). 2000. <http://globetrotter.berkeley.edu/people/Panetta/panetta-con0.html> (April 10, 2002).

"Leon Panetta, White House Chief of Staff." *Online Backgrounders, Online News Hour.* 2002. <http://www.pbs.org/newshour/bb/bio/panetta_bio.html> (April 13, 2002).

Panetta Institute home page. <http://www.panettainstitute.org/> (April 11, 2002).

JOHN PODESTA

Bailley, Peter. "Knox College Graduate John Podesta Named White House Chief of Staff." Knox College press release. October 16, 1998. <http://www.knox.edu/knox/knoxweb/news_events/releases_1998-99/Podesta_Feature.html> (April 5, 2002).

"Chief of Staff." *Inside the White House.* Fall 1999. <http://clinton3.nara.gov/WH/kids/inside/html/fall99/html/podesta.html> (April 5, 2002).

"Knox College Commencement Address." June 6, 1998. <http://www.knox.edu/knox/knoxweb/news_events/releases_1997-98/Podesta_Commencement.html> (April 5, 2002).

PodestaMatoon home page. 1998. <http://www.podestamattoon.com/home page1495/> (April 5, 2002).

ROGER B. PORTER

Lunny, Kellie. "Former Appointee Calls for More Top Jobs for Career Executives." *Government Executive Magazine.* July 10, 2001. <http://www. ksgcase.harvard.edu/case.htm?PID=1393> (April 3, 2002).

"1976 Footwear Import Decision." *Case Studies in Public Policy and Management.* 2001. <http://www.ksgcase.harvard.edu/case.htm?PID=1393> (April 3, 2002).

"Roger Porter Faculty Home Page at Harvard University." <http:// ksgnotes1.harvard.edu/degreeprog/courses.nsf/aba163361f7adf 748525676600686c40/dfbafa805411851a85256944000fa85b? OpenDocument> (April 3, 2002).

RALPH REED

"Ralph Reed." *The American Conservative Union.* <http://216.239. 33.100/search?q=cache:OwywJvJAw1MC:www.conservative.org/rerbi o.htm+ralph+reed+biography&hl=en> (March 15, 2002).

"Ralph Reed." *Conservative Speakers Program.* <http://www.yaf.org/speakers/ ralph_reed.html> (April 13, 2002).

"Ralph Reed." *Harry Walker Agency Biography.* 2002. <http://www.harry walker.com/speakers_template.cfm?SPEA_ID=184&CAT_ID=14> (April 3, 2002).

"Ralph Reed, Jr." *The Saguaro Seminar: Civic Engagement in America.* J.F. Kennedy School of Government <http://www.ksg.harvard.edu/saguaro/ reed.html> (March 15, 2002).

JOHN F. W. ROGERS

Rogers, John. Personal telephone interview with the author. (March 14, 2002).

EDWARD J. ROLLINS

Rollins, Ed. *Bare Knuckles and Back Rooms.* New York: Broadway Books, 1997.

PETER ROUSE

Congressional Yellow Book: Who's Who in Congress. Leadership Directories, 2002.

"Fabulous Fifty Congressional Staff." *Roll Call.* January 21, 2002. <http://www.rollcall.com/pages/features/01/fab50/> (March 17, 2002).

KAPIL SHARMA

Haniffa, Aziz. "Indian Behind Torricelli's Turnaround." *Rediff.Com.* August 21, 1999. <http://www.rediff.com/us/2001/aug/20us2.htm> (March 15, 2002).

"Kapil Sharma," *Salsa National Conference.* 2001. <http://www.wcl.american. edu/pub/organizations/salsa/salsaconference/government.html> (March 15, 2002).

GENE B. SPERLING

"Gene B. Sperling." John Ben Shepperd Public Leadership Institute home page. March 7, 2002. <http://www.utpb.edu/JBS/sperling.htm> (April 13, 2002).

"Gene B. Sperling." National Economic Council home page. <http://clinton3.nara.gov/WH/EOP/nec/html/sperling.html> (March 15, 2002).

"Gene Sperling, Chief Economic Adviser to President Clinton, Joins Brookings." <http://www.brook.edu/comm/news/0110sperling.htm> (March 15, 2002).

TED VAN DER MEID

Congressional Yellow Book: Who's Who in Congress. New York: Leadership Directories, 2002.

"Fabulous Fifty Congressional Staff." *Roll Call.* January 21, 2002. <http://www.rollcall.com/pages/features/01/fab50/> (March 17, 2002).

Friedly, Jock. "Witnesses Complain of Abuses by Ethics Committee." *The Hill.* October 14, 1998. <http://www.friedly.com/jock/kim101498.html> (March 15, 2002).

ANNE WEXLER

"Anne Wexler Biography." Wexler Group home page. <http://www.wexlergroup.com/bios.htm> (March 15, 2002).

Snow, Nancy E. "United State Information Agency." 2001. <http://www. foreignpolicy-infocus.org/briefs/vol2/v2n40usia_body.html> (April 10, 2002).

PAUL D. WOLFOWITZ

"Paul Wolfowitz Deputy Secretary of Defense." *DefenseLink*, Department of Defense. March 6, 2001. <http://www.defenselink.mil/bios/depsecdef_ bio.html> (March 15, 2002).
"Paul Wolfowitz, PhD." *Faculty Profile, The School of Advanced International Studies.* 2000. <http://www.sais-jhu.edu/faculty/profiles/wolfowitz.html> (April 13, 2002).
"President Bush Nominates Paul Wolfowitz Deputy Secretary of Defense." White House press release. February 5, 2001. <http://www.whitehouse. gov/news/releases/20010205-1.html> (March 15, 2002).

HOWARD WOLFSON

Congressional Yellow Book: Who's Who in Congress. New York: Leadership Directories, 2002.
"Fabulous Fifty Congressional Staff." *Roll Call.* January 21, 2002. <http:// www.rollcall.com/pages/features/01/fab50/> (March 17, 2002).
"Howard Wolfson, AB '89, Helps Hillary Clinton Meet Press." *University of Chicago Magazine Class Notes.* December 1999. <http://www.alumni. uchicago.edu/magazine/9912/class-notes/newsmaker.html> (April 10, 2002).

APPENDIX: RECOMMENDED READING/VIEWING

The following are some of the sources recommended for someone wishing to stay current with U.S. politics and hoping to gain more insights into how the process works.

NEWSPAPERS

Drudgereport. drudgereport.com. Scandal sheet that gives excerpts from many other newspapers.

Los Angeles Times. latimes.com. Often contains details and stories that other national papers don't have.

New York Times. nytimes.com. "America's paper of record."

USA Today. usatoday.com. A more generalist readership.

Wall Street Journal. wss.com. You have to subscribe to get it online. Conservative newspaper focusing on business.

Washington Post. washingtonpost.com. Similar to the *New York Times* in authoritativeness but concentrates more on Washington events.

Washington Times. washtimes.com. Washington's conservative newspaper.

SPECIAL PUBLICATIONS

Congressional Quarterly. Provides a number of first-rate, nonpartisan publications about Congress, politics, and public policy.
Frontrunner. Daily summary of political events around the nation.
The Hill. Newspaper focusing on Capitol Hill.
The Hotline. Daily summary of political events around the nation.
National Journal. Good source of political news; provides various services.
Roll Call. Newspaper focusing on Capitol Hill.

TELEVISION NEWS

ABC News
CBS News
CNN
C-Span
Fox News
NBC News

TELEVISION TALK SHOWS

ABC's This Week
Capitol Sunday
Face the Nation
Inside Washington
NewsHour with Jim Lehrer
Meet the Press
McLaughlin Group
Washington Week in Review

REFERENCE BOOKS

Barone, Michael. *Almanac of American Politics.* Washington, D.C.: National Journal, 2002.
Congressional Yellow Book: Who's Who in Congress. New York: Leadership Directories, 2002.
Nutting, Brian, and H. Amy Stern, eds. *Politics in America.* Washington, D.C.: Congressional Quarterly, 2002.
Patterson, Bradley H. Jr. *The White House Staff.* Washington, D.C.: Brookings Institution Press, 2000.

GOOD READS

Here are a few entertaining tales that, among other things, give glimpses into the mechanics of Washington jobs.

Brady, John. *Bad Boy: The Life and Politics of Lee Atwater.* Reading, Massachusetts: Addison-Wesley, 1997. A biography of the Republicans' first "rock-star" political operative.

Davis, Lanny. *Truth to Tell.* New York: Free Press, 1999. Davis tells about his attempts to manage the press during the Clinton administration.

Dean, John. *Blind Ambition.* New York: Pocket Books, 1976. The counsel to the president describes his activities during Watergate and in so doing tells how the White House operates.

McGruder, Jeb Scott. *An American Life: One Man's Road to Watergate.* New York: Athenaeum, 1974. The head of the Committee to Reelect President Nixon describes the campaign process and Watergate events.

Morris, Dick. *Behind the Oval Office.* New York: Random House, 1997. A close aide to President Clinton describes the behind-the-scenes activities he exerted to help reelect his boss. In doing so he reveals various anecdotes about how the campaign process and the White House work.

Redmond, Eric. *The Dance of Legislation.* Seattle: University of Washington Press, 2000. A classic account by a Hill aide who follows an idea through the legislative process from conception to final enactment.

Reich, Robert. *Locked in the Cabinet.* New York: Alfred A. Knopf, 1997. The secretary of labor in the Clinton administration describes his job and frustrations.

Rollins, Ed. *Bare Knuckles and Back Rooms.* New York: Broadway Books, 1997. Rollins gives an account of his turbulent life as a political operative.

Stephanopoulos, George. *All Too Human.* Boston, New York, London: Little, Brown, 1999. One of President Clinton's closest aides describes getting the president elected twice and working for him in the White House.

INDEX

ABOUT THE AUTHOR

B ill Endicott, a Massachusetts native, has held many of the jobs discussed in this book. He has been an aide to three congressmen: Jonathan B. Bingham (D-NY), Edward P. Boland (D-MA), and Berkley Bedell (D-IA). He led the Democratic National Committee's Talk Radio program and worked as chief of staff in the Communications Department of the U.S. Small Business Administration and as director of research and analysis in the White House Office of Political Affairs under President Clinton. He also served from private to captain in the U.S. Marine Corps Reserves.

Apart from political activities, Bill Endicott coached world and Olympic champions on the U.S. Olympic Team in whitewater canoeing and kayaking. (He is the author of five books on sports and was an NBC TV color commentator for the 1996 Olympics.) In business, he is active in several aspects of the investing world, including serving on the board of directors of Avalon Capital, a mutual fund.

Bill Endicott is a graduate of the Phillips Exeter Academy, Harvard College, and Harvard's John F. Kennedy School of Government. He is also a Mayflower descendant and related to two Massachusetts governors, a U.S. senator, and a secretary of war. He is married to Abigail Bingham Endicott, a professional singer and voice teacher. They reside in Bethesda, Maryland, and have one son, Sam, also a creative musician.